PENNY JUNOR is a well-known biographer, writer and broadcaster. The author of many books, she is known principally for her biographies of the Royal Family including *Diana, Princess of Wales*, *Charles: Victim or Villain?*, *The Firm*, *Prince William* and *Prince Harry*. She is married with four children and seven grandchildren, and lives in Wiltshire.

D0280002

90710 000 346 760

ALSO BY PENNY JUNOR

ROYAL BIOGRAPHIES:

Diana, Princess of Wales
Charles
Charles and Diana: Portrait of a Marriage
Charles: Victim or Villain?
The Firm: The Troubled Life of the House of Windsor
Prince William: Born to be King
Prince Harry: Brother, Soldier, Son

OTHER BIOGRAPHIES:

Richard Burton: The Man Behind the Myth
Margaret Thatcher: Mother, Wife, Politician
John Major: From Brixton to Downing Street
Wonderful Today (with Pattie Boyd)
My Life, My Way (with Sir Cliff Richard)
The Man Who Lives With Wolves (with Shaun Ellis)
Home Truths: Life Around My Father

PENNY JUNOR

THE DUCHESS

The Untold Story

WILLIAM
COLLINS

William Collins
An imprint of HarperCollins*Publishers*
1 London Bridge Street
London SE1 9GF

www.WilliamCollinsBooks.com

First published in Great Britain by William Collins in 2017

This William Collins paperback edition published in 2018

1

A catalogue record for this book is
available from the British Library

ISBN 978-0-00-821103-5

Printed and bound in Great Britain by
CPI Group (UK) Ltd, Croydon, CR0 4YY

MIX
Paper from
responsible sources
FSC
www.fsc.org   FSC C007454

This book is produced from independently certified FSC paper
to ensure responsible forest management

For more information visit: www.harpercollins.co.uk/green

For Luna

CONTENTS

INTRODUCTION

For much of the final decade of the twentieth century, one story regularly dominated the news across much of the developed world. It was the unravelling of the marriage between Charles, Prince of Wales, heir to the British throne, and his beautiful, charismatic princess, Diana. This real-life drama had all the ingredients of a blockbuster: money, sex and monarchy. Month after month, the public was privy to the betrayals and infidelities, to snippets of life behind Palace doors, even to snatches of intimate, late-night telephone conversations between lovers; it was better than the best fiction and it gripped the millions who followed its every excruciating twist and turn in the pages of the tabloid press.

In the midst of it all was a woman in her forties: Camilla Parker Bowles, the Prince's long-term mistress, the married woman whom Diana squarely blamed for the failure of her marriage to Charles and for fifteen years of unhappiness. She claimed her husband had been obsessed by Camilla, that he had slept with her the night before their wedding, that they'd connived together to continue their affair behind her back. She called Camilla 'the enemy' and 'the Rottweiler' and it was she to whom Diana was referring when she famously said in a lengthy interview on British television, 'There were three of us in this marriage, so it was a bit crowded.' That was the ultimate salvo in what was known as 'The War of the Waleses'. Diana's mother-in-law, the Queen, finally intervened. She called time and insisted the couple seek an early divorce.

Yet whatever she might have said – and believed – Diana's claims were false. Camilla was not the sole reason the royal marriage fell apart, and she and Charles certainly did not sleep together the night before his wedding; there were many other factors that explain what went wrong. However, there is no denying that the Prince did always love Camilla – in the way, perhaps, that we all carry a torch for our first love – and when the marriage had irretrievably broken down, he did turn to her for solace. By this time Diana had lovers of her own, but she still obsessed over his reunion with Camilla.

Today, Camilla is known in England and Wales as the Duchess of Cornwall, and in Scotland as the Duchess of Rothesay. She is what the Prince refers to as 'My darling wife', and when he's with her, you can see why. Everything about him, from the grin on his face to the relaxed body language, tells you that he adores her, depends upon her – she is a strong woman, far stronger than he – and that with her in his life he feels complete, I suspect for the first time. They are a compelling and well-matched couple, fired by the same ideals, tickled by the same sense of the absurd. They are friends, companions and soulmates, and in the fullness of time, by whatever name, she will be by his side to support him when he becomes king.

How Camilla came to play such a pivotal role in British history is an extraordinary story of human frailty, of love, loss and great sadness. There was no simple happy ever after. A heavy price was paid for her happiness with Charles and even now it is compromised by forces beyond their control. Like all stories, over the years the facts have been distorted – either by prejudice or ignorance – and I think can bear retelling. As a writer I've been close to the protagonists for over thirty-five years, but this is the first time I have focused on Camilla. For more than a year I have followed her on her official engagements in Britain and abroad. I have watched her work, observed the impact she has on the people she meets and listened to her chatting to them; and I've chatted to her myself many a time, although I've not interviewed her. I've also spoken to friends, family and the people who work with her – all of them very special people who have been with her for years. She is utterly charming to everyone, whatever their age, ethnicity, sexual orientation or importance, and invariably has a confidential little aside for them all, making each one of them feel they are special. If she's being taken past the receptionist behind a desk who she's not been introduced to, or a cleaning woman, or a kitchen porter, she will stop to say hello. She chats to all the familiar reporters and photographers who follow her, always allows them to get the shot they want, and is happy to pull a face, or to be photographed eating a tricky canapé. This is by no means how every member of the Royal Family behaves. Camilla has such a twinkle in her eye that you feel the world is a better place after a couple of moments in her company. The last member of the Royal Family who had such a compelling effect on the people she met was the Queen Mother.

The Prince of Wales adored the Queen Mother too: he was closer to his beloved grandmother during her lifetime than any other member of his family. And there are some people who think Camilla is rather like her.

In my view, when history comes to judge her, Camilla will not be seen as the woman who nearly brought down the House of Windsor. I think she will be recognised as the woman who shored it up.

The Queen has been loved and admired as a monarch for more than six decades, but in these turbulent times, there are no guarantees for the future. After the death of the Princess of Wales in 1997, Charles was destroyed, his popularity through the floor. Camilla made considerable sacrifices to rehabilitate him, and to support and bolster him – and when they finally married she was sensitive as a stepmother. His sons and heirs, William and Harry, could have badly lost their way. There was no certainty they would turn into such well-grounded, responsible, likeable young men, or that they would embrace their unenviable destiny. She could have driven a wedge between father and sons. Instead she was the glue that has kept them together. Those were dark and dangerous times for the institution and for the family, but they have come through them, and so long as Britain continues to want a monarchy, its future will be in safe hands.

Camilla will never be universally loved because of the early scandal. Some people find adultery unacceptable in any circumstances, while others are so loyal to Diana's memory that they will not entertain the possibility that she had any of the frailties that make us human. But fortunately most people are more forgiving and more open-minded. Camilla came into Charles's broken marriage and gave him something to live for when he was in despair. It obviously wasn't an ideal scenario, but the Prince wasn't the first person to have made a mistake in marrying the wrong woman, and he won't be the last. He tried hard to make the Princess happy, to make their marriage work – harder, I suspect, than many people in the same situation would do – but he failed and he will live with that sense of failure for the rest of his life. Yet, for the most part, the media and the public were unforgiving.

Camilla is warm, she's funny, she's friendly, and she's fun to be with. When things go pear-shaped, she doesn't panic or allow others to panic around her. Her first instinct is to laugh, and that has been her saving grace throughout all the years of heartache. She's also a terrible giggler. When you see that twinkle in her deep blue eyes, you know she'll be up for anything. Equally, she's the sort of woman whom you know has real depth underneath the froth and the laughter, and if you were in a jam you would want her with you because you know she would calmly cope.

She has compassion too, but she can be tough – some would say ruthless – when needs be. She is nobody's fool and won't be pushed around by anyone. That said, she is not ambitious, she's not moody or temperamental – although the eyes can flash and she can get cross – and she's finely attuned to other people and their needs, in a way that her husband is not. And perhaps most endearing of all is that her family is paramount. She put them through hell because of her relationship with the Prince and now she's making amends.

Her sister, Annabel, eighteen months younger, is very different in character but probably her closest friend and confidante. They did everything together as children and although they have different friends, they speak on the phone three times a week as they always have done; they still holiday together and still see one another regularly. Likewise, her two children, Tom and Laura, who are both married with small children of their own, are all very close and very protective of one another. Camilla is particularly close to her daughter, Laura – and Laura is the only person she's afraid of. She utterly dotes on her five grandchildren and sets aside most weekends for them, as well as taking regular holidays in Devon and Scotland. She has kept the house in the country that she had before she married the Prince and goes there as often as she can, and she is joined there by her family. She cooks, she gardens, she reads, she relaxes, preferring the normality of her old home to the formality of the Prince's house half an hour away. Often the Prince quietly joins her. Normality is not something he has had much experience of in his life.

Spend two minutes with Camilla in the flesh and you will understand what Charles sees in her. But why he walked away from Diana and into her arms, why he risked everything, even the institution of monarchy, to have her in his life, is more complex.

The stammering George VI was unprepared and ill-equipped to be king when he was thrust into the role by his brother's abdication in 1936. By good fortune he had a strong wife, Charles's grandmother, Queen Elizabeth. Without her, Bertie, as he was known, could never have done the job. As it was, he died at the age of fifty-six, and she would claim it was the stress of the job that killed him. He was a good and popular king and left the monarchy in a healthy condition for his daughter, who was just twenty-five when he died. Intellectually, Charles will be the best prepared heir who has ever ascended the throne – he is cultured, well-informed, well-travelled, well-read, and he knows more about how people live and work in Britain than most politicians. He has spent the last forty years heavily involved in everything from architecture and inner city deprivation to interfaith dialogue, the rural economy and conservation. He's not afraid to put his head above the parapet if he thinks he can be of use. But emotionally he is less robust. She will give him the strength and the confidence to do the job.

She has already transformed him, as everyone can plainly see. Before she came into his life in the dying days of his marriage, he was lonely, depressed and angst-ridden, under-appreciated for his tireless charity work, and widely despised for his infidelity. Today he is happy, laughing and fulfilled. That makes him a better prince, a better father and a much more productive and popular figure. And when the time comes, it will make him a confident, capable and I believe much-loved king. Without her, there might have been a very different outcome.

But more than that. To the surprise of everyone who knew her before she married the Prince of Wales, Camilla has turned into a formidable worker and a very serious advocate for women, unafraid to put her name to issues like rape, sexual violence and domestic abuse. She is also tackling the widespread problem of illiteracy and encouraging people of all ages to read and enjoy books – something she herself has done since childhood. The advantage of coming to the role later in life is that she has nothing to prove. She is a grandmother, she has been around the block, she is not jostling to make her mark in the world, to look thirty years younger, or to steal the limelight, so nobody feels threatened or intimidated by her. She is happy to be herself, and if she can make a difference here and there to people's lives, so much the better. Her calmness, warmth, good humour and approachability – and her ability to be very tough when the occasion demands – are everything the nation could want in the uncertain years that will follow the death of such a popular and long-reigning Queen.

THE DUCHESS

1

The Problem

Thick early morning fog had slowly lifted and given way to a sunny but cold autumn morning in the English county of Dorset. The countryside was looking glorious, at its green and pleasant best, as I headed for the experimental new town of Poundbury; the leaves on the trees were the colour of rich orange marmalade. It was the perfect day to witness a rare event. The Queen, the Duke of Edinburgh, the Prince of Wales and the Duchess of Cornwall were to visit the town where Charles has implemented all his unorthodox ideas about urban planning. It's not often that you see the four senior members of the British Royal Family on a public engagement together – and it's almost unprecedented for the Prince's parents to visit and thereby tacitly endorse one of his achievements.

Poundbury is undeniably an extraordinary achievement, one which has been in the making for nearly a quarter of a century. Charles was hoping to impress his parents, but after a lifetime of disappointment in that hope, he was not holding his breath. The Prince of Wales has been trying to win his parents' approval his entire life, but he is not the son his father wanted – he is way too sensitive – and he has never felt he was good enough, never felt he came up to their expectations, never felt truly loved or appreciated. The Queen has many wonderful qualities and as a sovereign she has been peerless, but she is not emotionally demonstrative – and the Duke, for all his talents, is a bully. Charles grew up with everything he could want materially, but very few of his emotional needs were satisfied, and no amount of wealth and privilege can make up for the damage of that early emotional deprivation. The only person who made him feel good about himself, until Camilla came along, was his grandmother, the Queen Mother, who died in 2002 at the age of 101. And he was here today to officially open the central square that he has named after her.

Charles has put heart and soul into Poundbury. He has gone against accepted wisdom and practice, and for all the years of contempt and ridicule he has been proved right. The buildings in Queen Mother Square are designed for mixed use, all neoclassical in design – one bears a striking resemblance to Buckingham Palace – and most are named after the Queen Mother's favourite racehorses. After a tour of some of the buildings, and some speeches, the Queen was to unveil a bronze statue of her mother that stands imposingly, three metres high, in the centre of the square.

I parked my car in a field, the designated car park for the day, and made my way on foot through long wet grass and stinging nettles to the centre of Poundbury, a five-minute walk away. I was two hours early but the square was already full of police and well-wishers, hundreds of them, a crowd that would swell to thousands. Since it was half-term, excitable children had joined parents and grandparents, all of them wrapped up against the cold. When the royal convoy finally arrived, the spectators were standing six deep and more behind crowd barriers, waving flags and taking photos on their mobile phones. This was a day that they would remember for many years to come. The family is not normally seen together other than at weddings and funerals, at Christmas and Easter, when they all go to church, or on ceremonial occasions, like Remembrance Day and Trooping the Colour on the Queen's official birthday. With the Queen and the Duke now both in their nineties, there are no guarantees that these four will share an event again.

The centre had been cordoned off and security was tight – sniffer dogs would have been round earlier and there were no doubt snipers on the roofs – but everyone was good-natured and jovial. They usually are when royalty comes to the countryside. The Royal Family is in the feel-good business; it is important that security is never too heavy-handed.

The town feels like no other I have ever visited. I was last there in 2004, when I was given a guided tour by the development manager; it has more than doubled in size since then and still has two more phases to go. It is not to everyone's taste, but I have to confess I was impressed. Charles set out to challenge the reliance on cars that had dictated most urban planning of recent decades, where shops were mostly built in one out-of-town zone, industry in another, and residential in yet another. This has meant the car is not an option for most people but a necessity. Poundbury also set out to challenge the belief that if you put rich and poor alongside one another, it automatically depresses house prices.

Here humans triumph over cars. As I discovered on my first visit, you can't drive at much more than a crawl if there is no knowing who has priority. And it is one big social mix, so there are no rich enclaves and no poor ghettos. Thirty-five per cent of the housing is social, but you would scarcely know from looking at it – so tenants tend to take pride in their homes and look after them. And residential buildings are mixed up with businesses, factories, shops, pubs, restaurants, schools and leisure facilities – in the way that communities that grew organically once were – so that no one needs to get into their car to go about their daily life. Cars are banished to courtyards behind the houses and pedestrians take precedence in the streets; it's safe for children to walk on their own to school or play outside their front doors, and employment is on the doorstep. It's a town where there are fountains, flowers, trees, grass and water features, but no street furniture or road markings, no visible satellite dishes and no telephone wires. The buildings are unashamedly traditional, with chimneys for open fires and tasteful front doors; they're a hotchpotch of different designs and sizes, some detached, some terraced, with space and walkways between them, with everything on a human scale.

What I found most remarkable about Poundbury, though, was the vision of the man – and the bravery. He swam against a torrent of opposition to put his ideas into practice. They were deeply controversial ideas and the whole massive project could have gone catastrophically wrong. The social housing experiment might not have worked, the factories might have created problems, or they could have had a jobsworth of a planning officer who insisted on bollards, road markings and standard street lighting. But they didn't. His critics have mocked it – they've called it 'toy-town', a 'retro-kitsch fantasia'. Taxi drivers call it 'Charlesville'. But for all the sniping, it's now a thriving community of three thousand people, over two thousand of them in work. Crime is low, accidents are few and house prices are buoyant. What's more, it's had a major impact on urban planning, and not just in the UK. Council engineers, traffic experts, highways officials, architects, developers and planners arrive by the coachload from all over the world to look and learn from the experiment.

Charles has been an outspoken critic of modern architecture since the early 1980s, famously calling one high-profile project – the proposed extension to the National Gallery in Trafalgar Square – 'a kind of vast municipal fire station … like a monstrous carbuncle on the face of a much-loved and elegant friend'. That design was scrapped and over the years, contracts on other major projects have also been cancelled after his intervention. He has divided opinion as a result, both amongst architects and the public. He's been accused of abusing his position – a common refrain about the Prince of Wales – of being unconstitutional, a cranky elitist, and for setting himself up as an authority on a subject he knows nothing about. So when in 1987 Dorchester District Council first talked about requisitioning 400 acres of open farmland belonging to the Duchy of Cornwall, owned by the Prince, for an extension to the town, it was an opportunity for him to put his money where his mouth was.

The Queen and the Duke of Edinburgh visited the project eighteen years ago, five years into phase one. They were there for twenty minutes, without the Prince, and offered him no opinion, either good or bad, after the visit. But it was early days, with only 500 people living there; maybe this was too early for them to offer an opinion. This time around, they surely would. Whatever their views on the style of architecture, you would think they must be fiercely proud of Poundbury and all of the Prince of Wales's achievements.

This time his parents spent longer in Poundbury; they were there for seventy minutes. The family group had travelled from London on the royal train to Dorchester, where they were met by the Lord Lieutenant in all his finery, and by cheering crowds. They then travelled in a convoy the few miles to Poundbury, the Queen and Duke in her specially adapted Bentley which carries on its roof her crest and the Royal Standard, the Prince and Duchess following in a Rolls Royce. All four got out of their respective cars and were into a civic line-up before a tour of the main buildings. First was a branch of Waitrose, the upmarket supermarket chain that sells the Prince's organic produce under the Duchy label, where they were each presented with hampers, then on to a reception in the Jubilee Hall, then to the Royal Pavilion to meet the architects and hear Charles explain the development. Next, a fleeting look at The Duchess of Cornwall, the pub that he has named in his wife's honour, and onto the dais for the formal bit and the unveiling. Andrew Hamilton, the development director, spoke first, praising the Prince's vision in challenging the accepted orthodoxy of planning and development in the UK.

Then the Prince spoke, his voice unusually croaky. He had a bad cold but it may also have been nerves. He is never easy around his parents: 'It is a great honour Your Majesty is able to be with us today,' he began before listing all those to whom he was indebted for helping him turn his dream into a reality. Then he invited his mother to unveil the statue in memory of his 'darling Grandmother' and to declare her Square open.

If either of his parents were proud, it wasn't immediately obvious. For most of the ceremony there was not a hint of a smile, not an admiring look; they might have been sitting with strangers. Only when the cloth cover was successfully off the statue did the group show any animation or chat to one another, but it was brief. Then, after greeting a handful of the people who had waited so patiently for this moment, the Queen and the Duke of Edinburgh prepared to leave. As he got into the car, the Duke put his hands together a couple of times by way of a congratulatory clap to his son and said, 'Well done.' It was as rare as it was unexpected. His only other remark was that there was no echo in one of the rooms they'd been in. His mother smiled but offered nothing.

And so it has been throughout his childhood and his adult life. If he has a successful foreign tour, visits Tottenham after the riots, or offers comfort at a disaster scene, he hears nothing; if he makes a good speech, or launches an interesting initiative, there is silence. The last time the Queen and Duke showed any public interest in anything he has done was in 2012. During the Queen's Diamond Jubilee tour of the country, the Prince's office had an unexpected call from Buckingham Palace to say that she and the Duke would like to visit the north country town of Burnley, once the world centre of the cotton industry, where six of the Prince's charities have worked hard to revitalise the town. They wondered whether the Prince might join them. When Charles was told he thought there must be some mistake. 'The Queen wants to visit my project in Burnley? That can't be right.'

The person who has given Charles the courage and the encouragement to do half of the things he has done in the last few decades is Camilla, and whether she will be called Queen or Princess Consort is immaterial. What matters is that, finally, he feels loved and supported by someone close.

2

Debs' Delight

The Prince of Wales first met and fell in love with Camilla Shand in the summer of 1971. They were introduced by a mutual friend, the glamorous Chilean historian Lucia Santa Cruz. Lucia and Charles had met in 1968 shortly after he began as an undergraduate at Trinity College, Cambridge. Lucia was not a student; she already had a degree from Oxford and was a few years older than Charles. She was working as a research assistant to Lord Butler, the distinguished former Conservative minister who was then Master of Trinity, and was writing his memoirs, *The Art of the Possible*. Rab and Mollie Butler were good friends of Lucia's parents, the Chilean ambassador and his wife, and they invited her to dinner at the Master's lodge to meet the Prince, thinking they might enjoy one another's company. They did; they became lifelong friends – but never in a romantic way. Lucia has repeatedly been credited with being the Prince's first lover but this could not be further from the truth. She already had a serious boyfriend, the man who is now her husband, Juan Luis Ossa Bulnes, and they have children and grandchildren together in Chile. Charles is their eldest son's godfather.

Lucia's parents went back to Chile in November 1970, after Salvador Allende became president, bringing in a Marxist government and bringing an end to her father's time at the embassy. It was a difficult period for her but because of the political uncertainty, she stayed on in London to fend for herself, living at Stack House, a block of flats in Ebury Street, Belgravia. She was on the first floor and her neighbour in the flat below was Camilla Shand, then sharing with her friend the Hon. Virginia Carington, whose father was the Conservative politician Lord Carrington.

Lucia and Camilla already knew one another socially – they moved in the same circles – but as neighbours they became good friends and Camilla took Lucia under her wing. They were in and out of each other's flats every day, borrowing clothes, going to the same parties and dances – and at weekends Camilla would take Lucia down to her parents' house in the East Sussex countryside. Lucia spent that first Christmas with the family and woke up on Christmas Day, as all the young did, to a pillowcase full of presents at the end of her bed, delivered by Father Christmas. And downstairs there were more presents. Every time she went, she was made to feel at home; they were always welcoming and generous to friends, and with her own parents so far away it meant a lot. One of her most treasured memories was asking Camilla's father, Bruce, about the Second World War, whereupon he described to her some of the experiences that led to his capture by the Germans. He went on to write a book about it, *Previous Engagements*, published in 1990, but at the time his family had never heard him speak about it.

Camilla was dating Andrew Parker Bowles, and Lucia inevitably knew all about him. They had first met in March 1965 at her 'coming out' party as a debutante – a cocktail party for 150 people given by her mother at Searcy's, a smart venue behind Harrods in Knightsbridge. He was twenty-five and a rather beautiful officer in the Household Cavalry; she was seventeen but remarkably self-assured. She was good company, well read and intelligent – but neither university nor serious work had ever been in her game plan. She wanted nothing more than to be an upper-class country wife with children and horses and an enjoyable social life.

Being a debutante is a custom long gone – some would say mercifully – but the upper classes once used to launch their seventeen-year-old daughters into society in the hope of finding them an eligible husband. For the season, a year, they partied seamlessly night after night, weekend after weekend. Each party was a concentration of privilege and titles, all chronicled in two glossy magazines, *Tatler* and *Queen*. The highlight, and the glitziest of the lot, was Queen Charlotte's Ball, a huge charity event held at the Grosvenor House Hotel on Park Lane, a confetti of conspicuous wealth. And if nothing else, that season ensured these young women would have connections and invitations for life. The men were known as 'debs' delights' and while the girls could only do one season, the boys – so long as they were bachelors – could carry on reaping the benefits of other people's hospitality year after year. All they needed to ensure the invitations kept coming was access to the right kit – namely a white tie – and an ability to charm the mothers.

The whole thing dated back to 1780 when King George III held a ball in honour of his wife, Queen Charlotte, to celebrate her birthday and to raise money for the maternity hospital which bears her name; the centrepiece was a large cake. It became an annual event at which several hundred nubile girls were formally presented at court – and it was held at Buckingham Palace until 1958, when the Duke of Edinburgh pointed out that the whole thing was 'bloody daft' and his sister-in-law, Princess Margaret, said that 'every tart in London was getting in'. By the time Camilla came out, Queen Charlotte's Ball was held at the Grosvenor House, and the 'Queen' to which the girls were presented was nothing more regal than a giant cake.

Andrew was a debs' delight *par excellence*. One of his partners in crime was Nic Paravicini, a fellow officer and polo-playing friend who later became his brother-in-law and business partner, being married to Andrew's sister, Mary Ann. The couple subsequently divorced, but Andrew and Nic remain good friends. Footloose and fancy-free in those early days, and based with their regiment at Knightsbridge Barracks, they were geographically at the centre of all the action, and were two of a kind. Andrew was charming, smooth talking and debonair, and thanks to his Army training and riding he was slim and fit in every sense of the word. All the women were after him, some of them married – and he knew it, and reaped the benefits. He was one of the most attractive young men on the deb circuit, and a good catch too: he has noble blood coursing through him and connections with royalty going back generations. His parents, particularly his father, Derek, were close friends of the Queen Mother and in 1953, at the age of thirteen, he was a page boy at Queen Elizabeth II's coronation. Camilla may have had a boyfriend at the time of her coming out party – she was hugely popular with boys from an early age – but she noticed Andrew that night, and he her.

Soon afterwards he disappeared to the other side of the world to be aide-de-camp to the Governor-General of New Zealand, Sir Bernard Fergusson. They didn't meet again until 1966, at a dance in Scotland, shortly after his return. She was looking very pretty, as usual, and the centre of attention, as usual, so he went over to her and simply said, 'Let's dance.' They danced, and she fell in love. It was the beginning of a long and torturous romance – torturous because she became a puppet on a string. He was hugely fond of her, and she was nominally his girlfriend – she spent innumerable weekends with him at his parents' house near Newbury with all his siblings and their friends, but he couldn't resist other women, and what was particularly hurtful was that many of them were her friends.

Occasionally she retaliated. One night she spotted Andrew's car parked outside the flat of one of her best friends, so she wrote a rude message in lipstick on the windscreen and let all the air out of his tyres. But curiously, for such a strong, confident and intelligent woman, she put up with his behaviour – possibly because as well as being strong and confident, she has also always been determined and stubborn, and once she had made her mind up that she wanted to marry Andrew, nothing was going to stop her.

Lucia decided her friend needed to meet the Prince of Wales, who had no satisfactory girlfriend, and so she contrived to introduce them to one another. It happened on an evening in 1971 when Lucia and the Prince had arranged to go out together; she told him to come early, she had 'just the girl' for him and described Camilla as having 'enormous sympathy, warmth and natural character'. Charles had recently been in Japan and had brought a present for Lucia, a little box, and knowing he was to meet her friend Camilla, he'd brought a gift for her too. As Lucia made the introductions she joked, 'Now you two be very careful, you've got genetic antecedents' – referring to Alice Keppel, Camilla's great-grandmother, who had famously been a long-term mistress of King Edward VII, Charles's great-great-grandfather. 'Careful, CAREFUL!'

In Lucia's first-floor flat that evening, there was an immediate attraction between the two of them and an instant rapport; Charles loved that she smiled with her eyes as well as her mouth, and laughed at the same silly things he did. He also liked that she was so natural and easy and friendly, not in any way overawed by him, not fawning or sycophantic. He was very taken with her and after that first meeting he began ringing her up. Then they met and he continued to feel easy in her company. But it was a busy time for him and he was seldom at home.

Charles was young and shy, only twenty-two, and in the midst of intensive military training. He had just qualified as a jet pilot with the Royal Air

Force, and was about to embark on a career in the Royal Navy. He loved flying – he had taken it up at university and had a natural aptitude for it – but the Navy was a family tradition, and boats were deemed safer for the heir to the throne than jets, so that was where he was ultimately headed. He passed out of RAF College at Cranwell having earned his wings in just under five months – rather than the normal twelve – with the highest commendation, and having won membership of the exclusive Ten Ton Club by flying at more than 1,000 mph. He was in the back seat of a Phantom, scrambled from RAF Leuchars in Fife on a training exercise; they climbed to 35,000 feet in two minutes, almost vertically, launched a mock attack on an enemy aircraft, and flew twice over Balmoral, the Royal Family's home in the Highlands of Scotland, at 400 feet, causing seven locals to phone the police in protest, before going supersonic over the North Sea. He had also scared himself half to death by jumping out of an aircraft at 12,000 feet with a parachute that wrapped itself round his feet. Fortunately he had the presence of mind to disentangle himself and descended harmlessly into the sea at Studland Bay in Dorset. The press was full of praise for his derring-do and started billing him as Action Man. At that time, the country's most eligible bachelor could do no wrong.

After the freedom of flying, Dartmouth Royal Naval College, where he started in September 1971, was like going back to boarding school all over again, and he hated it. He did an intensive 'fast stream' six-week course, again half the length of the normal course. Yet when he graduated, top in navigation and seamanship, neither of his parents came to the ceremony. The only member of the family who showed was his beloved great-uncle, Louis, Earl Mountbatten of Burma, the man who had been Supreme Commander in South East Asia during the Second World War, the last Viceroy and first Governor-General of India, First Sea Lord and finally Chief of the Defence Staff. Mountbatten was the man Charles called his honorary grandfather. He had been devoted to him since he was a small child. Realising at the last minute that no one else would be there to watch the graduation, Mountbatten flew down to Devon from his home in Hampshire in a helicopter for the occasion. Weeks later, Charles flew out to Gibraltar to join his first ship, the destroyer HMS *Norfolk*.

Charles was with *Norfolk* for nine months, some of which was spent on shore-based training courses in Portsmouth. Mountbatten's home, Broadlands, was less than half an hour's drive away and so Charles was a frequent visitor, and this was the time when the two men became especially close. Mountbatten had realised some years earlier that Charles was adrift; his relationship with his parents left a lot to be desired and he needed confidence and guidance in his future role. It was Mountbatten who told him, in regard to women, that it was important 'in a case like yours, the man should sow his wild oats and have as many affairs as he can before settling down, but for a wife he should choose a suitable attractive and sweet-charactered girl before she has met anyone else she might fall for … I think it is disturbing for women to have experiences if they have to remain on a pedestal after marriage.'

In the late autumn of 1972, Andrew Parker Bowles was away with his regiment and Charles was on dry land for long enough to hook up with Camilla. They saw one another whenever the opportunity presented itself. This was quite often at Smith's Lawn, the Guards Polo Club in Windsor Great Park, where both Charles and Andrew played, for a time in the same team. Camilla had been a regular sight at polo matches for years, watching Andrew and his friends play – and the father of one of her friends was chairman of the club. So she could go and watch Charles play without arousing particular attention. The Prince had not taken up polo until the age of sixteen, but he became a fanatical player, raising vast sums of money for charity in the process. The Duke of Edinburgh was president of the club and a very able player, as was Lord Mountbatten, who had written the definitive book on the sport. Both had been very keen that Charles should play.

By this time, Andrew was serving in Northern Ireland in the aftermath of the Bloody Sunday massacre – a seminal event in which the British army, at the height of the Troubles, fired on unarmed civilians engaged in a peaceful protest and killed twenty-six of them. After Ulster he was posted to Cyprus, so for most of 1972, Charles had Camilla to himself, and the two of them spent very happy times together, quite often at Broadlands, which was a safe place away from the prying eyes of the press. But while Mountbatten was only too happy to play host to the pair, he made it abundantly clear that this relationship could never go anywhere in the long term. Camilla was not sufficiently aristocratic to be the Prince's wife, and she was not a virgin, which was a prerequisite.

The Prince was falling ever more deeply in love, and although far too reticent to say anything to Camilla was beginning to feel that, despite

Mountbatten's admonitions, he might have found someone he could share his life with. The only cloud on his horizon was that in the New Year he was due to leave for the Caribbean in the frigate HMS *Minerva*, which would take him away for at least eight months. He joined the ship three weeks before Christmas – and invited Mountbatten and Camilla both for a tour of inspection and lunch.

They were at Broadlands the weekend before he sailed, but he said nothing to indicate his strength of feeling, which was maybe just as well for his pride because Camilla may not have known how to respond. She was hugely fond of Charles, flattered by his attention, and they had had a very good time together, but she was in love with Andrew. To her fury, Andrew was also seeing Princess Anne, Charles's feisty younger sister. He had never been known to date just one girl at a time, but he seemed to be unusually smitten, and rumour had it that so was Anne. During their time together he was even invited by the Queen to join the family at Windsor Castle for Ascot week. So there was an element of tit-for-tat in Camilla's fling with Charles. She also enjoyed the historical connections – their great-grandparents' affair – which had always intrigued her. But her principal motivation was to have some excitement and make Andrew jealous. She knew it would never go anywhere, *could* never go anywhere.

Might she have felt differently if Charles had told her how special she was, how beautiful and funny, how warm, how sexy? If he had told her that he loved her above all things, that he couldn't live without her and that he would find some way of marrying her? It is impossible to know; not even those who know her best are convinced she would have said yes to him. Andrew was never very nice to her, never made her feel special, but she was stubbornly determined to marry him. His playing around had hurt her to the core, but her heart was still set on him. The fact that every other woman in London fancied him only made him more attractive to her. She adored him, and she had been dating him through thick and thin for seven years. She wanted to be Mrs Parker Bowles, wife of her handsome cavalry officer, not Princess of Wales, not Queen.

Andrew knew that his relationship with Princess Anne could never end in marriage. However much in love they may have been, he was a Roman Catholic and the 1701 Act of Succession – not changed until 2011 – expressly forbade an heir to the throne to marry a Roman Catholic. Princess Anne at that time was fourth in line and was not about to cause a constitutional crisis. She turned her attentions to a younger model, to Mark Phillips, a captain in the Queen's Dragoon Guards, and a three-day eventer who had just won a gold medal at the Montreal Olympics in 1972. Anne was herself a talented three-day eventer – she had won a gold medal at the European Eventing Championships the year before and been voted BBC Sports Personality of the Year in 1971 – and they had met on the eventing circuit. Theirs was a marriage made in the saddle, though apart from horses they had little common ground.

For a moment, Andrew must have thought he was about to lose both women. And so in March 1973, when Charles was thousands of miles away in the West Indies, Andrew asked Camilla to marry him and she agreed. She wrote to Charles herself to tell him. It broke his heart. He fired off anguished letters to his nearest and dearest. He has always been a prolific letter-writer. It seemed to him particularly cruel, he wrote in one letter, that after 'such a blissful, peaceful and mutually happy relationship' fate had decreed that it should last a mere six months. He now had 'no one' to go back to in England. 'I suppose the feeling of emptiness will pass eventually.' He did have one last-ditch attempt to get Camilla to change her mind, however. He wrote to her the week before the wedding asking her not to marry Andrew. Nevertheless, the wedding went ahead. Her mother, Rosalind, was not entirely happy about it – she didn't think Andrew treated her daughter very well – but Camilla was determined. She foolishly believed that leopards can change their spots.

3

Medals Not Money

Camilla was the eldest child in the family. She was born with exceptional confidence, and it was that confidence, plus the support of her family, that would see her through the nightmare years. Both her parents and her two siblings would stare at one another in mystification. 'Where did this come from?' they would ask. Maybe it was being the first-born, maybe it was because she felt so safe in her small world, maybe it was in the genes, inherited from great-grandmother Alice Keppel, another strong and confident woman. Whatever it was, no one else in the immediate family, confident characters though they were, felt they had anything that approached Camilla's.

As a little girl she marched happily into school without looking back. She galloped her pony, and flew over jumps without an anxious thought. She charged into the sea and laughed at the waves. She was a natural leader, the one everyone wanted as their friend; a pretty, sunny child with fair curls and a calm disposition that everyone liked. She wasn't rebellious – she left that to her sister Annabel, eighteen months younger. Annabel was the one with all the daring ideas. If ever they hatched a scheme – once it was tying rope across the road outside the house and waiting for cars to drive into it, another time dialling random numbers on the telephone and daring one another to say 'You're smelly!' to whoever answered – Camilla would be in the thick of it, but never the instigator. The two girls were different then and are different now. As they grew older, Camilla was the funnier of the two but Annabel was the one who got things done – and she is the one who has always had a career. Their little brother, Mark, was closer to Annabel in age, and he grew up to be the biggest rebel of the three. As a family they wanted for nothing. There was plenty of money, their parents were devoted to one another, and all three children had supremely secure and happy childhoods.

Major Bruce Middleton Shand and the Honourable Rosalind Maud Cubitt, as she then was, had married in 1946, the year after his liberation from a German prisoner-of-war camp where he had spent two years. Having lived for a year in London, where Camilla was born, they set up home together in the small village of Plumpton, at the foot of the South Downs, near Lewes in East Sussex, a culturally rich part of the world within easy commuting distance of London. Bruce took the train from Lewes to his office in Mayfair most mornings.

Camilla hero-worshipped her father. She adored him without qualification, and he adored her. She loved her mother too, and her mother loved her, but her bond with her father was that very special one that sometimes exists between fathers and daughters, a relationship that lasted from her birth for the remainder of his long life. Her passion for horses came from his, and his passion for books became hers. He was the one who read stories to her when she was a little girl. He was a gentle soul, never judgemental, never sharp or disagreeable, but wise and thoughtful, and funny, and always there for her.

The same could not be said for Bruce's father. Philip Morton Shand, known professionally as P. Morton Shand, was a prolific writer and critic before the war. A very clever man who spoke French and German fluently, his own father had also been a writer and a barrister, and his mother's family were all doctors. P. Morton was a colourful figure, a good friend of John Betjeman, the poet and architectural critic. He loved food and wine and in the preface to *A Book of Food*, published in 1927, he wrote, 'This is frankly a book of prejudices, for all food is a question of likes and dislikes. One may be tolerant about religion, politics, and a hundred and one other things, but not about the food that one eats.' His great-grandson, Tom Parker Bowles, Camilla's son, who never knew him, would become an equally prolific and entertaining food writer.

P. Morton's main subject was architecture and for most of his professional life, he championed the modernist movement. He was friends with many of its key figures at that time, including Walter Gropius and Le

Corbusier. By the end of his life he'd had a complete change of heart; as he wrote to Betjeman, 'Contemporary architecture = the piling up of gigantic children's toy bricks in utterly dehumanized and meaningless forms.' Interesting that more than twenty years after his death, the Prince of Wales, the man so in love with P. Morton's granddaughter, would be expressing the very same thoughts. Bruce scarcely knew his father, because amongst his other talents, P. Morton was a serial adulterer. Three years after Bruce's birth in January 1917, he divorced Bruce's mother, Edith Harrington, and disappeared from his son's life. Bruce's mother remarried Herbert Tippet, a golf course designer, and they moved to America, where they lived for some years in Westbury, Long Island. They returned to England when Bruce was ten, and thereafter his paternal grandmother, of whom he was very fond, had a big say in his upbringing. She had hopes he would become a doctor like her father, or a banker. But rather than sending him to Eton, P. Morton's old school, she chose Rugby, in Warwickshire. 'Rather illogically, and I think unfairly,' he wrote about the boycott of Eton, 'she attributed the plethora of wives, four in all, that my father collected to the influence of that seat of learning.'

Rugby, where the game of rugby football originated, was not a success. He spent 'not necessarily unhappy but infinitely drab years' there and left 'having learnt very little and having made practically no friends – on the whole a pretty unsatisfactory boy, rather indolent, self-conscious and inveterate'. But he did develop a love of books at Rugby and discovered horses, so rather than attempt medicine or money, it was tacitly agreed within the family that he should go into the Army for a few years.

After a short spell in France, cut short by his grandfather's death, he crammed for the entrance exam to the Royal Military Academy Sandhurst, which he passed with flying colours in 1935 'despite having become, rather like my great-great-uncle, "imprudently" drunk on the second night of the exams'. His great-great-uncle had died young, having 'been imprudently drinking too much before going out into the hot sun'. Bruce passed out of Sandhurst and joined the 12th Royal Lancers in 1937, having made a lot of friends; he declared he would always be grateful to that establishment 'for putting some life and backbone into a rather amorphous and disorganised adolescent'.

He had met his father just once in all those years, briefly, when he was eighteen, at his grandmother's funeral. He didn't see him again for another twenty years, by which time Bruce had a wife and three children, and his father was on his fourth and final marriage. One of his half-sisters is Elspeth Howe, the former chair of the Broadcasting Standards Commission and wife of the former Conservative minister, Geoffrey Howe.

Bruce was a gentleman – in every sense of the word – and he came home from the war a hero, but he was not an aristocrat and not a wealthy man. What money he had came from his late grandfather, and from his job in the wine trade, topped up by his military pension. He had been a very brave soldier. By the age of twenty-five, in 1942, he had won the Military Cross twice and been wounded and taken prisoner at the battle of El Alamein in North Africa in 1942.

At the outbreak of war in 1939, he'd been part of the British Expeditionary Force sent to France; and he was in Belgium when the Germans invaded in May 1940. It was there he won his first MC for his courage in covering the withdrawal of a column of lorries and guns under fire from four German tanks. That same month, he and his men covered the withdrawal of troops to the beaches and port of Dunkirk, after the Allies had been cut off and surrounded by the German army. Over eight days, 338,226 soldiers were evacuated by a hastily assembled fleet of 800 boats of all shapes and sizes that had come to the rescue from the south coast of England. Bruce was assigned the job of embarkation staff officer at the seaside resort of La Panne, which was being continuously bombed, and through a combination of resourcefulness and good luck escaped from Dunkirk in a cement ship, landing after an uncomfortable night at Margate on the morning of 1 June.

The second MC, or bar, was awarded in Libya, where he was wounded in the second battle of Alamein, when his vehicle was hit by enemy fire. A German bullet passed through Bruce's cheek and into his radio operator, who was killed instantly. Their driver managed to turn the car but they were hit again by a 'tremendous blow' and he slumped over the wheel, dead. As the car began to burn Bruce climbed out of the top and lost consciousness briefly. He next remembered trying to clamber onto another vehicle, but was then hit in the knee and lost his grip. As he said, 'A buzz of German voices greeted my return to consciousness.' After a month in hospital in Athens, he was taken by train to Spangenberg Castle, near Kassel, a prisoner-of-war camp where he spent the final two years of the war with three hundred or so other British officers. The security personnel guarding them were mostly schoolteachers with good English; their chief,

Hauptmann Seybold, was a man who prided himself on his knowledge of the idiomatic use of the language. 'He was reputed to be the originator of the classic saying, after a satisfactory morning's search for a radio, "You British think that I know fuck nothing, I tell you that I know fuck all."'

Bruce came back from the war a distinguished but broken man. His injuries had made him unfit for active service, he was retired from the Army the year Camilla was born in 1947, and after a false start marketing educational films, he went into the wine trade. The father he scarcely knew had written books on the subject. Bruce became a partner in the long-established Mayfair firm Block, Grey and Block of South Audley Street, which specialised in supplying wine to Oxbridge colleges – and he had an enviable cellar beneath the kitchen of the family home. Many years later, when the company ran into difficulties, he joined Ellis, Son and Vidler of Hastings and London, where he worked until he retired – while always combining the job with his duties and interests elsewhere. He was Master of the Southdown Fox Hounds for nearly twenty years, hunting several times a week from the end of August to April. He also reviewed military books for *Country Life* magazine, and later on became a servant of the Crown and a member of the royal household. He was a passionate historian, and a voracious reader of biography and memoirs. He had been kept sane during his years of incarceration by what he described as 'a very adequate library' at Spangenberg Castle that had provided him with all of these as well as 'the great Victorian authors, notably Thackeray and Trollope', to whom he remained loyal all his life.

Years later, when Camilla was caught in the midst of a very different type of war, she too read books to keep a hold of her sanity. Books, horses and the support of this very special father helped see her through some very dark times.

4

History

It was Rosalind's family that had the money. In 1947, the year Camilla was born, Rosalind's great-grandfather died and her father, the Hon. Roland Calvert Cubitt, became the 3rd Baron Ashcombe and inherited the family fortune. He'd grown up with no expectation of it but three older brothers were killed in the war, all in their twenties. The fortune had been amassed by his great-grandfather, Thomas Cubitt, a pioneering master builder born in Norfolk of humble origins in 1788. Cubitt revolutionised the building industry in the nineteenth century, designing and building great swathes of London including Camden, Islington, Bloomsbury, Stoke Newington, and in the heart of the West End, Belgravia and Pimlico. He also built Osborne House, Queen Victoria's favourite retreat on the Isle of Wight, and won the contract to extend Buckingham Palace. He became close friends with the Royal Family and after his death of throat cancer at the age of sixty-eight, Victoria said, 'In his sphere of life, with the immense business he had in hand, he is a real national loss. A better, kindhearted or more simple, unassuming man never breathed.'

Towards the end of his life, Thomas Cubitt bought Denbies, an estate of 3,900 acres outside Dorking in Surrey, where he built himself a grand three-storey mansion with nearly a hundred rooms, similar in design to Osborne House. After his death, the estate passed through his sons – at one time it employed as many as 400 people – but the fortune was decimated by death duties, and the house was billeted with troops during the war and fell into disrepair. Rosalind's father didn't have the money to restore and run it, so he converted a couple of other buildings into something more manageable and the big house was demolished in the early 1950s. By this time much of the land had been very profitably sold for development, and the remainder is now owned by Denbies Wine Estate, one of the largest producers of wine in the UK. (By a happy coincidence, Camilla is now the president of the United Kingdom Vineyards Association.) Rosalind grew up there but by the time she married Bruce, her mother had divorced her father had moved to West Meon in Hampshire.

Rosalind's mother, Sonia Keppel, was also well-known in society, but for rather different reasons. She was the daughter of Alice Keppel, who'd been famous at the turn of the century as a dazzling society hostess and as the long-term mistress of King Edward VII.

Alice Keppel was married to the Honourable George Keppel, son of the 7th Earl of Albemarle, when she met Edward, or Bertie, as he was known, in 1898. She was twenty-nine years old, the youngest daughter of a Scottish baron, Sir William Edmonstone. Bertie was fifty-six and still Prince of Wales; he didn't become king until Victoria's death three years later, but he fell soundly in love with Alice and she remained with him and loyal to him, lightening his darker moods, until his death in 1910.

Alice was ambitious and her husband was a third son. Despite his charm, good looks and titled lineage, he didn't have the wherewithal to meet her ambitions. So, being a strong and determined woman, she swiftly embarked on a series of affairs with rich men to keep them both in the style to which she aspired. She worked her way up the social scale until she came into the future king's orbit. Within a matter of weeks she was his official mistress, ousting Daisy, Countess of Warwick. George Keppel, it would seem, was happy to share his wife and enjoy the proceeds of her numerous and varied lovers. Bertie was particularly generous in his largesse; he organised a job for George and membership of the gentleman's club he coveted. In return, when Bertie came to call on his wife at 30 Portman Square, every day at tea time, George tactfully left.

Morality aside, Alice Keppel was an intelligent, cultured and highly likeable woman, known for her tact and good humour, who inspired affection and admiration from all who knew her. She was outspoken, witty, generous, kind and utterly discreet, a winning quality in a royal mistress. Physically, she was very beautiful, with alabaster skin, blue eyes, chestnut hair, a small waist and large breasts. Her eldest daughter, Violet, wrote of her, 'As a child, I saw Mama in a blaze of glory, resplendent in a perpetual tiara. I adore the unparalleled romance of her life ... She not only had a gift of happiness, but she excelled in making others happy. She resembled a Christmas tree laden with presents for everyone.'

The bearded Bertie was charming, informed, intelligent, beautifully mannered and meticulously dressed – an arbiter of men's fashion – but by 1898, he was not, physically, the most attractive of men. He was fat and bronchitic, a chain smoker with a 48-inch girth, who had always liked his pleasures in excess, including other men's wives. He was a leading figure in London society and spent his time eating, drinking, gambling, shooting, sailing and playing bridge. At weekends he went to grand country-house parties, where he enjoyed more of the same.

When he finally became king, after his mother's reclusive forty years in widow's weeds, he would revitalise the monarchy, but he did no work to speak of during his years in waiting. He performed ceremonial duties and was the first to make public appearances as we know them today, opening for example the Thames Embankment, the Mersey Tunnel and Tower Bridge. He also successfully represented Britain abroad, most notably in India; but Queen Victoria disliked him, disapproved of his playboy lifestyle and blamed him for his father's death. Prince Albert's death in 1861 had come just two weeks after he journeyed to Cambridge University to repri- mand Bertie for bedding an actress. As the Queen wrote to her eldest daughter, 'I never can, or shall, look at him without a shudder.' She refused to let him have an active military career and wouldn't allow him to partic- ipate in affairs of state. So he had too much time on his hands – not a crit- icism that could be levelled at the current Prince of Wales, although the lack of parental approval rings loud bells.

It wasn't that Bertie had an unhappy marriage. He loved his wife Queen Alexandra and she loved him – she referred to him as 'my Bertie' – but he had a voracious sexual appetite and thought nothing of taking other men's wives. They were different morals for a different age. Although not *de rigueur* today, adultery was rife amongst the upper classes in Edwardian times and a delicious source of gossip, even though any hint of indiscretion was instant social death.

Alexandra tolerated her husband's affairs. Not only was she a product of the time, she thought jealousy an ignoble quality, 'the bottom of all mischief and misfortune in this world'. When Bertie took up with Alice, she welcomed her as a great improvement on Lady Warwick, who had caused public scandal. She received Mrs Keppel at Windsor Castle, as well as Sandringham, the Royal Family's estate in Norfolk, and sometimes made use of Alice to keep the King happy. Like his great-grandson, Charles, the King had a fearsome temper and Alice was the only one who was able to calm him.

For the next twelve years, Mrs George Keppel was a regular sight beside Bertie at all the social events he favoured. Dressed in fabulous floor-length gowns, with collars of diamonds and ropes of pearls, she was with him at the casinos in Biarritz and Monte Carlo; grouse shooting at Sandringham, yachting at Cowes, horse racing at Ascot, on trips to Paris and the fashionable Czech spa town of Marienbad, and to the endless rounds of high-voltage country-house parties, where she was welcome in all but a few. The King even had the temerity to sit her next to the Archbishop of Canterbury at dinner.

Her two daughters were in awe of their mother. The younger, Sonia, who became Camilla's beloved grandmother, wrote in her autobiography, *Edwardian Daughter*:

Mamma used to tell me that she celebrated the Relief of Mafeking sitting astride a lion in Trafalgar Square. And that I was born a fortnight later. I never doubted her story. From my earliest childhood, she was invested for me with a brilliant, goddess-like quality which made possible anything that she chose to say or do. It seemed quite right that she should bestride a lion. Europa bestrode a bull, but the large, blonde Europa of my mythological picture-books in no way resembled my mother. In my extreme youth she drove a tandem of mettlesome ponies in a dog-cart. Had she decided to emulate Europa and ride a bull, she would not have let it take charge of her; she would have controlled it; and competently too; on a side-saddle. But somehow a bull was too plebeian a charger for my mother; a lion seemed much more fitting.

And of her mother, after Sonia's birth:

I can picture her as she lay back among her lace pillows, her beautiful chestnut hair unbound around her shoulders … And I can see the flowers sent as oblations to this goddess, the orchids, the malmaisons, the lilies. Great beribboned baskets of them, delivered in horse-drawn vans by a coachman and attendant in livery. They would have been banked in tall, cut-glass vases about her bed.

Mrs Keppel turned adultery into an art form. In *Mrs Keppel and Her Daughter*, Diana Souhami wrote:

She dazzled and seduced. Her demeanour and poise countered 'whispers, taints and horrible noxious suspicions'. Clear as to what she wanted – prosperity and status – she challenged none of the proprieties of her class. Even her enemies – and they were few – she treated kindly which, considering the influence she wielded with the Prince, indicated a generous nature. She invariably knew the choicest scandal, the price of stocks, the latest political move; no one could better amuse the Prince during the tedium of the long dinners etiquette decreed.

Lord Hardinge of Penshurst, Head of the Foreign Office, who travelled with the King and wrote many of his speeches, made the following note in his private file after Bertie's death:

I would like here to pay a tribute to her wonderful discretion, and to the excellent influence which she always exercised upon the King. She never utilised her knowledge to her own advantage or to that of her friends; and I never heard her repeat an unkind word of anybody. There were one or two occasions when the King was in disagreement with the Foreign Office, and I was able, through her, to advise the King with a view to the policy of the Government being accepted. She was very loyal to the King and patriotic at the same time.

It would have been difficult to find any other lady who would have filled the part of friend to King Edward with the same loyalty and discretion.

The parallels are remarkable. When Edward died in 1910, Alice Keppel discreetly took herself, her two daughters, their nanny and five travelling companions on a trip around the world in a ship. They were gone for a couple of years before she quietly resumed her position in London society from a new house in Grosvenor Street. Some years later she and her husband bought a beautiful Italian property, Villa dell'Ombrellino, in the hills overlooking Florence, where she spent the rest of her life – apart from the war years – and continued to entertain the great and the good. Winston Churchill was one such visitor; he set up an easel on the terrace to paint the view of the Duomo. When Alice died in 1947, Violet Trefusis inherited the house and lived there writing novels and memoirs until her own death in 1972. Annabel used to love going to stay with her great-aunt. Violet, who had no children of her own, was fond of Rosalind and her young family and determined that Rosalind would have the bulk of her estate when she died.

None of Rosalind's children ever knew their Keppel great-grandmother, but they knew the story from their grandmother, and Camilla was the one who was always fascinated by it. Sonia called Edward 'Kingy' and would sometimes find him having tea with her mother when she came down from the nursery at six o'clock. She described it in her memoir:

> On such occasions he and I devised a fascinating game. With a fine disregard for the good condition of his trouser, he would lend me his leg, on which I used to start two bits of bread and butter (butter side down), side by side. Then, bets of a penny each were made (my bet provided by Mamma) and the winning piece of bread and butter depended, of course, on which was the more buttery. The excitement was intense while the contest was on. Sometimes he won, sometimes I did. Although the owner of a Derby winner, Kingy's enthusiasm seemed delightfully unaffected by the quality of his bets.

George Keppel's name was on the birth certificates of both Alice's daughters but there was speculation that their biological fathers were more likely to have been other men. Violet, born in 1894, was rumoured to have been the child of MP William Becket, while Sonia, born in 1900, was said to resemble George Keppel but was more probably Bertie's. Either way, Sonia loved the man she believed to be her father and wrote very warmly about him, but as a child she accepted that sometimes holidays didn't include him. At

Easter, she and Violet, plus the ubiquitous Nannie, travelled through France by *wagon-lit* to spend two or three weeks in Biarritz with Kingy, as guests of Sir Ernest Cassel at the Villa Eugenie. Sonia repeatedly confused Sir Ernest with the King and would dutifully bob to him: 'gradually I came to realise that Tweedledum was quite easily distinguishable from august Tweedledee. For one thing, Tweedledee laughed more easily and, as I already knew, he could enter into nursery games with unassumed enthusiasm. Always he was accompanied by his dog, Caesar, who had a fine disregard for the villa's curtains and chair-legs, but a close personal regard for me.'

Easter Sunday at Biarritz was an occasion for giving beautiful presents, and not just to the grown-ups. Throughout her life, Sonia had a collection of little Easter eggs given to her by Kingy and Sir Ernest. One was 'exquisitely midget' in royal blue enamel, embossed with a diamond 'E' and topped by a tiny crown in gold and rubies.

After present giving, they would set off for a mammoth picnic:

Kingy liked to think of these as impromptu parties, and little did he realise the hours of preliminary hard work they had entailed. First his car led the way, followed by others containing the rest of the party. Then the food, guarded by at least two footmen, brought up the rear. Kingy spied out the land for a suitable site and, at his given word, we all stopped, and the footmen set out the lunch. Chairs and a table appeared, linen table-cloths, plates, glasses, silver. Every variety of cold food was produced, spiced by iced cup in silver-plated containers. Everything was on a high level of excellence, except the site chosen. For some unfathomed reason, Kingy had a preference for picnicking by the side of the road.

Violet, six years older than Sonia, grew up to a notoriety of her own after she fell in love with Vita Sackville-West. They had met as children with a mutual enthusiasm for books and horses, and at fourteen, when they went with their governesses to Florence together to learn Italian, Violet had declared her love to Vita and given her a special ring. Not many years later they became lovers.

Although homosexuality between women was never illegal it was still scandalous; but, like adultery, it was less so if conducted within the respectability of marriage. Both women went on to marry but they continued to be lovers, frequently going abroad together for months at a time. In 1913, Vita married Harold Nicolson, the diplomat, diarist, author and politician, with whom she had two children and a devoted but open relationship – he had homosexual lovers of his own. Violet married in 1919, but she did so under pressure from her mother, who was worried about the scandal affecting Sonia's chances of a good marriage. The marked man was Denys Trefusis, the soldier son of an aristocrat, a cavalry officer with The Blues who'd fought heroically in the First World War and was left with what today would be called post-traumatic stress disorder. Sonia didn't much like him to begin with and thought Violet had made an odd choice – he was neither literary nor artistic, which were the sort of people her sister liked to be around, but she warmed to him 'when I discovered that he had a sense of the ridiculous very much like mine'. But Violet never did – and the lack of feeling was mutual. Alice threatened to stop Violet's allowance unless she married Denys and she bankrolled him for some time, repeatedly refusing to let the pair file for an annulment. When Violet finally accepted that her affair with Vita was over, she and Denys moved to France, but they became completely estranged. She had a lengthy affair there with the Princess de Polignac, formerly Winaretta Singer, a daughter of the American sewing machine millionaire Isaac Singer. Her husband, Prince Edmond de Polignac, was a discreet homosexual.

Sonia Keppel's marriage was infinitely happier than her sister's – although it did end in divorce. She met Roland Cubitt in 1918. 'Rolie's greatest charm,' she wrote, 'was his gaiety. With his bright eyes and inexhaustible capacity for enjoyment, he looked like an alert fox terrier, eager for exercise … I began to invest Rolie himself with practically every romantic quality: Adonis's beauty; the chivalry of Sir Lancelot; the fidelity of Leander; the heroism of King Arthur. Being an essentially simple person, had he realised this he would have been extremely embarrassed by it … In his happy way he took people as he found them and he expected them to do the same about him.'

They were unofficially engaged for a year before she was invited to spend a weekend at Denbies, the family seat, to meet his parents. She was terrified and had been warned in advance that Lord Ashcombe led family prayers every morning, Lady Ashcombe didn't like fashionable girls, she liked them to look natural and to wear gloves at all times, and no one was allowed to smoke in the drawing room or to play cards on Sundays. She lowered the hem of her dress specially in preparation for the visit and used only minimal face powder.

Throughout tea, on the afternoon of their arrival, Lady Ashcombe referred to Sonia in the third person singular. "'Will the young lady have sugar in her tea? Will the young lady have a scone and some home-made strawberry jam?" Half dead with fright, I had a feeling that, by these indirect references, she was inferring that I had been deprived of my passport.' It wasn't until Monday morning that she detected anything approaching a thaw. 'Still terribly nervous, somehow or other my restless hands got hold of a piece of knotted string which, unconsciously, I began to unravel. As she watched me, with sudden warmth in her voice, Lady Ashcombe commented: "I like young ladies who undo string!" Dared I hope by that remark that she had decided to return me my passport?'

His parents insisted the couple were too young to marry, but in reality were not keen on their son, and now heir, marrying the daughter of the King's mistress. Alice expressed concerns too, but not about their age. 'It isn't that I don't like Rolie,' she had said, 'I think he's very nice. But if you marry him, you'll marry into a world you've never known, and I'm not at all sure that you'll like it.'

In comparison to the exotic and exciting world Sonia had known for the first twenty years of her life, the Ashcombes' world was certainly very conservative and oppressive. Sonia had always been chaperoned but she had been allowed a great deal of freedom, and she was a brave, fashionable and feisty young woman. When a general, a big broad man, who had promised her mother he would act as her chaperon, made a sudden lunge for her in the back of a brougham between the Ritz Hotel and the Albert Hall, heading for the first big event of the 1919 London Season, she scratched his face. "'What a little tigress it is!" he exclaimed delightedly. "Quite able to fend for itself really, without a chaperon!"' With silent intensity she fought him all the way, and by the time they arrived at the ball, her dress was torn, the powder gone from her nose and her shoulder had a big bruise. The general, on the other hand, had a face criss-crossed with red scratches and a swollen left thumb that clearly bore teeth-marks where she had bitten him. 'As the brougham drove up to the entrance, he looked at me and burst out laughing. "Never enjoyed a drive so much in my life!" he exclaimed. "Now, run along, and tidy up, before I hand you over."'

And when her parents took her off for a three-week winter sports holiday in Switzerland, to the Palace Hotel in St Moritz, home to the famous Cresta Run, she had not been there for twenty-four hours before she'd taken up bobsleighing and agreed to take part in the Bobsleigh Derby, the big event of the bobsleighing calendar. She joined two teams of complete strangers; in one she was with a crew of four men, in the other with two men, and she was to do the steering. They had bumped into some old friends in the hotel, the Duke of Alba and the Duke and Duchess of Santona, and it was Jack Santona's suggestion. Her mother pointed out that Sonia had no experience of bobsleighing, but having established that she was not frightened by the prospect of racing downhill through a deep ravine of ice, with steep banks and corners, at up to 70 mph, neither she nor her father let their own misgivings spoil her pleasure. Sonia not only survived, her team won the race in which she steered and she came away with the Vlora Cup. One of her fellow steerswomen was not so lucky; when she took one of the bends too high, the boblet flipped over and crushed her leg so badly it had to be amputated.

After two years of unofficial engagement, Rolie's parents finally came round to the marriage. He and Sonia officially announced it in the spring of 1920 and were married that autumn at the Guards Chapel of Wellington Barracks. In the intervening time, Alice negotiated her daughter's marriage settlement. Lord Ashcombe had demanded a meeting with her husband, George, but arrived to find just Alice waiting to speak to him. She played the interview like a poker hand, luring Ashcombe into bidding very much higher than he had originally intended. She won, and 'When, still shaken, he had expressed the hope that this (expensive?) marriage would last, grandiloquently Mamma had answered: "My dear Lord Ashcombe, neither you nor I can legislate for eternity."'

5

The Foundation Years

Bruce and Rosalind were a golden couple who seemed to have everything: good looks, charm, class, money, healthy children and a happy marriage, one that did last an eternity. Bruce was a genial, cultured man who loved art and music as well as his horses. He was courteous, immaculately dressed, scrupulously polite, always smiling; a man to whom people immediately warmed. So was Rosalind. She was big-bosomed, big-hearted, generous and tactile. She too dressed smartly in skirts and suits, with bright red lipstick, but she was less conventional than she looked. She invariably had a small cigar in one hand, and liked her children's friends to call her by her first name, which was unusual in the 1950s. She was a strong woman from a long line of strong women.

Rosalind could be sharp – she didn't appreciate being called Ros – but she was very funny and famed for her throwaway lines. When a teenage Camilla and her friend, Priscilla, were dressed up to the nines, ready to hit the town of Brighton for the evening, she said, 'My God, Camilla, you look just like Mandy Rice-Davies with spots!' For all that, she was hugely caring. Every Wednesday for seventeen years she went to Chailey Heritage, a school for the disabled outside Lewes, where she worked as a volunteer with thalidomide children. She only stopped when the pain of her osteoporosis made it impossible to make the journey.

The house in East Sussex where they settled after Camilla's birth, a seven-bedroom former rectory, called The Laines – initially they rented it

– is not classically beautiful. But its position, nestling at the foot of the South Downs with not another building in sight, is hard to beat, and the garden that Rosalind created, like a series of rooms, is still beautiful. The main section was built in the eighteenth century in the local style of flint and red brick, with later additions; the ivy-clad house sits on a slight incline at the end of a gravel driveway, in complete seclusion, surrounded by five acres of garden, with fields belonging to the neighbouring farm beyond. It's big but not grand, essentially a comfortable family home, with light, airy rooms, high ceilings and open fireplaces where log fires crackled in winter. Like all old houses with rattling windows – royal ones included – it could be very cold.

The kitchen did not play a part in family life, as it might do today. Tucked away in the servants' wing behind a green baize door, it was small and dingy, as kitchens so often were at that time, even in the smartest houses, and was the domain of the cook. Rosalind didn't cook. She preferred the growing and eating of food and left the cooking to Maria, the female half of a devoted Italian couple who were with the family for many years. Her husband waited at table. Another couple lived in a cottage at the end of the drive: David was an oddjob man-cum-gardener and chauffeur, and Christine was the cleaner and housekeeper.

It was a house for living in, for wonderful meals with friends, for children and dogs, not a status symbol – but it was filled with beautiful things, particularly paintings. Rosalind had a good eye and was a great home-maker, as her daughters are. She used warm, earthy colours and pretty fabrics. The furniture was a mix of old and new, of comfortable modern sofas and chairs and antique chests, desks, tables and mirrors; there were plenty of objets d'art scattered about, bits of silver, table lamps and framed photographs. Many of the better pieces were heirlooms, mostly from Rosalind's side of the family. The dogs were Sealyham terriers.

Although they didn't use the kitchen, food and drink played an important part in the family's lives. They gathered round the dining-room table for noisy meals, with their framed ancestors looking down at them from the walls, and ate simple but delicious fare with vegetables fresh from the garden. It was the scene of many a lively dinner party too. Guests would afterwards repair to the drawing room, an elegant formal room, but when it was just the family they used a smaller sitting room, to which in the 1970s they added an orangery that Rosalind filled with plants. Or there was the library, with a club fender around the fireplace. Books were everywhere; Bruce's study, where he sat for many hours reading and working, was lined with them.

Camilla's bedroom was always a mess. It was above the drawing room, with a bathroom next door that she shared with Annabel, whose room was beyond. There were four bathrooms but none of them were en suite – few were in those days – although each bedroom had a washbasin. The house was often full. Friends and family came from all over to stay or spend weekends. They would come to attend events at Glyndebourne, the great opera house that was just a fifteen-minute drive away – the Christie family who ran it were good friends – or there was the Theatre Royal in Brighton, where shows were trialled before moving into the West End of London, and there was horse racing at Plumpton just along the road. Hunting friends would come for a day out with the Southdown and in the summer, the beach was no more than half an hour away.

Bruce and Rosalind were a sociable pair at a time when people living in the countryside enjoyed an active social round, before the breathalyser put an end to drink-driving, and while domestic staff were still present to make entertaining easy. It was a time when people dressed up for the theatre and changed into evening wear for dinner, when the ladies withdrew afterwards to powder their noses, leaving the men to talk, smoke cigars and pass the port. But although they lived in one of the biggest houses around, they were refreshingly modest – even after Bruce was appointed Deputy and then Vice Lord Lieutenant of East Sussex in the early 1970s. He also became an officer in the Queen's Bodyguard (the Yeomen of the Guard), whose headquarters are at St James's Palace. This elite group is the oldest British military corps still in existence, and has all sorts of arcane titles. Bruce was invited to join it in middle age, and when he retired at the age of seventy he had reached the rank of Clerk of the Cheque and Adjutant. It was a career, he joked, that involved dressing as if to fight the Battle of Waterloo – and one that Rosalind hadn't been able to take too seriously. 'Oh God, Bruce, do you have to?' was her reaction. She may have been upper class to her bootstraps, but you would never have known it from her conversation or her lifestyle – and class was a word she abhorred. She never actually voted Labour, but she certainly flirted with the idea; she was a thoroughly egalitarian woman who took everybody at face value no matter what their background. There was never a hint of snobbishness or entitlement from any of them. Every year they opened their garden to the public, they held fund-raising events and parties for the hunt and the pony club. All the children's friends came to swim in the pool. Everyone was welcomed with the same warmth, and when Bruce left the village after Rosalind's death, having lived there for forty-five years, locals had nothing but good words to say about them.

Camilla, Annabel and Mark could not have had more perfect child-hoods, as they have all at various times said. These extraordinary parents filled the house with merriment, boosted rather than criticised them and made them feel valued, safe and loved. They encouraged them to be their own people, to seize life with both hands. To believe that the world was a good place with good people in it, that life was to be enjoyed – and that there would always be a welcome at home, no matter what. They were a tight-knit bunch who had each other's backs covered and who respected one another.

Until her teens, Camilla's life was about ponies. She rode them, she drew pictures of them, she read books about them and her bedroom was full of rosettes she had won at the local gymkhanas. Her favourite pony was a piebald called Bambino, who lived in a field at the bottom of the garden that they rented from the next-door farm. She loved it to bits and looked after it meticulously. Annabel rode but was never as keen as Camilla, while their mother didn't ride, although her own father had been a master of foxhounds so she'd grown up around horses. Mark had no interest – he preferred elephants.

Camilla rode on the Downs, the range of rolling chalk hills that extend for about 260 square miles from the Itchen Valley in Hampshire to the white cliffs of Beachy Head, near Eastbourne. And covering the entire area is a network of public footpaths and bridleways. The main bridleway, the South Downs Way, is 100 miles long, but there are over 2,000 miles of other tracks. For a little girl in love with ponies, it could not have been more idyllic, and a childhood roaming free in such an expanse explains why Camilla is at her very happiest in the countryside.

Her great childhood friend, Priscilla Spencer, was also pony mad. Almost exactly the same age, Priscilla moved into a house across the fields when they were both eight, and went to the same school. For a while, she and her younger sister Judy, Camilla and Annabel all had riding lessons together with a fierce, ex-military man called Mr Stuckle. He took them up onto the Downs and bellowed at them until Annabel refused point blank to go again. After that they went riding by themselves, day after day. Often they'd be gone all day, riding for miles, flying over the wooden jumps known as tiger traps and dodging defence installations left over from the war. They took sandwiches in little leather boxes attached to their saddles. And sometimes, they would sleep overnight on the Downs, out in the open. This was long before mobile phones. Everyone wanted a mother who was as easy-going and relaxed as Rosalind.

The children never had nannies. Rosalind was a full-time, hands-on mother. Sometimes David in the cottage might ferry them to school but it was usually Rosalind, and she'd be there for the plays and concerts, the fetes, the fairs. On summer afternoons after school, she would take them down to the beach at Hove for a swim in the sea – something Camilla loves to this day. But most of the time she just let them do their own thing. She was strict about manners and hot on discipline – she would get furious with Mark for trashing her lawn with his go-cart – but she gave them the freedom to fly and in their different ways, they did. Bruce was never the disciplinarian in the family, and her mother would have said he let Camilla get away with murder.

Their friends loved coming to stay at The Laines, and it was as much to see Rosalind and Bruce as it was to be with them. As Priscilla says, 'Sometimes you come across somebody who really is exceptional and Rosalind was that person. She was very like Camilla. A bit sharper of tongue but funny – the most amusing person you'd ever, ever meet. I absolutely adored her. And Bruce was the best looking man you've ever looked at in your life, urbane and charming.'

One very special feature of The Laines was the garden. It was Rosalind's domain and her passion. With the help of well-known landscape gardener Lanning Roper, she created formal lawns, made rose gardens, planted hedging, shrubs, flowers and specimen trees, all of which are now fully mature. Outside the kitchen she put in a fig which she and Bruce brought back from the Garden of Gethsemane, in Jerusalem, and at the bottom of the garden she planted an oak sapling that they bought on the 900th anniversary of the Battle of Hastings. It was said to have come from the very oak tree in which King Harold's mistress, Edith the Fair, sat to watch the battle in which he was slain. And in the walled garden she grew vegetables, and espaliered fruit trees along the walls.

Camilla did eventually inherit her mother's love of gardening but growing up, if she wasn't doing something horsey, she would be lounging around the swimming pool with her friends. Or she would be at school.

6

The Stuffed Stoat

At the age of five, Camilla went to Dumbrells, a little village school in Ditchling, about three miles from her home. The pupils – the school was attended by both girls and boys – were housed in three classrooms and there was a dairy farm next door. The children either loved it or loathed it, sank or swam – and the difference was almost entirely down to whether the headmistress, a terrifying figure called Miss Knowles, rated them or not. She liked quick-witted children and if their intelligence wasn't immediately evident, she had no interest in finding the key to unlock their potential. The result was swingeing favouritism. To her favourites she was the most extraordinary, exciting and inspirational teacher, who gave the lucky ones a passable education, a zest for the outdoors and a moral code for life. Camilla was one of those lucky ones, and her six years at Dumbrells were some of the happiest of her life.

The school was named after the three sisters who founded it 1882, the three Misses Dumbrell – May, Edith and Mary. Having fallen on hard times, with their widowed mother, they brought in a tenant farmer to run their farm and turned their home into North End House Home School, a boarding establishment for young children whose parents were in India. By the time Camilla arrived in 1952, the name had changed, there were no boarders, two ugly prefab wooden classrooms had been added, and the only Miss Dumbrell left was the very elderly Miss Mary, a tiny figure dressed in a long grey gown and mittens, out of which her tiny fingers peeped. Miss Knowles was in her fifties; she had been a pupil at the school, returned as an assistant teacher in 1924 and was there until it closed down in 1982. It is now a private house again. The front drive has been rerouted and an estate of sheltered housing has encroached on much of the garden that the children used to play in, but many original features remain – though not, alas, the alarming stuffed stoat in a glass case that used to greet the children as they came through the front door each morning. It appeared to be gazing in terror at a stuffed bat on the other wall.

French was taught from an early age, and at lunchtime one of the three long tables in the dining room – to which the children were summoned by a loud gong – was a 'French' table. Everyone who sat at it was expected to speak French to the teachers who presided. Translating spotted dick and jam roly-poly, two favourites, into French was quite a challenge, and during Camilla's time the convention was abandoned. Lunch began and ended with the saying of grace. There was always a choice of two main courses with vegetables and two puddings – one a milk pudding, the other baked – but it was Hobson's choice. To make sure there was enough of everything to go round, each child had to have something different from his or her neighbour, so if you hated rissoles or tapioca the clever thing was to sit next to someone who loved them. The food was generally delicious, and all freshly cooked – most of the vegetables came from the garden. No one was allowed to start until they had all had been served, nor finish until the teachers had finished. And anyone who didn't finish their food had it taken into the Big Schoolroom, where they had to eat it later in front of everyone under the eagle eye of Miss Knowles. Everyone had to use a knife and fork and hold them properly with their first finger on the shaft – not like a pen. There was no speaking or drinking water with one's mouth full, and no shouting. And neighbours had to look after each other and pass them what they needed. At the end, everyone stood while grace was said again.

Miss Kempton, the cook, was an eccentric woman with a harelip. The children were scared of her and because of the lip, found her very difficult to understand. For some reason Camilla and Priscilla could make out what she was saying better than anyone else, so every day Miss Knowles sent the two of them off to the kitchen, missing the last lesson of the morning, to help Miss Kempton prepare the lunch. Across the corridor was a little room, not much bigger than a cubbyhole, which permanently smelt of sour milk. It was where the maid, Sarah, poured the milk that was obligatory at break time. It came directly from the farm, a stone's throw away, which was run by a jolly red-faced fellow called Mr Holman. He had a celebrated herd of Guernsey cows, so the milk was rich and creamy, even though most of the children hated it. The farm had not been mechanised until just before the war. All the cows had been milked by hand, and a big white carthorse called Blossom used to pull the plough. They now had a tractor, but Blossom lived on and the children loved her. They would watch her from one of the windows in the Big Schoolroom that looked out over the farmyard.

The Big Schoolroom was Miss Knowles' domain. There, all the children, a great mixture of ages, sat at old-fashioned wooden desks, each one with a little china ink pot, while Miss Knowles repeatedly drummed into them the finer points of English grammar, throwing pencils and books at anyone bold enough to misbehave. The room doubled up as a gym, so there were wall bars behind her desk, ropes coiled up near the ceiling and fittings for parallel bars on the walls; and it was where morning prayers were held at the start of the day. The afternoons were the best part of every day. Miss Knowles would read a story, everyone sitting in rapt attention as she read *Ivanhoe, Kenilworth, Barnaby Rudge* and *Treasure Island* – classics by Sir Walter Scott, Charles Dickens and Robert Louis Stevenson, all unabridged – which would be impenetrable for most of today's eight- and nine-year-olds. She read unemotionally but accurately, bringing the books to life by richly impersonating all the characters, while narrative poems also formed part of her repertoire; *Hiawatha* was one of her favourites. In summer, she would sometimes read to the children in the garden. When the soft fruit was ripe, they would sit cross-legged on blankets on the lawn, topping and tailing gooseberries and blackcurrants while Miss Knowles read the story.

Miss Knowles had a ruddy face that had never seen make-up, big blue eyes and wavy chestnut hair tied into an untidy bun at the nape of her neck. Day in day out, she was in the same clothes: a navy V-necked frock with a cream blouse underneath, and when it was cold, a navy jacket over the top. The outfit was finished off with black stockings and plain black court shoes, which made a very distinctive clacking sound in the corridors that ensured she never arrived unannounced. Josephine Ferguson, a pupil at the school in the 1940s, wrote about it in her book *The Stuffed Stoat*, saying Miss Knowles had once explained that an aunt had left her twenty-nine pairs of stockings and umpteen dark blue frocks and that being hard up, she had felt obliged to wear them to save money. History doesn't relate whether she was still working her way through the same twenty-nine pairs of stockings in the 1950s, but her daily outfit was identical.

For her pupils, though, there was no uniform. Most of the girls, Camilla included, wore dresses; and she had long white socks that miraculously always stayed up, while other people's slid down to their ankles.

What everyone loved best of all were nature walks, when the children roamed the countryside collecting as many different wild flowers as possible, putting them into jam-jars for Miss Knowles to identify before they were pressed and pasted into books. There was a prize at the end of the term for the child with the best collection. Sometimes the walks simply crossed the farmland at the back, sometimes they took the children further afield – walking along the road in a crocodile holding hands, two by two – to the orchid woods or the Downs.

There was very little competition in the school – and some would say very little learning. Sports day was low-key and showing off in any way was forbidden. There was a nativity play in the Christmas term, in which Camilla and Priscilla once sang 'We Three Kings of Orient Are', and every year a big Christmas tree was installed in the schoolroom, decorated with real candles that were lit. Today's health and safety inspectors would have had a fit. But the big event of the year was the summer play in which all the bigger children had a part, and which they rehearsed for weeks.

Miss Knowles was a stickler for manners, and not just at the lunch table. She taught the children how to introduce people to one another correctly, and before the summer play everyone had to introduce their parents to those of their friends if they hadn't yet met. It was a given that they should look people in the eye and shake hands politely, and should be just as polite to Sarah, the maid, and Cherryman, the gardener, as they were to other people's parents.

Miss Mary died in 1962, and twenty years later Miss Knowles retired and went to live in a cottage in a nearby village. Josephine Ferguson summed up Dumbrells in the following terms:

> unfortunately for posterity, there will never again be a school like it, and there will probably never again be such remarkable and dedicated characters as the Dumbrell sisters and Miss Knowles, who devoted their lives to teaching just a few of us, out of four generations, to have

not only an erudite and resourceful outlook on life, but a compassionate manner towards our fellow beings, at the same time saving us from being priggish goody-goodies by their delightful sense of humour, which they passed on to us. They were unique women, but would never have thought themselves so.

By the time the school closed Camilla was married and living in Wiltshire, but she often came back to Plumpton to see her parents and would occasionally go and visit her old teacher. It was an indication of just how much she'd enjoyed Dumbrells and how much she owed the school for her happy start in life. Miss Knowles had followed her progress in the meantime, as she had no doubt followed that of all her favourite pupils. When one of Camilla's contemporaries was picking up a nephew from the school in 1973, Miss Knowles excitedly showed her a copy of the *Tatler* with photographs of Princess Anne's wedding to Mark Phillips. There in the line-up was Camilla.

7

Swinging Sixties

Quite a lot of little girls who are in love with ponies during their pre-teens transfer their affection when they hit puberty to boys – and their ponies are left to languish in the paddock with matted manes. Not so Camilla's; she merely spread the love. Her ponies were replaced by bigger ponies and then horses, but she never lost her passion for them – and they were an important link between her and her father. As Annabel's enthusiasm for horses ebbed away, it was increasingly just the two of them who shared this passion.

But there was room in her heart for boys too. She discovered the attraction of the opposite sex in her early teens. It was all perfectly innocent, but Pony Club dances in Lewes Town Hall and friends' parties suddenly became way more exciting. When the lights dimmed and the tempo changed, everyone started dancing slowly, kissing and doing a bit of exploratory groping. Girls from good, stable families may have read about sex, thought about it, giggled about it with their friends and developed passionate crushes on boys – they may even have fallen in love with one or two of them – but even so, not many girls like Camilla lost their virginity before the age or seventeen or eighteen. And she was no exception, although she did have a first kiss at just twelve or thirteen. She was a pretty girl with a shy dimpled smile and boys found her very attractive.

By her early teens, Camilla was only at home at the weekends and in school holidays. In 1958, at the age of eleven, she had become a weekly boarder at a fashionable London school in Kensington, named after the street in which it was situated, Queen's Gate. The difference between the two schools could not have been more extreme. At Dumbrells, the ambient noise was birdsong and farm animals. At Queen's Gate it was the rumbling of traffic and the bustle of the capital. There were no sheep or cart horses to gaze at out of the window, no gardens to run into at break times, no orchid woods. The nearest open space was Hyde Park, a fifteen-minute walk away across busy roads and through the filth of traffic fumes. But there was a host of museums and other cultural centres on the doorstep. The Natural History Museum, the Science Museum and the Victoria and Albert Museum were just a short walk away; the Royal Albert Hall and the major theatres and galleries were not much further.

Like Dumbrells, Queen's Gate had started off in the founder's home, in Stanhope Gardens, in 1891, but a year later the school moved round the corner into a leased building at 132 Queen's Gate. Its founder was Miss Eleanor Beatrice Wyatt, but she was principal for no more than eight years. The woman who took the school into the twentieth century was Miss Annabel Douglas, an American who had come to the UK as a student. She took the lease of the house next door, no. 133, doubling the capacity, and her own replacement in 1919, Miss Spalding, enlarged it still further by buying no. 131.

Two more houses have been added since then for the junior school but to this day, the school still has its premises in this elegant Victorian terrace, in one of the most sought-after residential areas of London. It is a warren of staircases, mostly small rooms and narrow passageways on five floors. On the face of it, the site is utterly impractical for a school that today has more than 500 pupils, with no playing fields on site and no parking – although who needs playing fields with all those staircases? Yet it has been successfully educating privileged young ladies for 125 years and everyone seems very happy there.

Nowadays, Queen's Gate is as academic as the next school, and in February 2016, the Duchess made a return visit to officially open an impressive new science laboratory in the basement. But in the late 1950s and early 1960s, when she was there as a pupil, there was no real expectation that any girl would go on to university after school or have a career. There were no high-tech science labs – like most public girls' schools at that time, there were wooden benches with bunsen burners, and maybe a diagram of the alimentary canal and a frog or two to be dissected in the biology lab. Girls in all but a few fee-paying schools were very disadvantaged compared to their sisters in state grammar schools. In the private system girls were being prepared for marriage and motherhood – a smattering of European languages, a readiness to do good deeds in the community and an ability to cook and sew were deemed more important than academic qualifications. Girls' education has undergone a revolution in the intervening years, and Camilla just missed it.

Girls who worked hard in those days, moreover, the swots, were definitely not cool. The cool kids mucked about, smoked, drank and bunked off lessons, and they were the ones that had the friends. Camilla was never short of friends and she couldn't have been less interested in the idea of a career. She wasn't itching to travel or see the world and had no desire to go to university. She wasn't ambitious, and she wasn't influenced by her more aspiring contemporaries. She wanted the life her mother and so many of her mother's county friends had. She wanted no more from life than to be happily married to an upper-class man and live a sociable life in the country with horses, dogs, children and someone to look after them all and do the hard graft.

'I cannot believe that Queen's Gate has been going for 125 years,' she said after she'd unveiled a plaque marking her visit in 2016. 'I feel like it's 125 years since I was here. I wish I could say I was a head girl, or even a prefect or captain of games – I was none of those, I might have been in the swimming team. But I do remember I was a boarder here, which I hear now is abolished. I was a weekly boarder and lived right at the top of the school, quite cold, I think we were always made to have the windows open – fresh air.

'I did leave when I was sixteen, I didn't go on to the sixth form. I think in those days we weren't encouraged to go to university. I think the very, very clever girls went on but nobody seemed to give us much inspiration to go on. So we went off and explored the university of life, and Paris and Florence and London.'

She only boarded for the first couple of years. In 1960, Rosalind bought a flat round the corner in Queen's Gate Gardens so Camilla could become a day girl while she and Annabel, who followed her to Queen's Gate, had somewhere to live. To look after the girls, and effectively to chaperone them, she installed an unmarried friend called Cecilia Hay, an interior decorator – and who was nearly sent to an early grave by the experience.

Camilla would often travel up on the train from Lewes at the end of the weekend with Lord Shawcross, who as Sir Hartley Shawcross, KC had made his name as the brilliant chief British prosecutor at the Nuremberg War Crimes Tribunal in 1945–6. He and his wife, Joan, and their children, William (who at that time was very smitten with Camilla), Joanna and Hume, all of a similar age to the Shand children, were close family friends who lived on the other side of Lewes. Joan was herself mad about horses and hunted with Bruce, and the families were regularly in and out of each other's houses. By the end of the 1950s, among Hartley's roles was a directorship of Shell Petroleum, and Joan was invited by the company to launch a new tanker called *Aluco* that had been built in Newcastle. They turned it into a two-family outing, and so grown-ups and children all piled into a Pullman train for a very luxurious journey north, where they stayed in an equally luxurious hotel – one which the love-struck William remembers well.

Camilla left Queen's Gate in 1964 having learnt how to fence, but with just one O level, which given her ability was surprising. Miss Knowles must have wondered what on earth had gone wrong. There were perhaps advantages to having nothing more distracting than Blossom and a herd of Guernseys outside the schoolroom door.

She went home to the country for the summer holidays and, along with Priscilla, took a short cookery course with a former teacher from Constance Spry's domestic science academy who taught from her own house near Lewes. Then, after their birthdays in July – there was just ten days between them – they learnt to drive with the local driving instructor, 'a dreadful old man' who developed piles and had to give up. But not before he had got them both through their tests – which were taken in Brighton – on the second attempt. There followed long lazy days with friends, gossiping by the swimming pool at The Laines, where the roses were all in bloom. Kirsty Aitken, granddaughter of the newspaper baron Lord Beaverbrook, was another schoolmate and close friend. Camilla was never short of friends – or boyfriends. That part of East Sussex had an unusually lively social circle, particularly in the horsey world. A lot of the girls she knew had older brothers, and even if they weren't especially horsey a lot of them had been members of the pony club as children, and had been to all the pony club dances. Camilla attracted them like bees to a honeypot and always had several gangly teenagers pining for her.

The elegant seaside town of Brighton, with its Regency terraces, wide pebble beach and amusement piers, was the local hotspot. They used to go there to the cinema and the theatre, or to hang out in the coffee bars and pubs and buy new releases from the record shops. Camilla was never really into the Beatles but loved the Rolling Stones. Brighton had once, when the railway was built linking it to London in Victorian times, been a very fashionable resort and it was still a lovely town – and since Sussex University had opened there in 1962, it had become younger, more vibrant and edgier. Before anyone could drive, a parent would take them, but when Camilla acquired an admirer a few years older than her, Richard Burgoyne, who owned a snazzy sports car, he drove them. The Shands didn't drive showy cars. Bruce had a little white van with no seats in the back; the children would all pile in, sitting on the metal floor and sliding around. No regulations about seats or seatbelts in those days.

At the end of the summer Camilla was sent off to finishing school in Switzerland, to a place called Mon Fertile on the banks of Lake Geneva – just one of many such schools at that time. It was the standard next step for well-heeled teenagers who were neither destined to go down the academic path nor yet old enough to be launched into the marriage market. Parents who might have been anxious about letting their daughters go abroad on their own at such a young age were reassured by the solid stability of the Swiss and the multilingual culture around Lake Geneva. So for nine months, they were packed off to learn to ski, to perfect their French, and to learn the finer points of etiquette while having fun in a picturesque environment.

Such places have mostly long gone but at that time, they were seen as a crucial step in completing a girl's education. Girls learnt flower arranging, how to cook and sew, dress the table for a formal dinner party and taste wine, as well as basic first aid, child care and domestic accounting. Deportment was also an important part of the curriculum. From Switzerland Camilla went to Paris, to the Institut Britannique, and came away after six months having had a lot of fun but with a lifelong terror of lifts. She was stuck in one, she told me, for seven hours with a friend and two Frenchmen. Her team knows better than to try and put her in one. She will walk up any number of stairs rather than be incarcerated in a lift ever again.

But learning to speak idiomatic French was useful. She made a short speech in the language on her first solo foreign trip, to Paris in May 2013, in her capacity as patron of Emmaus UK, a charity founded in the French capital after the Second World War to help homeless people rebuild their lives. She travelled from London on the Eurostar train, to the surprise of fellow passengers, and joked that it was her first official trip without her husband and may be her last. She took some Emmaus companions, formerly homeless themselves, and in typical style told them how she was dreading the speech. 'If it all goes wrong then I will need you to clap loudly and disguise it,' she said. 'I'll give you all signs to hold up too.'

The signs were not needed. 'I hope you will forgive my rusty French,' she said to a crowded room, 'but it is fifty years since I was a student at the Institut Britannique in Paris.' Speaking slowly at first, she appeared to grow in confidence as she got into it. The verdict was that her pronunciation was very English but her French was faultless.

Camilla never embraced the Swinging Sixties wholeheartedly, as her sister, her brother and most of her contemporaries did, but when she returned to London fully 'finished' in 1965, there was no more exciting place to be. The austerity of the post-war years was finally over, the baby boomers had come of age, they had disposable income, they had ideals and they were wanting a different world from their parents. They were seizing the day and having fun. They marched for CND to ban the bomb; they made love not war; they had student sit-ins and demonstrations; they made their own psychedelic music – the Beatles, the Rolling Stones, the Beach Boys, the Animals, the Hollies, The Who; they bought *Oz*, Richard Neville's countercultural creation, and *Private Eye*, started by Richard Ingrams and friends, two magazines that offended and challenged the Establishment; and they questioned all the conventions that had been drilled into them in their youth.

The men grew out their short back and sides and partings, while men and women alike threw out the conservative clothes their parents wore and dressed themselves in pretty, colourful fabrics, beads, bell-bottoms, culottes, wide belts that were purely decorative, thigh-length boots, floppy hats and shaggy Afghan sheepskin coats. It was Mary Quant who had started the fashion revolution – she became the first person to design specifically for the young and we flocked to Bazaar, her iconic shop in the King's Road, for miniskirts – but others like Ossie Clark, Alice Pollock, Celia Birtwell and Barbara Hulanicki quickly followed, and suddenly fashion was affordable and fun. At the same time Jean Shrimpton, Celia

Hammond, Pattie Boyd and Twiggy – a new breed of model – were showing us how to wear it, how to wear make-up and style our hair. We didn't sit in rollers under great dome dryers as our mothers did; we had our hair cut and blown dry by a new breed of stylist – Leonard of Mayfair, Daniel Galvin and Vidal Sassoon.

London was buzzing. Boutiques and markets sprang up all over but most of the action was in the King's Road in Chelsea and Carnaby Street in Soho. Clubs and coffee shops also opened, places for young people to hang out and meet their friends and listen to up-and-coming musicians and pop groups. Some of Camilla's favourite haunts with her friends were the Stock Pot in the King's Road – where you could eat for peanuts – the Builders Arms in Cale Street and a nightclub in a basement at the bottom of Park Lane.

Camilla was right there in the midst of it all, but remarkably untouched by it. She was never a hippy, but she was no goody-goody; she and her friends had a wild time. She smoked like a chimney, drank her fair share, and loved to party. Priscilla remembers being thrown off a bus by the conductor because she was wearing such a short miniskirt that her knickers were visible. 'The clippy said it was "disgusting". It was before the age of tights and I had on stockings and suspenders. It's now the most embarrassing thing in my life, but that was the era, and of course we didn't mind a bit, we couldn't have cared less. We all went to parties and we all behaved badly all the time. The Sixties music was more fun than anything.'

But Camilla was never into flower power or drugs, and her style of dressing remained surprisingly conservative, given the cornucopia of variety that was out there. Bohemian she was not. The year when the real partying began was the year she came out, and the year she met her cavalry officer, who was eight years older than her and never the sort of man who would have been influenced by the counterculture. Thereafter, she was locked into a very conservative world; and she felt comfortable there. She found herself a couple of temporary jobs, one of them more temporary than she intended. She joined Colefax and Fowler, the exclusive interior design company, as one of several well-bred assistants, and didn't last the week. When she turned up late for work one day her boss, Tom Parr, a difficult man prone to explosions of rage, sacked her on the spot. Imogen Taylor, now in her nineties, who had considerably more sticking power – she was head designer for fifty years – wrote in her memoirs, *On the Fringe*, 'There were a lot of debutantes working for us, including Camilla. She worked for us for a moment, but then got the sack.' She wasn't alone. 'He would shout and bellow so the building heard every word. He'd roar: "Get out, you silly b***h. Go – leave at once! I can't have people like you in the firm!" when some poor girl had merely folded something the wrong way or done something very minor. The Duchess of Cornwall was one assistant who fell victim to his tantrums – she came in late having been to a dance.'

Camilla couldn't have cared less. But what made everyone at Colefax and Fowler laugh was that she was living at Claridges, hardly a minute's walk away. Her grandmother, Sonia, a very wealthy woman, permanently kept a suite in the luxurious hotel and Camilla had been drying her hair in the window and fallen asleep.

By then, her grandfather was dead and the family fortune had gone to Henry Cubitt, Camilla's uncle and godfather, known as 'Mad Harry', the 4th Baron Ashcombe. He also inherited Denbies. When Rolie died in 1962, the Cubitts were the largest landowners in London after the Westminsters and Cadogans. They owned the whole of Pimlico; there were also vast estates in the South of France and Canada, but Harry was an alcoholic and virtually lost the lot. He moved in glitzier circles than his sister and in the good times had a house in Barbados, where Camilla went for some sunshine in the winter of 1971, taking her friend Virginia Carington with her. Harry was forty-seven and divorced; Virginia was twenty-five and fell for his charms. To everyone's surprise, they married in 1973, but were divorced in 1979. Virginia now works at Clarence House running Charles and Camilla's private diaries.

Harry finally got on top of his addiction and was married a third time to another, much younger, woman, Elizabeth Dent-Brocklehurst, the Kentucky-born widow of his friend Mark. Mark Dent-Brocklehurst had died seven years earlier at the age of forty, leaving her two small children, Henry and Mollie; Sudeley Castle, a large 1,000-year-old property in Gloucestershire; and hefty death duties to be paid. Harry, who had never had any children himself, sold his own house, moved into Sudeley and spent the rest of his life helping to restore the castle, where Henry VIII's widow Katherine Parr died, and turn it into a tourist attraction while working with addiction charities. He died in 2013.

8

Mrs PB

Camilla married Major Andrew Parker Bowles on 4 July 1973, shortly before her twenty-sixth birthday. The summer had been cooler than usual but 4 July was one of the hottest days of the month, with temperatures reaching 27 degrees Celsius. The big, lavish society wedding, with a guard of honour and trumpeters, was held at the Guards Chapel, where her parents had been married, and afterwards at St James's Palace. The guest list included the most illustrious names in the country, amongst them Queen Elizabeth, the Queen Mother, Princess Margaret – the Queen's sister – and Princess Anne. Camilla looked glorious in a traditional long white dress, with a ten-foot train, by Bellville Sassoon, one of her favourite designers. Many of the evening dresses that had passed between her and Lucia Santa Cruz at Stack House were by Bellville Sassoon. Her bridesmaids wore mini-versions of the bridal gown, while the page boys were in nine-teenth-century Blues uniforms. The groom wore a morning suit. He had had a punishing stag party at White's a few nights earlier, which resulted in so much breakage the club couldn't serve lunch the following day.

Camilla and her family had dined and spent the night before the wedding at the Berkeley Hotel in Knightsbridge. And it was from there that she and her father made their way to the chapel the next morning. Bruce was fond of Andrew and made him a director of his wine business, but Rosalind had her reservations. She thought him a snob – he enjoyed his association with the Royal Family a little too much for her taste, and his friends all seemed to have double-barrelled names or titles or baronetcies somewhere in the family. Rosalind was no great lover of royalty – the tales she'd heard from her mother about her own childhood with Alice Keppel and the King were enough to put her off all things upper class and royal for life.

The Prince of Wales was invited to the wedding but didn't come. He was still in the Caribbean and that day he had a commitment in Nassau, representing the Queen at celebrations marking the end of British rule in the Bahamas. He denied it, but it has long been assumed that he stayed away because he couldn't bear to watch the person he loved walk down the aisle with someone else.

In the summer of 1973, Camilla's heart belonged to Andrew, the man so many women had wanted but whom she had successfully bagged. She thought he was everything she looked for in a man and he would give her everything she had dreamed of. He was thirty-three, an alpha male, sophisticated and experienced. She liked the fact that he was a cavalry officer, as her father had been, and that like her father he was brave. He hadn't fought Rommel's tanks, but in 1969 she'd watched him ride in the 129th Grand National, on a horse called The Fossa. It is one of the most dangerous and challenging races over jumps in the world, and out of a field of thirty that year, only fourteen finished. He was eleventh. By comparison, Charles at twenty-four was still a work in progress and would never match Andrew's confidence or his masculinity. It is no surprise that at the time she found him the more appealing.

The newlyweds left for the South of France that afternoon and by way of a short honeymoon spent several idyllic days at Cap d'Ail, staying at La Capponcina, a villa owned by Andrew's uncle, Sir Max Aitken, chairman of Beaverbook newspapers. Afterwards they settled down to married life and a routine of weekdays mostly apart, with Andrew in London, and weekends normally together. Their first house, which they rented for a year while Camilla hunted for something suitable to buy, was near Newbury in Berkshire, not far from Andrew's parents who had recently downsized to White Oak House at Highclere.

After seven years of courtship, Camilla knew the whole family well. She was particularly fond of Andrew's father, Derek Parker Bowles, a former soldier with the Royal Horse Guards, a landowner, Justice of the Peace and High Sheriff of Berkshire. Derek was great-grandson of the 6th Earl of Macclesfield, and a thoroughly likeable man, charm personified. The same could not be said of his wife. Dame Ann was Commissioner of the Commonwealth Girl Guides Association, and was nicknamed 'Rhino', for obvious reasons; she kept Pekingese dogs, and in the early Seventies, Camilla had a relative of one of them called Chang that she loved dearly. Dame Ann was the daughter of the millionaire racehorse owner Sir Humphrey de Trafford, 4th Baronet, and descended from an old English Roman Catholic family. She was a difficult woman who displayed no great love for her eldest son. Andrew nevertheless inherited from her side of the family his passion for horse racing, which has been a lifelong fascination, as a jockey, breeder and spectator – and he took her religion.

Donnington Castle House, where Andrew grew up and the family were living when Camilla first knew him, was an imposing seventeenth-century brick house with a beautiful garden, built as the lodge to a now-ruined fourteenth-century castle. Newbury racecourse was on the doorstep, with more racing at Ascot, polo at Windsor, Goodwood and Cowdray Park, and rowing at Henley – all the traditional upper-class sporting playgrounds an easy distance away – as well as local pheasant shoots. At weekends, the house was invariably filled with Parker Bowles children and their friends, and great fun was always had by all. Derek was a brilliant cook and had two kitchens, one for himself to use and the other for the cook they employed, but the meals everyone remembers were those created by Derek himself. He was also a very good gardener and was a nephew of the great horticulturalist, plantsman and writer, E. A. Bowles. Sadly, Parker Bowles senior had suffered badly from tuberculosis in earlier life and had only half of one lung, and he died in 1977 at the age of sixty-one. Dame Ann lived on for another ten years.

Andrew was the eldest of four; next was his brother, Simon, who also went into the Army and then the wine trade, before founding Green's, the well-known restaurant and oyster bar in St James's. The only girl, Mary Ann, married Nic Paravicini, who after the Army became a merchant banker and dabbled in the property business with Andrew. Their son is the blind, autistic musical genius, Derek Paravicini. Rick, the youngest, was a bloodstock agent and great character but sadly became an alcoholic, and died in 2010 at the age of sixty-three.

Camilla and Nic both loved Derek Parker Bowles and got on with him famously, but neither of them could cope with their mother-in-law, and it became a running joke about which of them was more in favour. Camilla would say, 'You're leading at the moment, I'm right at the bottom.' But the next time they saw each other their status would be reversed. She would laugh her deep laugh about it and pull faces; laughter is her way of coping with every difficulty.

Camilla found a house to buy near Chippenham in Wiltshire, about an hour west from Newbury, and she and Andrew moved there in 1974, when Camilla was pregnant with their first child. Tom Henry Charles was born on 18 December 1974. Bolehyde Manor was a big medieval property in the village of Allington, just south of the M4 motorway. It was ideal for Andrew, with London less than two hours away by car and a fast, mainline station nearby. There were good schools in the locality, and they had friends in the area. But a big attraction for Camilla was that it was just inside Beaufort country, the oldest and biggest fox hunt in England. Andrew hunted occasionally but he didn't find it particularly interesting – his enthusiasm was for racing and polo – but Camilla had hunted since she was a little girl with her father. And like her father, if she wasn't curled up with a good book, she wanted to be on a horse.

Bruce had learnt to ride at Rugby but his hunting career began as a young cavalry officer, in the pre-war years when there was a good railway network and people travelled all over the country in pursuit of sport – even more than they do today. Strong friendships were forged at Sandhurst, and in soldiering generally – and the upper classes at that time still had large country houses and sporting estates, where friends congregated for weekends. Bruce frequently found himself at Dauntsey Park, in north Wiltshire, where his friends Hugh and Joyce Brassey lived. Brassey was a fellow officer and hunting enthusiast and the house was in the heart of the Duke of Beaufort's hunting estates. After the war, in 1949, they had moved from the big house, but were still living in north Wiltshire and the friendship and the visits continued. When Camilla and Andrew moved to Bolehyde, her father no longer needed the Brasseys' as a base – he stayed and hunted with his daughter instead – but they often came to dinner with her father afterwards.

Camilla gave great dinner parties – her time in Switzerland had not been wasted. A house filled with friends, good food and good wine was what she had grown up with and what she loved, and Andrew was the same. Initially they started off rather grandly with a Portuguese couple doing the work, but after a year they decided it was a waste of money. Unless it was a big dinner party, when she would bring in a cook who lived in the neighbouring village of Tockenham, Camilla thereafter did the cooking. She was good at it – her roast chicken is legendary. But she sticks to what she knows, which is mostly plain English fare with lots of home-grown vegetables. And there was a big, productive vegetable garden at Bolehyde to raid, as well as an enviable fruit garden.

Bolehyde was centuries old, with a resident ghost. Camilla was typically unfazed. She would joke about how she'd be sitting on the sofa watching television, and the ghost would come and sit beside her and would change the channels. She never saw it, but she could feel it next to her, and she would laugh about how she and the ghost always wanted to watch different programmes.

The house was Grade II* listed, which meant it was of significant historic value, originally dating back to the early fourteenth century. There had been later additions but none were much later than the seventeenth century, so it's not surprising the ghost felt proprietorial. For a house of its size and importance, the approach to it was insignificant – the driveway was no more than 20 yards long, and the front of the house was clearly visible from the lane. But it was an imposing house nevertheless, built of Cotswold stone with three front gables, mullioned windows and a distinctive square stone porch with a stone balustrade above it. There were four reception rooms, each with stone-flagged floors and big open fireplaces, but the kitchen – designed, like that of The Laines, for staff to work in – was tucked away at the back with no view. Upstairs there were eight bedrooms – with a further three bedrooms in an annexe where, after Tom was born, a nanny lived. She was the only live-in help they had after the Portuguese couple left. The first nanny, Georgina, didn't last, but Mary, who replaced her, was with them for years and is still a good friend. She comes to the party Camilla gives at Clarence House every June for her grandchildren and the children and grandchildren of friends.

The house had 200 acres of land, stables, a big distinctive garden, a swimming pool, a tennis court, a seventeenth-century stone dovecot, outhouses and two stone summerhouses that flanked the original driveway. It was a magnificent place to live, steeped in history, but it was big and expensive to run, constantly in need of maintenance and repair – and the listing meant that nothing either inside or outside could be altered without planning permission. The garden was a great feature of the property –

beyond the formal gardens and stone-slabbed pathways there were sculpted yew hedges, statuary, and expanses of manicured lawn leading to lovely views over open countryside – but it was divided up by a patchwork of stone walls, which couldn't be moved because of the planning restrictions, so there was very little scope for change and, like the house itself, it took a great deal of maintenance.

Camilla didn't have the gardening bug when she was growing up but, when they moved to Bolehyde, it became her therapy. Andrew was already a gardening enthusiast and he prided himself on his greenhouse and the houseplants he cultivated. He would say Camilla didn't do much more than dead-head the roses – and only then because, when he went off to London for the week, he would leave her lists of things to do in his absence. She and her friends used to laugh about the lists – most of which she ignored.

Camilla was not built for work in those days – she did the bare minimum she could get away with – but she was a good homemaker and an excellent mother. Like the kitchen, the rest of the house was dark inside because of the leaded windows and low ceilings, an effect intensified by the profusion of oak panelling, but she had a good eye for colour and brightened it up. She furnished it as her own childhood home had been furnished, with a mixture of antique and modern pieces, using pretty fabrics, plenty of table lamps and good rugs. There were books everywhere, and dozens of prints, paintings, cartoons and photographs on the walls, while silver boxes, framed photographs and other knick-knacks covered all available surfaces. Vases of fresh flowers and pot plants were a regular feature. Definitely shabby-chic rather than – to use her expression – 'tickety boo', it was a comfortable and happy home for her own children to grow up in.

What's more, she made sure that Tom and his sister Laura Rose, born on 1 January 1978, had the security of living in one place. Most Army families move from pillar to post and live on military bases, uprooting their children from schools and friends every time they are transferred. But Camilla was not a regular Army wife. She refused either to live in married quarters or to move from one posting to another, which may not have done much for Andrew's progression up the regimental ranks but did ensure that they all had a happy home life.

And to most outsiders, they did appear to be a very happy family. Everyone who knew them well was aware of Andrew's serial unfaithfulness to Camilla, but it was passed off as a bit of a joke. One friend who sat next to him at dinner one night said, 'I'm really hurt, Andrew. I'm the only one of Camilla's friends you haven't made a pass at. What's wrong with me?' Those friends he did make a play for showed scant loyalty, yet she never seemed to blame them or make great scenes with Andrew. He and she were competitive with one another but there was never a tense atmosphere in the house, no barbed comments or bitter exchanges. They teased each other, and seemed to outsiders to have a good, healthy rapport. Andrew's affairs were just a fact of life and not something she often spoke about.

It was only those very closest to her who knew quite how standoffish and cold he could be towards her, and how deeply, bitterly hurt she was by his infidelity. She loved Andrew – for reasons that her family could never entirely fathom – and longed to be truly loved by him, and she didn't feel she was. There was always someone prettier, wittier, sexier, waiting to take him away from her. And because he spent his weekdays in London, he was never short of the opportunity to do as he pleased. Today, looking back, he would admit there is truth in that. If blame was to be apportioned for the way the marriage ended, he would feel obliged to take a full 80 per cent of it. Love her though he does, he would also admit that Camilla was more in love with him than he was with her.

For some years, when they were both in the Army, he and his brother-in-law Nic Paravicini shared an office, and a flat too – the same flat off Ebury Street that Camilla had shared with Virginia Carington. Although they were both married, they led a bachelor existence, and had a code involving empty milk bottles. Arranged in a certain way outside the door, these meant 'Do not disturb.' Nic would say Andrew arranged the milk bottles more often than he did. And still, as often as not, the women Andrew was seeing were Camilla's friends.

For all the hurt, it would never have occurred to her to divorce him. She had been brought up to believe that you stuck at things, you didn't give up. And so she found ways of coping. Hunting was one way; galloping amongst a cavalcade of horses, any one of which might bite or kick or take a tumble, left no time for thinking. And in the summer when the hunting season came to an end, her escape was to bury herself in her garden. She saw friends and family, and there were the children to keep her busy as she took them to and from nursery and then school, to parties and the cinema, to see their grandparents in Plumpton or Annabel and her children, Ben, Alice and Catherine Elliot, in Dorset.

Bruce and Rosalind were tremendous grandparents and the cousins loved going to stay with them. The initials of each of them, crafted out of round stones, are cemented into the path in the vegetable garden at The Laines to this day. They went there at Christmas and Easter, and every summer Bruce and Rosalind paid for the entire family to spend a fortnight in the Grand Hotel Excelsior on Ischia, a tiny volcanic island south-west of Naples in Italy. Andrew was never keen on the sun and would spend his time, observed one of them cattily, inside writing postcards to duchesses and all his other titled friends. But the children loved it. Every day the routine was the same. They went down to the beach with their mothers for the morning, a doughnut for elevenses, back to the hotel to meet everyone for lunch, a general knowledge quiz, a siesta, a game of tennis on the clay courts, and back to find Bruce and Rosalind on their second Negroni. They did that every year until the children were in their teens.

Camilla never set out to be unfaithful to Andrew. She flirted for sure, because that was the way she was, a twinkly, sexy woman with a husky laugh that men adored. Everyone, indeed, adored her – men, women and children – because she was a life force and said outrageously funny things, but she no more wanted an open marriage than to fly to the moon. But as the years went by, she realised that Andrew would never change, would never love her and cherish her, never make her feel good about herself; and inevitably, the confidence that had been her hallmark throughout her childhood started to crumble. What had made her so strong as a child was the absolute certainty that her parents loved her and the absolute security that came from that certainty. She never, ever had that feeling with Andrew. She lived with a permanent knot of dread in her tummy, that one day he might leave her. It left her very vulnerable to the attentions of a suitor.

9

The Attentions of a Prince

Charles had been heartbroken when he lost Camilla, but however strong his feelings for her, life had to go on. He was a romantic, but he was not the first man to have been disappointed in love and not the first to have had to learn to live with it. He was young, he was attractive, he was eminently eligible and he took out a succession of pretty girls, some of them suitable, some not – and some too sensible to want a future under the spotlight. He proposed to Amanda Knatchbull. Mountbatten had been urging his grand-daughter on Charles since she was a teenager, but they knew each other too well. She turned him down. He wasn't surprised; he knew that any girl he married would have to make huge sacrifices. Even those he dated risked having their past raked over in the tabloids. The press were obsessed by his love life: they chronicled every sighting, every dinner date, every holiday companion, every girl who showed up to watch him play polo. One news-paper exclusively reported his engagement to Princess Marie Astrid of Luxembourg, whom he had never even met.

He hated it. He resented the intrusion and he despaired of ever finding someone. He knew she would have to meet the strict and increasingly rare criteria his position demanded. More than a decade after the advent of the contraceptive pill and the era of free love, the pool of unmarried, aristo-cratic Anglican virgins available was diminishing by the day. In 1975, he had said, 'I've fallen in love with all sorts of girls and I fully intend to go on doing so, but I've made sure I haven't married the first person I've fallen in love with. I think one's got to be aware of the fact that falling madly in love with someone is not necessarily the starting point to getting married.' But he had made the mistake of saying he thought thirty might be the right age to settle down. As he approached the magical age, the scrutiny and the madness and his despair intensified.

If he was seen with women married to his friends, however, or old girlfriends who were now married, no one seemed to turn a hair. Not unlike in Edwardian times, they slipped beneath the radar, and although the press had their suspicions about some and were certain about others, they never pursued them in the way they pursued single women. One of those was Dale (later Lady) Tryon, a vivacious Australian he'd met at a school dance at Timbertop in Australia when they were both seventeen. He'd nicknamed her Kanga. She was the daughter of a rough and ready Melbourne printing magnate, so she was rich but not marriage material. She moved to London and in 1973 married the merchant banker Anthony Tryon, one of the Prince's oldest friends and sometime financial adviser. He was ten years older than Dale, a far more sober character who would become the 3rd Baron Tryon. His father had been Keeper of the Privy Purse, a key member of the royal household and, like Andrew Parker Bowles, a page boy at the Queen's coronation. Charles became godfather to their elder son, also named Charles, born in 1976. They had another son and two daughters. As well as a house in London, they owned a 700-acre estate in Wiltshire and rented a fishing lodge in Iceland. Charles was a frequent visitor to all three. Dale called him the 'Bonny Prince' and whenever he telephoned to say he was on his way to see her, she cleared the house.

One year, Anthony had gone ahead to Iceland with a mutual friend, Timothy (later 5th Baron) Tollemache. Dale and the Prince flew separately in an Andover of the Queen's Flight and were so engrossed with each other in the private compartment, where they had asked to be left undisturbed, that they failed to notice the plane had landed at Reykjavik and that outside a red carpet and a civic reception awaited, complete with Icelandic military band. Kanga kept their affair secret from no one and had an open line to Nigel Dempster, the *Daily Mail*'s famous gossip columnist, who was a fellow Australian. She started up a fashion label in 1980, selling one-size-fits-all dresses, and constantly promoted them and herself by selling stories about her royal connections.

In the end this was her undoing. Charles started ignoring her, and she became almost demented with the pain of losing him – and she hated Camilla, whose star was in the ascendant. 'Kanga adored him,' says a close friend in the fashion industry who helped launch her brand. 'Whenever he rang the office she would disappear. She was very funny and completely outrageous and unbelievably naughty sexually. When she was nice she was fantastic and when she was nasty she was horrendous. She was like a spoilt child, living on the edge, everything was extreme and there was always drink in the equation.'

Camilla was none of those things. Charles spent many a weekend with the Parker Bowles family. It was inevitable that they would continue to see one another. They had so many friends in common, and they went to so many of the same sporting and social gatherings. And, of course, there was polo. Charles and Andrew still played in the same team and were friends, and since a lot of the matches were held in the Wiltshire/Gloucestershire area, it was logical for Charles to stay the night at Bolehyde, when as often as not Camilla would get together a party of his friends for dinner. Because of Andrew's royal links, there were often invitations from the Queen and the Queen Mother as well as from the Prince himself. The couple went to stay at Sandringham and Balmoral, they went racing at Ascot and Cheltenham, and they were always invited to the lavish parties the Queen Mother used to throw at Royal Lodge in Windsor Great Park or to her Scottish homes, Birkhall and the Castle of Mey, way up in the north. Andrew was a great favourite of the Queen Mother, and she approved of his new wife. So did the Queen; Camilla got on famously with Elizabeth. Their mutual love of horses and dogs was a winning formula.

When Tom was born, Andrew and Camilla asked the Prince to be their son's godfather, which further cemented the relationship between them all. The christening took place at the Guards Chapel, and they specially arranged the date to fit in with the Prince's naval schedule so he could be there. Charles left the Navy in 1977 having commanded his own ship, HMS *Bronington*, hunting mines in the North Sea. It was the year of the Queen's Silver Jubilee, and the beginning of his full-time royal duties.

It was also the year he dated Diana's eldest sister, the fiery, red-haired Lady Sarah Spencer. They had met at Windsor Castle, whither she'd been invited by the Queen for Royal Ascot. The Parker Bowleses had also been invited – Camilla was pregnant with Laura for most of that year. And it was while Charles was shooting at Althorp, the Spencer family's estate in Northamptonshire, in the autumn, that he first consciously met Diana, who was just sixteen and home from boarding school. She said later, 'I kept out of the way. I remember being a fat, podgy, no make-up, unsmart lady but I made a lot of noise and he liked that and he came up to me after dinner and we had a big dance … for someone like that to show you any attention – I was just so sort of amazed. Why would anyone like him be interested in me? And it *was* interest.'

That was the moment when she first started to dream about marrying the Prince of Wales. Her sister's relationship with Charles came to an abrupt end. 'He is fabulous as a person,' announced Sarah, 'but I am not in love with him. He is a romantic who falls in love easily … Our relationship is totally platonic. I do not believe that Prince Charles wants to marry yet. He has still not met the person he wants to marry. I think of him as the big brother I never had … I wouldn't marry anyone I didn't love, whether it was the dustman or the King of England. If he asked me I would turn him down.'

Publicly bruising comments like that did nothing for the Prince's fragile ego. And where better to seek solace for life's knocks, setbacks and dilemmas than with Camilla, who might laugh and tease him but would do so gently and kindly, almost in a maternal way, and who was loyal to her bootstraps. He would speak to her on the phone for hours, pouring his heart out, or write her long expansive letters – all of them handwritten with a fountain pen in black ink. His head was always buzzing with ideas and torturous thoughts about life and his curiously ill-defined role in it. They always had plenty to talk about, as they always would; conversation came easily between them and they shared the same sense of the ridiculous. She didn't falsely flatter him, she wasn't angling for anything, and she was one of the few people who'd never been in awe of his status. She treated him like a normal person, as she had when they were together, and if ever he behaved badly, or was selfish or thoughtless, she wasn't afraid to tell him so. She was a proper friend.

When they'd first known one another, Charles didn't hunt, but in the intervening years he had discovered the sport and found it thrilling. The Queen never hunted – her interest, like her mother's, was racing – but her father, King George VI, had been a great enthusiast, as was his father, and on back through the generations. Charles on the other hand had grown up playing his father's game, polo. He absolutely loved it, but it is a summer sport; and so, encouraged by Lieutenant Colonel Sir John Miller, the Queen's Crown Equerry, he wrote to the Duke of Beaufort in 1974, asking if he could join his famous hounds for a day.

The Duke of Beaufort's foxhounds are one of the few remaining private packs of hounds in the country, although since the ban in 2004, they now set out to follow trails and not foxes. They are also the most prestigious. They live very luxuriously in kennels on the Badminton House estate, the Duke's magnificent ancestral home in Gloucestershire, where hounds have been kennelled since 1640, and have pedigree records dating back fifty-four generations to the mid-1700s. They hunt over 760 square miles of south Gloucestershire and north Wiltshire, much of it owned by the Duke – and while they are deadly for a fox, they are some of the softest animals you will ever come across.

The 10th Duke laid on an extra meet with some friends specially for the Prince's benefit. He found it 'exciting', 'challenging' and 'dangerous', an 'extraordinary thrill', and became passionate about it. The Queen's advisers were anxious he would upset the anti-bloodsports lobby, but she thought him old enough to make up his own mind, and so Charles continued to hunt. After the ban in England and Wales, neither he nor Camilla, nor his sons, could be seen to break the law and none of them has hunted since. But for many years before that, he and Sir John travelled the country in search of the best packs to ride out with – always unannounced. He didn't want to antagonise the saboteurs, so he seldom attended the meet. He would make arrangements with the Master to join the hunt five or ten minutes after they had moved off, and rather than jostle alongside the rest of the field, he would get special dispensation to ride up at the front with the huntsman.

The polo season was all over by September, when the polo ponies were turned out to grass for a well-earned rest, and the hunters that had spent the summer idly munching grass were trotted round the lanes to get them fit for the hunting season. This started with cub hunting in August, which allowed the huntsmen to train inexperienced young hounds to follow the scent. Proper hunting began in October and ran through the winter until March or April, leaving just a month before the polo season began again.

Hunting is a highly dangerous sport and because of that inspires great camaraderie, so that even if Camilla went hunting alone she would always be amongst friends, everyone looking out for one another. Horses are heavy, strong and unpredictable. A hundred and one things can go wrong, and it takes just one to consign a rider to a wheelchair for the rest of their days, or worse. It's no wonder they start the day with a stirrup cup of sloe gin before moving off. And there is a social side to hunting that has nothing to do with horses; it includes an annual hunt ball, which is the highlight of the season and an opportunity for great drunkenness and for all the simmering sexual tension built up in the saddle to find an outlet.

Camilla is a highly competent horsewoman. She has no fear on a horse, she is completely at one with the animal and apart from once falling and breaking her collar bone, she has never had any serious accidents, but she's never been a risk-taker. As in life, so in hunting. She would take the day at a gentle pace and never leap blindly over any obstacle that presented itself. She jumped if it was necessary, but if something looked dangerous and there was the option of an open gate instead, she would take it. And she only ever hunted one horse, so she would go home when her horse was tired, usually in the early afternoon.

Charles was a very different rider, as men often are. He rode his horses hard, pushing himself and his mounts to the limit. He went for the biggest and most difficult jumps, and because he came to the sport so late in life, he took a lot of falls in the early days. He needed to feel the fear and worked off a lot of his demons on the back of a horse. He invariably had a fresh animal waiting at the rendezvous point halfway through the day, by which time his first horse would be very tired.

Charles rode his polo ponies in the same way, taking risks and sometimes suffering terrible falls. And on the ski slopes he was no different. He always went for the most difficult routes down a mountain, pushing himself to the limit – only feeling truly alive, perhaps, when the adrenalin was pumping. It is all part of his complexity. He is who he is by accident of birth; he is famous, he is revered, he attracts crowds of people wherever he goes, but not because he's the fastest man on earth or the highest jumper, the most talented actor, the most gifted singer or the most astonishing chef. He is famous because he is the Queen's son and he will one day be King, and no matter what he does with his life, he will be remembered in history books and studied in centuries to come. He happens to have done a huge amount of good in his adult life – building Poundbury is just one small part of it – and there will be plenty to fill those history books, but that is not why he is famous. His fame is entirely vacuous – that is his curse – and something with which he has always struggled to come to terms and one of the reasons, no doubt, why he has constantly sought approval.

10

An Education

Charles's parents have always been remote. The Queen acceded to the throne when he was just three years old, and as a young mother she had no choice but to demote her family to second place. Thanks to the demands of the job, she and her husband were abroad for months at a time and there was no thought of taking their children with them.

Times have changed and lessons have been learned. Charles's grandchildren, Prince George and Princess Charlotte, often travel with their parents, William and Kate, the Duke and Duchess of Cambridge, and they are a star attraction; but in the 1950s, this seemed impractical and unthinkable. Charles and his sister Anne, two years his junior, were left behind with their nanny, the terrifying Helen Lightbody, in the care of their grandmother, Queen Elizabeth the Queen Mother. This is how the Prince of Wales developed such an enduring affection for his grandmother and why his relationship with his mother and father is more distant. And the Duke of Edinburgh was tough on Charles.

Prince Philip had his naval career taken away from him on the death of King George VI in 1952. From that day forward he has played second fiddle to his wife – something that did not come naturally. He has made the most of it, working tirelessly to support the Queen, and he has a raft of achievements under his belt, not least the Duke of Edinburgh's Award Scheme, which recently celebrated its sixtieth year and is now run in forty-eight countries. He has also been a prime mover in the field of conservation and technology and is responsible for cutting waste and helping to streamline the monarchy. He is often thought of as an irascible and reactionary old fool who always puts his foot in it, but he is about as foolish as a fox; and has been known to reduce grown men to tears with his cutting remarks and bullying attitude. Charles's sister Anne was a tough proposition and the apple of her father's eye. But Charles, the eldest, the heir, a small, shy and sensitive child, was often a victim and was easily bullied; he was a disappointment.

In private, Philip's role was more traditional. As paterfamilias, he modernised and managed the estates at Windsor, Sandringham and Balmoral, and he made the decisions about the children's education. He decided that Gordonstoun, his own alma mater, would toughen Charles up. So rather than sending him to Eton, across the bridge from Windsor Castle, where he would have been with friends and close to home – his grand-mother's choice for him – he was dispatched at the age of thirteen to the north of Scotland, to a notoriously spartan and harsh regime on the banks of the Moray Firth, where he was hundreds of miles from home and utterly miserable. He slept in a large dormitory with no carpets on the floor and no creature comforts. He went on early morning runs, whatever the weather, dressed in nothing but a pair of shorts, and into a cold shower at the end. At night the windows had to be kept wide open, so boys whose beds were close by would sometimes wake up with rain or snow on their covers. He was bullied by the other boys – kicked and punched on the rugby pitch, where he never excelled, and hit by his roommates in his dormitory at night for snoring. And he was picked on by the assistant housemaster, who was no great lover of the British monarchy. Apart from Norton Romsey, a cousin who was in a different year and whom he scarcely knew, he was friendless. As he wrote in a heartbreaking letter, 'I don't like it much here, I simply dread going to bed as I get hit all night long ... I can't stand being hit on the head by a pillow now.' And in another the same year he wrote, 'It's absolute hell here most of the time and I wish I could come home.'

His father was unmoved by Charles's plight, and seldom saw his son during term time. Gordonstoun had been the making of Philip when he was growing up and he was convinced it should be the making of Charles. He had given instructions to the headmaster and housemaster that Charles was to be treated just like every other boy, allowed no special dispensations.

Philip's childhood had been difficult and punctuated by loss, and he had no patience with his son who had grown up with the security and comforts that he himself had never known.

After two long unhappy years, Charles did eventually come to terms with Gordonstoun and make a few friends – he would occasionally cycle to Elgin on a four-seater bicycle with his cousin and a couple of older boys, singing lewd songs – but he was always a misfit. He was square, to use an old-fashioned term, old for his years and far more comfortable in the company of adults than boys of his own age. He didn't swear, he wasn't crude, he wasn't loud, rowdy or physical as most of the others were. He wore his hair in a neat parting to the side, when most people had floppy Beatles styles, and he was not into pop music or sport or any of the things that interested the other boys. He liked classical music, and while others were fiddling around with guitars and drum kits, Charles took up the cello. What he did discover, however, was a talent for acting, and he was a brilliant mimic. His all-time favourite radio programme was the comedy show *The Goons*, with Peter Sellers, Spike Milligan, Harry Secombe and Michael Bentine, and he could imitate the lot of them to perfection. He also learnt to mimic some of the members of staff at Gordonstoun to good effect. Those were the only times, when pretending to be someone else, that he lost his awkwardness and spoke with confidence and presence.

At seventeen, his A level course was interrupted while he spent six months in the Australian bush to allow the Commonwealth to play some part in the future King's education. It was another baptism by fire for the awkward, shy Prince, but as Sir David Checketts, who travelled with him, said on their return, 'I took out a boy, I came back with a man.'

Charles never lost the dread he felt at the beginning of each term but – call it Stockholm syndrome, perhaps – he was able to speak well of the school, looking back, and it was no doubt a big influence on the man he is today. It may even explain why he and Camilla have such different views on the ideal temperature for a room. She lights fires and he goes around opening windows.

It was the character of the general education there – Kurt Hahn's principles; an education which tried to balance the physical and mental with the emphasis on self-reliance to develop a rounded human being. I did not enjoy school as much as I might have, but that was because I am happier at home than anywhere else. But Gordonstoun developed my will-power and self-control, helped me to discipline myself, and I think that discipline, not in the sense of making you bath in cold water, but in the Latin sense – giving shape and form and tidiness to your life – is the most important thing your education can do.

By the late 1970s, Bolehyde was the home Charles felt happiest in. Camilla had become quite simply his best friend. He drew from her strength and felt safe and comfortable around her. He loved that he could talk to her so openly and honestly about everything, knowing that it would go no further. She had no columnist on speed dial, she made him feel good about himself, as his grandmother did, and she was interested and encouraging about all that he was trying to do. In the years after the Navy, he'd struggled to find a role for himself – there is no job description for an heir to the throne – and he was pulled in different directions by the people advising him. The Palace establishment wanted to rein in his natural inclination to take an interest in social problems, while others were urging him to follow his instincts to support disadvantaged young people – he set up the Prince's Trust for this purpose – and to get involved in all that was going on outside the Palace gates. He agonised about how he might be most useful and had already discovered that his attempts to help were not universally appreciated.

Bolehyde was the place to which he could retire to lick his wounds. His friendship with Camilla was purely platonic. He simply enjoyed being in a normal home, being around her and her children. Friends of Camilla's would arrive at the house and find him sitting on the floor watching television with the children – and do a double-take when they realised who it was. He had always loved children, ever since his brothers, Prince Andrew and Prince Edward, eleven and fifteen years his junior, were small. It was for them he wrote *The Old Man of Lochnagar*.

Camilla became increasingly pleased to see him. It boosted her morale to be with someone who in turn was pleased to see her, who was kind to her and appreciated her. Charles has some blind spots but overall he is a sensitive character, much more in touch with his emotions than most men, much better able to express them, which is precisely what irritates his father so much. He is not the man the Duke expected his first-born son to be –

and six years of extreme hardship, morning runs and cold showers hadn't made him one.

Just as the Shand family jokingly wondered where Camilla had come from, the Royal Family must have sometimes wondered whether the Prince of Wales was a changeling. Compared with the rest of the family, he is a thoroughly Renaissance man, moved by beauty, music and art in a way that largely passes his parents, his siblings and his sons by. He may love dogs and horses, he may have been an enthusiast of hunting, shooting and fishing in his time, he may have done his share of playing Action Man, but his interests and his thirst for knowledge extend way beyond country and military pursuits. He's also deeply spiritual.

In the mid-1970s, he had fallen under the spell of the Afrikaner mystic and writer Laurens van der Post, who encouraged him in his spirituality and flattered him, something the Prince has always been susceptible to. The two men travelled to Kenya in 1977 and went walking in the Aberdare Mountains, locked in deep philosophical debate about the natural world and the 'old world of the spirit'. The seventy-year-old had been a friend and disciple of Carl Jung and introduced Charles to some of his writings about dreams and the 'collective unconscious'.

Van der Post was variously hailed a prophet and a charlatan, but as a storyteller he was mesmerising, especially on the subject of the lost bushmen of the Kalahari Desert. He was widely discredited after his death in 1996, but for the Prince he was the genuine article and had a profound influence on his young protégé. A line from one of his books, *The Heart of the Hunter*, particularly spoke to Charles: 'We suffer from a hubris of the mind. We have abolished superstition of the heart only to install a superstition of the intellect in its place.' He urged the Prince to withdraw from the world for a period, to cancel his public engagements so he might contemplate the inner life of the soul. The Prince's sense of duty prevailed – which was just as well, as this would surely have been the final straw for his bemused father – but he did continue his search for 'an inner world of truth', and Van der Post continued to be a close friend for the rest of his life. Despite his age, he was also invited to be one of Prince William's godfathers.

Camilla shared a lot of the Prince's enthusiasms, but this was never one of them. She is not a spiritual being at all; she is thoroughly grounded. Her element would surely be Earth, if she believed in the elements. According to one definition this 'Has cleaning power. It symbolizes prosperity, fertility, stability, orderliness, groundedness, sustenance, creativity, physical abundance, nourishment, solidity, dependability, security, permanence, intuition, introspection and wisdom.' She has all the properties, except perhaps the orderliness – and the introspection.

As time went by the nature of their relationship changed and in 1978 or early 1979, after the birth of Laura, they became lovers. This had not been in Camilla's game plan when she married Andrew. She was not a natural adulteress and there had been no other men in her life apart from the Prince of Wales in all the years she had been with Andrew, despite his flagrant adultery; but she was tired of sitting at home in the country while he played around with other women. It was high time he knew how it felt. When he discovered what was happening, Andrew didn't make a fuss. He was obviously in no position to complain, but there are some who would say that a part of him quite enjoyed the fact that his wife was sleeping with the future King; he might have felt differently had it been a travelling salesman.

Whatever the truth of that, Andrew wasn't overly worried about Camilla's affair. Everyone knew that Charles was sleeping with Dale and one or two others. He was not the jealous sort, and he assumed that there was never any danger that it might bring an end to their marriage, any more than his affairs would. He knew Camilla was flattered by the Prince's adoration, but he didn't think she was in love with him and knew perfectly well that Charles could never marry her. He needed a bride but not one who was a divorcee.

So life went on much as it had before. The Prince still came to stay with the couple, they all went racing together, to polo, to parties and dinners and balls. They all behaved in a typically upper-class fashion, as if nothing had happened. There were no rows in the house, nothing that upset the children or gave them any cause for concern.

The children were Camilla's priority and she was very discreet, but it wasn't long before other people had their suspicions. The Prince is cursed by the need to have personal protection officers (PPOs) with him at all times, and he also has a team of people to look after him, plan logistics and organise his diary, even his social diary. He can do nothing without someone knowing where he is and who he's seeing, and the royal court is a hotbed of gossip, as it always has been, and always will be.

Some of those closest to him began to voice their suspicions that Camilla had been added to the list of women who were more than just friends. Members of his own family picked up on it and warned that if news got out, it could be very damaging, not just to him as Prince of Wales but also to the institution. The days had long gone when princes could flagrantly exercise a royal droit de seigneur and sleep with other men's wives, as Edward VII had done, and the once compliant press could no longer be relied upon to protect the crown from scandal. The Royal Family had become the model for modern cohesive family life – even if it was, in reality, as fallible as the rest of society. The Queen had married for love and so had her father before her. The age-old convention of royal marriages of convenience and marriages arranged for dynastic reasons no longer applied. But Charles was too dependent to be warned off by the risk of discovery.

11

A Suitable Bride

The affair between Charles and Camilla changed nothing. Divorce was an even bigger taboo than having a past or failing to be quite blue-blooded enough. It had been Edward VIII's determination to marry a divorced woman, Mountbatten would remind Charles, that had caused such mayhem forty-odd years earlier. He was worried that Charles had a selfish streak like the Duke of Windsor, and had written to him warning against 'beginning on the downward slope which wrecked your Uncle David's life and led to his disgraceful abdication and his futile life ever after'.

Mountbatten was Charles's guide in all things, but in August 1979 that special relationship came to a terrible end. While out in a small fishing boat with his family off the west coast of Ireland, Mountbatten was assassinated by an IRA bomb. He, his fourteen-year-old grandson, Nicholas, and a young Irish boy who helped with the boat were killed instantly. His daughter, Patricia, and her husband John (Lord and Lady Brabourne), Nicholas's twin brother Timothy and Lord Brabourne's mother Doreen, Lady Brabourne, were horribly injured but alive. Lady Brabourne senior survived the night but died the next day.

Charles was in Iceland fishing with the Tryons when he heard the news, and wrote in his journal, 'A mixture of desperate emotions swept over me – agony, disbelief, a kind of wretched numbness … Life has to go on, I suppose, but this afternoon I must confess I wanted it to stop. I felt supremely useless and powerless … I have lost someone infinitely special in my life; someone who showed enormous affection, who told me unpleasant things I didn't particularly want to hear, who gave praise where it was due as well as criticism; someone to whom I knew I could confide anything and from whom I would receive the wisest of counsel and advice.'

If ever there was a time that Charles needed love, strength and support it was in the following days, weeks and months, and it came from many quarters. After the funeral, in Westminster Abbey, he took himself off to Balmoral with his grief. He went for long, lonely walks, drawing on his faith and all his inner reserves, desperately trying to make sense of the tragedy. Although Mountbatten wasn't ready for death, he had been nearly eighty and dreaded the frailty of old age, but what sense did it make for Nicholas, who was only fourteen, to lose his life when he had barely begun it? Norton Romsey and his fiancée, Penelope Eastwood, joined Charles, and although they had never been particularly close at Gordonstoun, the tragedy brought the cousins closer together. Amanda Knatchbull joined them too. Laurens van der Post and the Queen Mother proved great towers of strength but so too did Camilla, who easily slipped into the nurturing role of comforter and confidante. She was so much more than a lover and he leaned heavily on her.

It was a year later that he met Lady Diana Spencer once more, and some remarks she made about Mountbatten's death made him look again at her. They were both weekend guests of Robert and Philippa de Pass at Petworth in Sussex. Charles was playing polo at Cowdray Park and after the game everyone went back to the house for a barbecue. Sitting next to him on a hay bale, Diana said, 'You looked so sad when you walked up the aisle at Lord Mountbatten's funeral. It was the most tragic thing I've ever seen. My heart bled for you when I watched. I thought, It's wrong, you're lonely – you should be with somebody to look after you.'

Charles had just broken up with Anna Wallace. He'd taken her to two successive balls and then danced with Camilla for most of both evenings. Anna dumped him with the words, 'No one treats me like that – not even you.' He was now thirty-two. The press were on his case and so was his father, whom he wanted nothing more in life than to please. He needed a wife. It wasn't a matter of choice, it was duty. His life had never been his own, he had never been free to make real choices, or mistakes, like the rest of us. He was condemned by an accident of birth to a life of duty, like his mother. Of course there are huge privileges that go with being Prince of

Wales but there are even greater responsibilities, and one of those is to ensure the succession and future of the monarchy. Thirty years later, Charles's son and heir, Prince William, would be able to marry a commoner, Catherine Middleton, and very little fuss was made of either her background or her past. But by then things were different.

Lady Diana Spencer met all the criteria and more. She was born into high aristocratic circles, her father had been an equerry to King George VI and the Queen, her grandmother was a close friend and lady-in-waiting to the Queen Mother, and her eldest sister, Jane, was married to the Queen's assistant private secretary, Robert Fellowes. She was familiar with royal protocol, comfortable around the family. She had known them since she was small, having lived across the park from Sandringham House until the age of fourteen. She was innocent, shy and enchanting – and she seemed to like him. Charles has a weakness for people who are nice to him.

He invited her to watch him play polo at Cowdray Park with a group of friends, Camilla amongst them, followed by a ball at Goodwood House. She joined him aboard the royal yacht, *Britannia*, moored off the Isle of Wight for Cowes Week, the annual yachting regatta. They had fun and he confided in a friend that he had met the girl he intended to marry. Two dozen dark red roses were delivered to her doorstep in London, followed by an invitation to join a house party at Balmoral in the autumn. As usual, the Parker Bowles were amongst the guests. Charles wanted to take soundings from his friends in this, as in everything else, and everyone liked Diana. At nineteen, she was much younger than his regular associates, but she held her own in their company and seemed to enjoy the outdoor life and country pursuits as much as anyone. He taught her to fish in the River Dee, and there were the long walks and picnics that the family all love so much. She was comfortable around the Queen and other members of the family, and Charles's brothers competed with him to sit beside her at dinner. It seemed he had finally found someone who ticked all the boxes. She was apparently a happy-go-lucky, unaffected, unpretentious girl who made everyone laugh, who mucked in, and who was at ease in surroundings that many would have found intimidating. Patty Palmer-Tomkinson painted a lovely picture of her: 'We went walking together, we got hot, we got tired, she fell into a bog, she got covered in mud, laughed her head off, got puce in the face, hair glued to her forehead because it was pouring with rain … she was a sort of wonderful English schoolgirl who was game for anything, naturally young but sweet and clearly determined and enthusiastic about him, very much wanted him.'

It was when Diana was at Balmoral that the press first realised she was the new girl in the Prince's life. They spotted her, through binoculars, on the banks of the river with Charles while he fished, and it didn't take them long to work out where she lived. Thereafter, Coleherne Court, the flat in Fulham that she shared with three other girls, was besieged. Most days there were over thirty photographers on the street outside waiting for her to open the door in the morning. Some rented a room in the building opposite, so they could see into her bedroom. If she drove off in her car they chased her, if she walked down the street they chased her, running backwards, constantly calling out for her to look their way. Once, going to stay with the Prince at Broadlands, she climbed out of the kitchen window, which opened on to a side street, using her bedsheets as a rope to get away unnoticed. Reporters rang her at all hours. Some tried to get into the building by posing as tradesmen. She worked as a helper in a kindergarten in Pimlico and one photographer persuaded her to pose for a photograph with two of the children. She was wearing a light see-through skirt, and he took the shot with the sun behind her, giving the world its first view of her very beautiful legs. It was intimidating stuff for someone who had never been in the public eye. Diana was scrupulously polite but she found the pressure unbearable. When she got home, she said, 'I cried like a baby to the four walls. I just couldn't cope with it.' But because she was just a girl-friend, there was no mechanism to protect her.

Diana and Charles saw one other periodically throughout the autumn, but seldom one to one. It would be with friends, people like Nicholas Soames, Sir Winston Churchill's grandson, the Palmer-Tomkinsons, the van Cutsems, the Romseys, who since Mountbatten's death had lived at Broadlands, the Keswicks, the Tryons and, of course, the Parker Bowleses – all of whom knew one another. Both Camilla and Andrew thought Diana a sweet, funny girl, as indeed she was. Whenever he brought her to Bolehyde she helped around the house and was noticeably good with the children. Camilla liked her. She thought her young but funny and very sweet, and at first Diana liked Camilla and appreciated her friendship – a friendship that was genuine. One weekend they all went to watch Charles compete in the Amateur Riders Handicap Steeplechase at Ludlow on his own horse, Alibar. On another Charles took her to see Highgrove, the house on the other side of the motorway in Gloucestershire, which he'd just bought, and asked whether she would help him decorate it.

Highgrove was actually bought by the Duchy of Cornwall, the estate which provides the Prince of Wales with an income, as it has successive holders of the title throughout the centuries since it was created by Edward III in 1337 for his son, the Black Prince. It is an enormous estate, one of the largest in Britain: about 130,000 acres, of which 70,000 acres is on Dartmoor. The remainder is mostly agricultural land occupied by tenant farmers, much of it in Cornwall and the West Country, with some in Wales and Gloucestershire. The Duchy spans more than twenty counties and also owns forty-five acres in Kennington, south London, including the Oval cricket ground, home of Surrey County Cricket Club. Today it is thriving – and can afford experiments like Poundbury, the Prince's extension to Dorchester – but when Charles came of age in 1969, it had lain like a slumbering giant for thirty-three years, generating a fraction of the income it does today. And the Prince can only use the income, he can never touch the capital.

Highgrove, a couple of miles outside the pretty market town of Tetbury, was neither as large nor as grand a country property as a Prince of Wales might be expected to own, but it was affordable, it came with over 400 acres of land and it was everything he was looking for. It was close to his sister Princess Anne at Gatcombe Park, the estate the Queen had bought for her on her marriage, and to the Parker Bowleses. It was also in the middle of Beaufort hunting country and close to polo at Cirencester Park, the Beaufort polo club at Westonbirt, and all the other places he played. And it was midway between London and the West Country. But what he loved most about the house was the garden surrounding it, which was planted with mature trees and little else.

Of all his friends and advisers, only three raised a question mark about Diana, and they were not thanked for their concerns. Nicholas Soames thought the pair had too little in common and was worried about the intellectual gap between them. The Romseys agreed; Penny Romsey was worried that Diana was more in love with the concept than the man. In one conversation she had said, 'If I am lucky enough to be the Princess of Wales,' as if auditioning for a part rather than understanding quite what she would be taking on. She also seemed to rather enjoy the cameras while protesting at their intrusiveness. But what made all three of them suspicious was how

Diana had gone after the Prince so single-mindedly, and how she'd controlled the relationship. She had set her sights on him, flirting and flattering and being everything that he wanted her to be. Norton spoke to the Prince several times, on each occasion more bluntly, and had his head bitten off. Dale Tryon and Camilla were both in favour and their opinions were the ones he trusted most, although to Dale's fury, Camilla had more sway. Charles asked Diana to marry him.

A curious episode had prompted his proposal. The *Sunday Mirror* ran a story which no one has ever got to the bottom of. With the headline 'Love in the Sidings', it claimed that when the royal train had been parked overnight in Wiltshire with Charles aboard, a blonde woman, presumed to be Diana, had driven from London to join him secretly for a few hours, the clear suggestion being that they had slept together. Diana denied it but the editor, Bob Edwards, was so convinced the story was accurate that he published anyway and was shocked by the unprecedented reaction from the Palace. The Queen's press secretary, Michael Shea, called the story 'a total fabrication' and demanded a retraction, giving rise to speculation that this girlfriend must be special.

Some years later, Bob Edwards received a Christmas card from Woodrow Wyatt, the maverick politician and writer who was a close friend of the Queen Mother and knew the entire family. In the card, he simply said, 'It must have been Camilla.' At the time of the incident, Camilla had never been on the royal train and if someone had attempted to smuggle her on in the middle of the night, the train was guarded by so many British Transport policemen that someone would have leaked the story long ago. Years later, when Diana was angry with Camilla, she told Woodrow Wyatt that it was her husband's lover who had been on the train that night.

The upshot of the *Mirror* story was that Diana's mother wrote an impassioned letter to *The Times*, appealing to the editors of Fleet Street to stop harassing her daughter, and stop writing lies about her and attributing to her things she had never said. At which the Duke of Edinburgh wrote to his son to the effect that he must make up his mind about Diana. Either marry her or let her go; with all the media madness, it was not fair to keep her hanging on, and he was in danger of tarnishing her reputation. The Prince read it as an ultimatum to marry, although others who saw the note think this was the wrong interpretation. The note was, however, ambiguous and the two did not sit down and talk about it. Charles consulted others instead and confessed to one friend that he was in a 'confused and anxious state of mind. It all seems so ridiculous,' he said to another, 'because I do very much want to do the right thing for this country and for my family – but I'm terrified sometimes of making a promise and then perhaps living to regret it. It is just a matter of taking an unusual plunge into some rather unknown circumstances that inevitably disturbs me but I expect it will be the right thing in the end.'

His anxiety was that it was too soon. He liked Diana, but it had only been six months or so since they'd met and they scarcely knew each other. His marriage had to last for life. As he'd said before, this was the one area of his life in which he should be ruled by his head and not his heart, because for him 'marriage has to be for ever'. And 'A woman not only marries a man; she marries into a way of life which she's got a contribution to make. She's got to have some knowledge of it, some sense of it, or she wouldn't have a clue about whether she's going to like it. And if she didn't have a clue, it would be risky for her, wouldn't it?' He wasn't yet certain, but Diana was so perfect in so many ways that he couldn't risk losing her. He had always believed that love could grow out of friendship and so wasn't the most important ingredient; what really mattered was that his bride should know what she was taking on.

With all her links to the Royal Family, surely – at least in theory – Diana was that woman. But at nineteen, she had no notion of what being Princess of Wales would entail. She was head over heels in love and by her own admission, very immature. She was also very badly educated and naive. She lived in a romantic fantasy world of women's magazines and Barbara Cartland novels, which could not have been more divorced from reality; and she had never been in love before. If she had, she would have known that their courtship, which involved minimal touching and was constantly conducted in the presence of his friends, was not the way most people built a relationship. Charles was preparing to propose marriage to a girl he barely knew as a result of a misinterpreted memo from his father. It could not have been more catastrophic.

12

Dishonesty All Round

Lord Mountbatten would almost certainly have advised against the marriage, but he was no longer alive. Although the Queen offered no opinion, the Queen Mother was enthusiastic. She liked Diana and was pleased that she was the granddaughter of her old friend Ruth, Lady Fermoy.

Lady Fermoy knew that Diana was more complicated than she seemed, and she should have alerted the Prince of Wales. But she was socially ambitious for her granddaughter and so she said nothing. Years later in 1993, a month before she died, she apologised to both the Queen and Charles for failing to warn them. Diana, she knew, had been 'a dishonest and difficult girl'. Earl Spencer, who died in 1991, also admitted to the Prince that he had been wrong not to say something.

If anyone could be held responsible for the whole sorry story it is Ruth, Lady Fermoy. She is the one who prevented Diana's mother, Frances from getting custody of Diana and the rest of her children after she was divorced by their father. Frances had been in an abusive relationship with Johnnie Althorp, as he then was known. She already had two daughters, Jane and Sarah, before giving birth to a boy who died tragically after just ten hours. Diana was her next child, and three years later she had Charles, the son and heir that her husband so badly wanted.

Some time after the birth of Charles, Frances fell in love with Peter Shand Kydd. He was married but she saw an escape. So when Diana was six, she left for a trial separation, taking the two younger children and their nanny with her. She returned them to their father for Christmas and left them there, thinking it would be temporary, while she began divorce proceedings on the grounds of his cruelty. Johnnie contested the claim and had the top names in the country to vouch for him. Meanwhile Mrs Shand Kydd, who had taken a dim view of her husband's affair, divorced Peter for adultery, citing Frances as co-respondent. Johnnie had no difficulty, therefore, in divorcing Frances on the same grounds.

Frances didn't have a leg to stand on, but her adultery alone should not have prevented her keeping the children. It was rare in the 1960s for children so young to go to their father. What swung it was her mother. During the custody proceedings, which were held in camera, Ruth, Lady Fermoy, a terrible snob and appalled that Frances had run off with a man in trade, gave evidence against her own daughter, calling her a 'bad mother'. As a result, the four children stayed with their father and a succession of nannies. Frances had them for weekends in London.

Diana, at six, knew nothing about the custody battle. All she knew was that her mother had gone away and left her, and she would never get over the pain of being abandoned. She was haunted by it her whole life. Her father remarried when she was a teenager, exacerbating her sense of loss, and when Charles returned to Camilla in the dying days of their marriage it reawakened all the old feelings. Diana told Andrew Morton, author of *Diana: Her True Story*, published in 1992, 'I've always felt very different from everyone else, very detached ... I always had this thing inside me that I was different. I didn't know why. I couldn't even talk about it but in my mind it was there.' By the age of fourteen, she said, she had worked out that she had never been wanted, she was just a nuisance. Her parents had been desperate for a son and heir; after their first son had died, Diana arrived, a third girl – a nuisance – before the precious boy finally came along. 'I've recognised that now. I've been aware of it and now I recognise it and that's fine. I accept it.' She adored her father, but there was no stability with him because he was seldom at home and there was a fast turnover of nannies – most of them seen off by Diana and her brother for trying to take over their mother's position: 'we used to stick pins in their chair and throw their clothes out of the window.'

When Charles asked Diana to marry him, and she giggled and said yes without a moment's hesitation, he knew none of this about his bride-to-be. She had bent over backwards during the months of their courtship to be everything he wanted her to be. He had never seen the darker side of her nature – had probably never thought to ask – and had no reason to suppose that this cheery, easy, uncomplicated country-lover was not the genuine article. He proposed at Windsor in early February 1981, after steeling himself for the task while skiing with the Palmer-Tomkinsons in Switzerland.

The day the engagement was announced, the happy couple posed for photographers. It was the first time she had posed for a photograph since the see-through skirt incident five months earlier and yet she had since become the most photographed person in Britain. This time she was in a modest sapphire blue suit, and delighted to show off her ring, which she had chosen herself: a traditional oval sapphire surrounded by fourteen diamonds. Then there was a television interview in which they were asked all the obvious questions. No, the age gap wasn't a worry, yes, they had lots of things in common – their sense of humour and every outdoor activity, except riding, said Diana; and yes, agreed Charles when pressed, 'our love of the outdoors'. To sum up, how did they feel that day? 'Just delighted and happy,' said Charles, 'I'm amazed that she's been brave enough to take me on.'

'And I suppose in love?' ventured the interviewer.

'Of course!' said Diana, leaving Charles to mutter, 'Whatever "in love" means' – words that have so often come back to haunt him.

As soon as the engagement was made public, Diana moved out of her friendly flat and into Clarence House to stay with the Queen Mother for a few days, then to a suite of rooms at Buckingham Palace, where she stayed until the wedding in July. It rescued her from the media madness – but with hindsight, it was probably not the best move for her.

The modern monarchy is a working firm and Buckingham Palace is its headquarters. Several members of the family have apartments there, including the Queen and the Duke of Edinburgh – and at the time Prince Charles – but none of them thinks of it as home. It is like a small village with its own post office, travel agent and doctor's surgery. There are 52 royal and guest bedrooms, 188 staff bedrooms and 78 bathrooms and lavatories, as well as 19 glorious state rooms and 92 offices. The rest is given over to all the paraphernalia that goes with running a vast catering and hospitality operation: huge kitchens, store rooms, cellars, boiler rooms and a labyrinth of underground passages with great pipes and heating ducts. It has been where the last six monarchs have lived, and has been the focal point of the nation for more than 170 years. It was a far cry from a flat full of giggling, gossiping girls, and with no one of her own age to chatter to, Diana was desperately lonely. As her former flatmate said, 'She went to live at Buckingham Palace and then the tears started. This little thing got so thin. She wasn't happy, she was suddenly plunged into all this pressure and it was a nightmare for her.'

Diana told Andrew Morton she had known before the engagement that there was someone else in the Prince's life. 'I'd been staying at Bolehyde with the Parker Bowleses an awful lot and I couldn't understand why she [Camilla] kept saying to me, "Don't push him into doing this, don't do that." She knew so much about what he was doing privately and about what we were doing privately … if we were going to stay at Broadlands, I couldn't understand it. Eventually I worked it all out and found the proof of the pudding and people were willing to talk to me.'

She'd found a friendly letter from Camilla on her bed at Clarence House. 'Such exciting news about the engagement,' it said. 'Do let's have lunch soon when the Prince of Wales goes to Australia and New Zealand. He's going to be away for three weeks. I'd love to see the ring, lots of love, Camilla.'

It was a friendly gesture and Camilla remembered the lunch being just that – Diana was very excited and gleefully showed off the ring. Camilla knew how painful it was to have an unfaithful husband. She would never have wanted to inflict that on Diana or anyone else. She wasn't scheming. But over time Diana had come to see it as part of a conspiracy. She told Morton the lunch had been 'very tricky indeed'. Camilla had said, '"You are not going to hunt, are you?" I said, "On what?" She said, "Horse. You are not going to hunt when you go and live at Highgrove, are you?" I said, "No." She said, "I just wanted to know" and I thought as far as she was concerned that was her communication route. Still too immature to understand all the messages coming my way.'

The Prince had not handled things well. Instead of explaining to Diana at the outset that Camilla was an old girlfriend, he had presented her as nothing more than a friend. It didn't occur to him that she needed to know before someone else told her. Or that she might feel foolish, embarrassed or humiliated to have been chatting openly and girlishly about her feelings for him to someone who'd been a lover. He came clean after the engagement, admitting that she had been one of his most intimate friends, but

Bruce and Rosalind Shand on their wedding day in 1946. They were a golden couple.

Camilla (holding the lead rein) and her younger sister, Annabel. Their childhood was idyllic in every way.

Camilla aged 11 (left) on an outing to Newcastle with the Shawcross family in 1959. William Shawcross, 12, on the right, was very smitten. His sister Joanna is behind him and Annabel Shand is at the back.

Alice Keppel, Camilla's great-grandmother, who
was the long-term mistress of King Edward VII,
Prince Charles's great-great grandfather.

Opposite: Camilla in her late teens
painted by the society portrait artist,
Molly Bishop. The resemblance to her
great-grandmother is striking. Two
strong, confident women.

At a debutante party in the late 1960s, remonstrating, as she often did, with her boyfriend, Andrew Parker Bowles.

Lucia Santa Cruz, the Chilean ambassador's daughter, who introduced Camilla to Prince Charles and jokingly warned them to be careful.

Unlike her sister, Annabel Shand was a reluctant debutante.

Camilla courted Andrew Parker Bowles on and off for seven years and she got to know his family and friends well. With his cousin, David Bowes-Lyon, and a friend.

And below with his nephew, Charles Paravicini.

Her Pekinese, Chang, was a relative of Dame Ann Parker Bowles's dogs. Camilla was mad about the dog but less so about the woman who became her mother-in-law.

Camilla has always had a terror of flying. Today, she combats it by the technique known as 'tapping'.

November 1972, with Andrew at a shooting party in what was then Czechoslovakia. She was in the midst of a fling with Prince Charles – furious that Andrew was dating Princess Anne.

Hugh Pitman, Prince Charles and Andrew Parker Bowles on the same team at the Guards Polo Club in Windsor. Twenty-five years later, Andrew married Hugh's ex-wife, Rose.

Andrew Parker Bowles (number 2) with the Army polo team in Kenya in 1971, alongside a young Prince Charles. It is not surprising which of the two Camilla's heart was set on.

She may have been seeing Charles but it was Andrew she was in love with.

Camilla on her wedding day with her beloved father, Bruce. Prince Charles was in the Caribbean, his heart broken by her decision to marry Andrew.

It was a lavish society wedding. Back row: Andrew, Camilla and best man Simon Parker Bowles (Andrew's brother). Adults seated from left: Derek Parker Bowles, Dame Ann Parker Bowles, Queen Elizabeth the Queen Mother, Princess Anne, Rosalind Shand, Bruce Shand. Bridesmaids and pageboys were the couple's godchildren.

Early in their marriage at the Queen Mother's home at the Castle of Mey. Second from left is Lady Diana Spencer's grandmother, Ruth, Lady Fermoy, an old friend of the Queen Mother.

Laura Parker Bowles presenting a bouquet to the Queen Mother at her 90th birthday parade with her parents, and, right, Tom King, Secretary of State for Defence.

In the late 1970s, when Charles and Camilla were having an affair. With them is Lady Sarah Keswick who was and has remained a close friend of them both.

Camilla liked Diana and thought she was perfect for Charles.

With the two men in her life at the Guards polo club. Andrew knew what was going on but there was never any animosity between him and Charles, nor rows with Camilla. Once the Prince started dating Diana, the affair ended.

The famous balcony kiss that set the seal on the fairytale wedding.

Diana and Charles setting off for their honeymoon, escorted by a familiar face –
Andrew Parker Bowles, left, commander of the Household Cavalry.

The Princess of Wales took the world by storm. At the White House, she memorably took to the floor for 15 minutes with John Travolta.

But by the early Nineties, the pretence that Charles and Diana were happy was over.

The Parker Bowles family in 1984 at Buckingham Palace, the day Andrew received his OBE. At that time, Camilla's life was all about her children and her family. The Prince was no longer a part of it.

Camilla with her siblings and all the cousins. They were her life-support system. *Back row:* Andrew, Annabel Elliot, Ben Elliot, Simon Elliot. *Front row and seated:* Alice Elliot, Katie Elliot, Mark Shand, Camilla, Laura and Tom Parker Bowles.

reassured her that from now on there would be no other women in his life. He meant it. A close friend of the Prince's agrees: 'He made a huge mistake. You can sympathise with Diana, oh God yes. Put that way, he was the architect of the disaster. But you see, I think he feels that different standards apply to him because he wasn't allowed to marry the love of his life; he had to produce heirs so he had to do this for the nation. Also he wouldn't have had the sensitivity. I've always felt he lacked reading novels. He's very interested in objective things but not subjective, so he couldn't have understood the complexities of her feelings. He reads essays, history, no novels. He loves Shakespeare and that teaches you something, but I think if you are in a position like him, novels are a great antidote to your isolation.'

Shortly after the engagement was made public, they'd had dinner at Bolehyde. Amongst the other guests were the old Duke of Beaufort and John and Jane Irwin – Camilla and Jane hunted together and shared a school run. They'd met through mutual friends, the Hon. Patrick and Mary Howard when Tom and their son, Jake, were a few months old and the boys were like brothers. During dinner, Diana's necklace fell off. 'For God's sake, you can't go doing that sort of thing when you're at Buckingham Palace,' said John, and everyone laughed. They also discreetly discussed what she might buy Charles as a wedding present. John suggested a new super-lightweight fishing rod, but Diana knew the Prince liked his split-cane rod. It was a happy evening. As they sat round the dinner table, neither Camilla nor Charles was scheming to carry on an affair behind Diana's back. Once he had asked Diana to marry him, the physical side of their relationship was over, even if he hoped the friendship might continue.

Installed in Buckingham Palace, Diana shared an office with Michael Colborne, who had followed the Prince out of the Navy to be his right-hand man. Colborne had been a chief petty officer on board HMS *Norfolk* and a good friend, and he was the one person on the Prince's staff who braved his tantrums to tell him what he needed to hear. Indeed the Prince had made him promise not to change when he joined his household. 'If you don't agree with something, you say so,' he had said. Michael was a kind and wise man, married with a son and totally unmoved by wealth or privilege. He took people as he found them and quickly realised that Diana was ill-equipped for the life she was marrying into. She was a lovely girl but she was undisciplined, uneducated and so very young and insecure. He became a surrogate parent to her – she had no real support from her own; she wasn't close to her mother, and her father had been left a very different man after a brain haemorrhage. Michael was the one she turned to. She confided in him and they had many long, and sometimes tearful, heart-to-heart discussions. She told him all about herself, her family, her parents' divorce, her stepmother and her father's illness, and repeatedly quizzed him about the Prince's relationship with Camilla. He did his best in the months leading up to the wedding to prepare her for what lay ahead, but she had no concept of how her life would be and he feared for her.

Diana now had police protection, so she was no longer followed, but the stresses simply changed. She spent a weekend at Royal Lodge at Windsor, for example, but no one had thought to tell her that if she wanted to go for a walk in the Great Park, she needed to let someone know. She came back to find alarms going off and the place in turmoil. When she told Michael what had happened, saying she didn't know how she was going to cope, he explained the facts of life to her.

'This is going to be your life,' he said. 'And you're going to change. In four to five years you're going to be an absolute bitch, not through any fault of your own but because of the circumstances in which you live. If you want four boiled eggs for breakfast, you'll have them. If you want the car brought round to the front door a minute ago, you'll have it. It's going to change you. Your life is going to be organised. You open your diary now and you can put down Trooping the Colour, the Cenotaph service, Cowes Week, the Ascots. You can write your diary for five years ahead, ten years, twenty years. You're never going to be on your own again.'

13

A State of Mind

During those months before the wedding, the bouncy young girl so many people had encouraged Charles to marry changed radically. She lost weight. The blue dress she wore for the engagement was a size fourteen. Her waist was twenty-nine inches. By the time she walked up the aisle, her waist had shrunk to twenty-three and a half inches. But as worrying as the weight loss was her mental state – and the Prince wasn't the only one to notice her bizarre behaviour. The girl who had always seemed to be so easy, funny and cheerful, suddenly became moody, wilful and unpredictable. There were terrifying rages, temper tantrums and hysterical tears for no apparent reason, and her moods changed in a flash. She became jealous – obsessing about Camilla Parker Bowles – and suspicious, turning against people she had appeared to like, convinced they were out to get her, undermine her or spy on her. She was bored, she hated being alone and she resented the Prince working. She couldn't understand why his work had to take precedence over their being together.

The Prince had had no choice; as a working member of the Royal Family his days were mapped out six months in advance. He had relentless rounds of public engagements, meetings, receptions, dinners and paperwork, a lot of it out of London, as well as foreign tours and ceremonial commitments. She couldn't see why all this was so important, and was so insecure she took his absence as an indication of indifference. She was jealous of anyone he spent time with, including his mother. She thought their private conversations and correspondence were about her, little realising that as Prince of Wales he might share secrets of state with the Queen that no one else knew about, not even the Duke of Edinburgh.

Charles was as bewildered by the changes in Diana as everyone else, and put it down to nerves and stress, which he assumed would disappear once the wedding was behind them. No one realised that these were symptoms of the illness that had secretly taken her over. It is impossible to know exactly what it was that triggered Diana's eating disorder, but the sudden ascent to fame and the stress of being watched and followed and photographed and written about would have been a lot for even the most confident nineteen-year-old to handle. And this was accompanied by a massive change in lifestyle, her removal from everything that was familiar and safe in her flat-sharing days, and the slow realisation of what she had so hastily agreed to do for the rest of her life. And maybe, too, the fear that was not unique to her, that the man she was going to marry didn't love her as much as he'd loved his previous girlfriend.

After her childhood experiences, any or all of these things could have produced the turmoil in Diana's head that made her behave the way she did. Eating disorders have nothing to do with a desire to slim or to get fit, although they invariably go hand in hand with excessive exercise. They are severe mental illnesses that affect over 1.6 million people in the UK, and they are about control and coping with feelings or situations. Sufferers will say that they starve themselves (anorexia), or gorge and purge themselves (bulimia) because what they put in their mouths and do with their bodies is the one thing they can keep control of.

Mental health receives much more attention today than it did thirty years ago – and Diana's sons, who were as bewildered as everyone else by their mother's behaviour, have become leading advocates for a change in attitude. Through the Royal Foundation of the Duke and Duchess of Cambridge and Prince Harry, they launched a campaign in 2016 called Heads Together, which was the charity of the year for the London Marathon in April 2017. Speaking at a conference in December, Prince William said, 'The essence of the campaign is to help change the conversation on mental health. The rapid increase in poor mental health is one of the biggest challenges we face as a society and it is a challenge Catherine, Harry and I feel duty bound to tackle.

'All of us in this room have mental health, just as we have physical health, and we will all experience pressures on our mental health at some point in our lives. But for too long, held back by stigma, shame and fear, people have found it difficult to open up to others about those times when their mental health needs support.

'Catherine, Harry and I have been campaigning on this issue for only a few months now, but what we have observed already is that when we get our heads together – when we talk and listen to family, to friends and colleagues, we share the load; we reduce the problem; we realise we are not alone and we break down the barriers that prevent us from getting the help we need. It is really that simple: a problem shared is a problem halved.'

As soon as Camilla realised Diana had a problem with her, she kept her distance from Charles. If ever there was an invitation or a social gathering at which he might be present, she stayed away, saying 'Wales will be there.' But he did speak to her often on the telephone – sometimes, according to Diana, within earshot of her, which resulted in terrible rows; and when Camilla was ill with meningitis, he arranged for Colborne to send her some flowers, using the nicknames Gladys and Fred, which they'd called themselves when they needed to be incognito. Diana knew about the flowers – because she knew everything that went on in Colborne's office – and she wasn't happy about them. And when it came to choosing her attendants for the wedding, she vetoed Charles's suggestion that Camilla's son Tom, his godchild, be one of her page boys. She agreed to several of his other godchildren, but there was a big scene about Tom Parker Bowles and Charles backed down.

But what enraged her most of all was a bracelet destined for Camilla that she found on Michael Colborne's desk one Friday afternoon. Michael had been asked by the Prince to buy presents for all sorts of people, including jewellery for various women who had been special to him in one way or another during his bachelor years, namely Dale, Lady Tryon, Lady Sarah Keswick, Lady Cecil Cameron – and Camilla Parker Bowles. Charles is an inveterate giver of gifts, especially jewellery, as a way of thanking people and intended to see each of them individually to say goodbye. A package from the jeweller had duly arrived and Michael was investigating its contents when he was summoned by Edward Adeane, the Prince's private secretary. After their conversation, Adeane went looking for him to make one final point. As he reached his office door he was practically knocked off his feet by Diana rushing out at top speed, visibly upset.

Michael arrived moments later and realised what had happened. The lid was off the box with the bracelet inside it. When they next saw one another, on Monday morning, Diana confessed she had had a look at what was on his desk but said nothing further about it. I knew Michael Colborne for thirty years and he was as honest and straightforward as they come. Her account of the incident in *Diana: Her True Story* was embellished in the same way that those who witnessed other incidents say so many of the stories were. 'Anyway, someone in his office told me that my husband had had a bracelet made for her which she wears to this day. It's a gold chain bracelet with a blue enamel disc. It's got "G and F" entwined in it, "Gladys" and "Fred" – they were their nicknames. I walked into this man's office one day and said: "Oh, what's in that parcel?" He said: "Oh, you shouldn't look at that." I said: "Well, I'm going to look at it." I opened it and there was a bracelet and I said: "I know where this is going." I was devastated. This was about two weeks before we got married. He said: "Well, he's going to give it to her tonight." So rage, rage, rage! "Why can't you be honest with me?" But no, he cut me absolutely dead. It's as if he had made his decision, and if it wasn't going to work, it wasn't going to work. He'd found the virgin, the sacrificial lamb ...'

She did confront the Prince about it, but he didn't cut her dead. They had a very heated discussion – but he had had five months of heated discussions with Diana and her rages and was determined to stick to his guns. He had told her unequivocally that since their engagement there was and would be no other woman in his life, and he expected her to believe him.

The Prince of Wales is not a liar, but he gets no marks in this instance for empathy. He didn't try to imagine how an insecure nineteen-year-old might feel about him seeing the one old girlfriend she was fretting about. She had asked him if he was still in love with her and he had not given her a clear answer. It is small wonder that she became almost demented with suspicion and jealousy.

14

The Stuff of Nightmares

The wedding on 29 July 1981, at St Paul's Cathedral, had brought such promise. Britain was in the grip of a deep recession, struggling with social tension and rising unemployment. Almost three million people were without jobs, there had been violent riots in parts of London and several other cities. The wedding was a timely distraction, something to celebrate, the promise of love and hope that comes with every marriage.

Hers wasn't a rags to riches story – Lady Diana Spencer was a very wealthy young woman who'd grown up in one of the most magnificent stately homes in the country, filled with priceless paintings and works of art; her family had royal connections going back generations – but she was endearingly unsophisticated and the media created the impression that she was like one of us. The public quickly fell in love with her and watched, almost with pride, as their girl grew into the role. She lost her puppy fat and became lean and willowy. Her ordinary, everyday clothes were replaced by designer frocks. Her hair was beautifully cut, her make-up immaculate. The girl who might once have lived next door now clearly belonged in a palace. She even travelled to St Paul's with her ailing father, Earl Spencer, in a horse-drawn glass coach. Her train was twenty-five feet of billowing ivory silk taffeta. After years of searching, the handsome prince had found true love at last in an innocent young woman, who would not only be his wife but ultimately his queen. She was a real-life Cinderella who lived beyond the closing paragraph of the fairytale, and we became fascinated to see what 'happily ever after' really looked like.

St Paul's was packed. Most of the kings and queens of Europe were there, as were over 160 foreign presidents, prime ministers and their wives. Nancy Reagan, wife of the President of the United States, was amongst them. She had arrived in London with twelve security men and five hat boxes, and declared that the week she would spend in the capital would be the longest she had been away from her husband, Ronald, in twenty-nine years of marriage. A special chair had to be made for the 25-stone King of Tonga.

There had been a huge build-up to the day. The evening before, hundreds of beacons were lit on high ground all over the country to mark the start of the celebrations. In London, half a million people converged on Hyde Park for a massive fireworks display, with music, singing and cannon fire. People partied throughout the warm night, or curled up in sleeping bags to lay claim to a good viewpoint for the morning. By dawn there was no standing room within a hundred yards of St Paul's Cathedral.

Dawn ushered in a beautiful day. The sun shone, the bells pealed, thousands of well-wishers poured into the capital and thronged the streets, waving their Union flags. It was a day when everyone in the country, bar a few, was proud to be British, when strangers engaged with strangers and when only the most curmudgeonly were not caught up in the romance and the excitement. It didn't change the unemployment figures but it did briefly help lift the country out of its gloom; and the music and the goodwill were beamed around the world in the biggest and most expensive live outside broadcast ever mounted. Seven hundred and fifty million viewers in seventy countries were said to have watched the day unfold.

After the service, the Prince and his new Princess travelled to the wedding breakfast at Buckingham Palace in an open state landau pulled by four Windsor greys; they smiled and waved to the cheering crowds, looking for all the world as if this was the happiest day of their lives. The Queen and the rest of both families followed, all beaming and waving, and as the last of the carriages disappeared inside the famous black and gilt gates, the crowds surged forward for the traditional balcony appearance. They were so tightly packed there was not a patch of road or grass to be seen in the Mall or the surrounding parks. Impatient to be given a sight of the newly-weds, they started chanting 'We want Di, we want Di, we want Charlie.' Finally, the balcony doors opened and Charles and Diana stepped out, followed by the Queen and the rest of the immediate wedding party. The crowds were ecstatic and when, on their fourth and final appearance, Prince Charles bent forward and kissed his bride, they went mad; they roared and cheered, they burst into song, they danced and laughed and kissed strangers. It was the first time anyone had ever kissed on the balcony.

Charles was not convinced he was doing the right thing in marrying Diana but there was no way out and, bolstered by the hope that things would be different once they were married, he put a brave face on it. The night before the wedding, which Diana spent at Clarence House with her sister Jane, he sent her a note, along with a signet ring that bore the Prince of Wales feathers. 'I'm so proud of you and when you come up I'll be there at the altar for you tomorrow. Just look 'em in the eye and knock 'em dead.' That night she 'had a very bad fit of bulimia', ate everything she could possibly find and was 'sick as a parrot'.

She also had qualms. She'd told her sisters the day before that she couldn't go through with it now she knew Charles was having that last lunch with Camilla, but they'd said, 'Well, bad luck, Duch [the family name for her], your face is on the tea-towels so you're too late to chicken out.' They may have been making light of it, but they were right. This was not a simple family wedding with a hundred or so friends to disappoint. This was a full-blown state occasion. Two thousand, six hundred and fifty invitations had been sent out, ten thousand presents had been received, and forty-seven thousand letters; the day had been declared a public holiday. Hundreds of man-hours had gone into meticulous planning, not least the security for such a concentration of high-profile people under one roof; and transport provision had been made for so many extra visitors to the capital, and for road closures before and after the ceremony. The event could not be easily called off.

Although Tom Parker Bowles wasn't a page boy, he was there with his mother, standing on a chair at times to get a good look. Camilla was dressed in a grey suit and matching pillbox hat with a veil and was seated next to her sister. Andrew was on duty. He was commanding the Household Cavalry escort for the newlyweds. Charles looked over at Camilla as he walked down the aisle with a 'slightly plaintive, sad look' on his face. Their wonderful affair was over and this was reality kicking in. Camilla had lost the Prince, and Andrew was allegedly in the midst of an affair with Charlotte Hambro, Nicholas Soames's sister. They'd met in Rhodesia the year before, where Andrew was awarded the Queen's Commendation for Bravery, while working for her father, Christopher, Lord Soames, who was governor-general during the country's turbulent transition to the majority rule state of Zimbabwe. Camilla was unusually quiet on the family holiday in Ischia that August.

Meanwhile, Charles and Diana were on their honeymoon. It was a disaster, and only served to demonstrate how very little they had in common. After a few days at Broadlands, they flew to Gibraltar to join the royal yacht, *Britannia*, for a two-week cruise around the Mediterranean and Aegean before flying to Scotland for several more weeks at Balmoral. The Prince envisaged a wonderful holiday in the sun, swimming, reading, painting and writing thank-you letters. He had taken his watercolours and some canvases and a pile of books by Laurens van der Post, which he'd hoped they might share and discuss in the evenings. Diana was no reader and was offended that he should prefer to bury his head in a book rather than sit and talk to her. She hated his wretched books. She resented him sitting for hours at his easel, too, and they had many blazing rows. As she told Andrew Morton, her bulimia was rampant – but of course still secret. All he knew was that her mood swings were terrifying and her behaviour utterly bewildering. He had no idea what was wrong. One day, when he was sitting painting on the veranda deck, he went off to look at something for half an hour. He came back to find she had destroyed the whole lot.

Diana didn't tell Andrew Morton about that, but she did tell him about two other incidents. On one occasion they were consulting their diaries when a photograph of Camilla fell out of his, and another time, when they were in formal dress for dinner, she noticed the Prince was wearing a pair of gold cufflinks engraved with interwoven Cs. 'Got it in one. Knew exactly,' she said. '"Camilla gave you those, didn't she?" He said: "Yes, so what's wrong? They're a present from a friend." And, boy, did we have a row. Jealousy, total jealousy ...'

It's hard to believe that anyone as intelligent and well-read as the Prince of Wales could be so stupid, so utterly unable to imagine what a new wife might conclude if her husband carried a photograph of his old girlfriend in his diary, or chose to wear cufflinks bearing her initials, when he must have had dozens of others to choose from. But Charles was already way out of his depth. He had no idea how to treat a wife, how to look after her. He had no idea how to look after himself, he'd never had to do it. For thirty-two years, apart from his time at boarding school and university, he had been waited on hand and foot. He didn't even dress himself. And while he was famous for shouting at underlings, no one – with the possible exception of his father – had ever shouted at him before. He had no idea how to respond.

In Scotland they held a photo-call by the River Dee and, looking gloriously coquettish, the new Princess of Wales said she could 'thoroughly recommend' married life. 'It's a marvellous life and Balmoral is one of the best places in the world.' Nothing could have been further from the truth. She hated it. She hated the countryside, hated his family's passion for horses and dogs, hated the rain that poured down remorselessly; and she felt that her husband was avoiding intimate contact. She was raging, bingeing, vomiting and obsessing about Camilla – and getting no meaningful reassurance from Charles. And he was being driven away and ever deeper into himself. They didn't stay in the main house, but they had dinner with the rest of the Royal Family several times a week, and as usual his friends were invited – although not the Parker Bowleses – so there was very little chance for the sort of intimacy she'd hoped for on honeymoon. And with 21 naval officers, a crew of 256 men, a valet, a private secretary and an equerry all along for the ride, *Britannia* hadn't been much better. Charles couldn't see it, and if he could he wasn't prepared to change his ways. Balmoral was his favourite place on earth and he had thought Diana liked it too. She had said she did, but she'd said a lot of things she didn't mean during their months of courtship. He retreated to the hills and spent his days on solitary walks, or with his paints or books or fishing rod. He left dealing with Diana to others.

He rang Michael Colborne and asked him to catch a train to Aberdeen. 'I will be out stalking that day,' the Prince informed him, 'but I will see you before I go and I'd like you to spend the day with the Princess.' When he arrived at Craigowan Lodge, the small house where the newlyweds were staying, the Prince thanked him for coming and with no explanation left the house, accompanied by Norton Romsey. There followed the most shocking, distressing and draining day of Michael's life. For six solid hours, with no distraction beyond a plate of sandwiches at lunchtime, he sat there while Diana cried, paced around the room, kicked the furniture, ranted about everyone and everything to do with the place that she hated so much, and then fell into brooding silence before starting all over again. At five past four she suddenly said, 'I'm going upstairs,' and left the room.

Later that evening Michael was due to drive with the Prince to Aberdeen to board the royal train – he had an engagement the next day. He was waiting in the dark by the car outside the front door and could hear a monumental row taking place inside. Moments later the door flew open. The Prince came out shouting, 'Michael!' and threw something at him. It was Diana's wedding ring, which by some miracle he caught before it disappeared into the gravel. She had lost so much weight that it no longer fitted and she wanted him to take it back to London to be made smaller. The Prince was in a filthy mood and laid into Michael, in front of his detective and valet, all the way to Aberdeen, calling him every name under the sun for a catalogue of failings. Michael refused to engage and once on board the train ordered himself a treble gin and tonic. Before he could take the first sip, the Prince bellowed his name from down the corridor. For once he took his time. The Prince offered him a drink. 'Tonight, Michael,' he said, 'you displayed the best traditions of the silent service. You didn't say a word. I hear you've had a rough day.'

'Yes,' said Michael. 'I've had an awful day.'

For the next five hours or more they talked about Diana and all that had happened since the wedding. Charles was mystified and despondent. He didn't know what had gone wrong or how he was going to cope.

Soon afterwards Diana went to London. As she said, 'All the analysts and psychiatrists you could ever dream of came plodding in trying to sort me out.' But eating disorders were very poorly understood in the early 1980s and treatment very hit and miss. It is not much better today – but at least it's now known how serious these conditions are. Without treatment, up to 20 per cent of sufferers die from them and the continual vomiting characteristic of bulimia causes all sorts of internal damage. The conditions often go hand in hand with other psychiatric disorders, and judging by the behaviour that so many people reported over the years, Diana's almost certainly did too. Several experts have suggested Borderline Personality Disorder (BPD) or, as it is now often called, Emotional Unstable Personality Disorder (EUPD). Medical science still doesn't have all the answers to mental health problems but thirty years ago doctors were at even more of a loss, and BPD is notoriously difficult to treat. Minor personality disorders are common – they are seen in people who crave attention or adoration, and such people often find their way into politics or onto the stage without anyone ever knowing there is an abnormality. But severe disorders take their toll on the psychiatrists who attempt to treat those suffering from them as much as the relatives who attempt to care for and support the sufferers, partly because the symptoms are only displayed in private.

One of the friends Diana was closest to at the end of her life observed, 'She is like someone who has her nose pressed to the glass looking at the world outside, but never feeling that she is a part of it. She can't emotionally, psychologically cope with it.' Diana's condition was undoubtedly complex, but it's been hard for the public to accept because it was only really seen by the people who lived and worked with her. To the outside world, Diana was simply a beautiful, caring princess.

And the facts take nothing away from the tremendous good she did in her short life. She was a loving mother, a compassionate comforter of strangers, especially the sick, and she shone a light on issues to which society turned a blind eye. Millions of pounds were raised in her name and notice taken of important causes. To talk about her health problems is not to detract from any one of her strengths or achievements.

15

Princess of Wales

Charles had promised the people of Wales that when he married he would bring his bride to visit the principality from which she took her name. True to his word, it was the first place they went as a married couple. In October 1981, they spent three days in the country, covering four hundred miles, visiting seaside resorts, historic towns, country show grounds, leisure centres, hospitals, mining communities and industrial cities. It was a baptism by fire for Diana, but she was brilliant.

I was there, because I was writing a book about her, and I remember it vividly. It was as if she had reinvented herself. She still shyly held her head down – and she was pitifully thin – but she was no longer the girl next door; she was now a real beauty and a very skilled operator. Dressed in alluring outfits with stylish hats, she stepped out of their glass-topped Rolls Royce and headed towards the cheering crowds, again and again, like a long-legged filly finding its feet, her hands outstretched and a shy smile lighting up her face. Thousands of people had turned out to see her, waiting behind barriers for hours in the cold, the wind and the rain for what they knew would be no more than a fleeting glimpse and if they were very lucky a handshake and a word or two. But Diana didn't disappoint. She got wet, she got cold and had to hang on to her hat to stop it blowing off, but still she kept on smiling, kept on reaching out to people. She wiggled her wedding finger when people asked for a peep at her ring, she squatted down to talk to children, stroked blue-cold faces, warmed frozen hands between hers, and stretched forward on tiptoes to touch hands reaching towards her from the back. When a little boy shouted, 'My Dad says give us a kiss,' she said, 'You'd better have one then,' and bent down to kiss his cheek. She was a resounding success.

But what was noticeable about the tour was that the Prince of Wales was overshadowed by her and found himself apologising for not having enough wives to go round. At every stop they took one side of the street each, so it was pot luck which one of them the crowds met. Those who realised they were getting him rather than her audibly groaned in disappointment. The Prince made light of it and quipped that all he was good for these days was collecting flowers for his wife, but it was a new experience for him, and an uncomfortable one. She had not yet set out to upstage him – she said she was terrified and was simply trying to make him proud of her. Years later she would do it deliberately.

The Palace had assumed that media interest in Diana would die down after the wedding, but the prospect of a baby in June only served to heighten the public appetite for information – and a photograph of her on the front page of any publication sent its circulation soaring. Cheap copies of the clothes she wore were quickly on sale in the high streets, her hairstyle and jewellery were copied. Diana-mania had begun.

It was during her pregnancy with William that she had self-harmed, or as the *Sunday Times* had more dramatically said, 'was driven to five suicide bids by uncaring Charles'. At New Year, she threw herself down a wooden staircase at Sandringham. They'd had yet another violent quarrel and in the midst of hysterical sobs, she'd threatened to kill herself; he'd accused her of crying wolf and said he was going out for a ride. They'd quarrelled like this before, with threats and tears and tantrums, and the first few times he'd been very seriously alarmed. But he'd heard them too often and, not knowing what else to do, had started walking away. On one occasion she'd thrown herself against a glass cabinet, and she had cut herself several times with various sharp implements. They were not serious attempts to kill herself, as she was the first to admit; they were desperate cries for help, or more accurately for attention – *his* attention – but all she succeeded in doing with this behaviour was to push him further away.

Charles was dumbfounded. Everything about her was so far removed from the girl he first met. He had thought she was uncomplicated and easygoing, and that she liked his way of life – because that was the impression she gave him. He had assumed, therefore, that she would easily slot into that life with no need for him to change. He had turned thirty-three in November and his existence had a rhythm to it. There were valets to dress him and butlers to wait upon him, private secretaries to organise his workload, equerries to assist, and the household was expertly run by a team of staff. He worked long hours, and his sport and his hours of solitary reading and painting were important to him, as were his friends. Apart from being in charge of decorating Highgrove and later their apartment at Kensington Palace, there wasn't much left for Diana to do to feel part of it all. She resented the time he spent working, resented the horsey activities, resented the time he spent on his own and resented his friends, who were always around. She was jealous of them all for taking him away from her. She wanted his full attention – all the time. Since being abandoned by her mother at the age of six she had craved that all-encompassing love and attention that she'd lost. And in the fantasy world of trashy romantic novels in which she'd lived, that's what happened when you married a prince; you kissed, you fell in love, and you lived happily ever after. But, as he had said all those years ago, any wife of his 'would marry into a way of life'. He couldn't devote twenty-four hours a day to her. He was Prince of Wales; his life was one long round of duty and commitment – and the sport and the time out was a necessary antidote.

Lucia Santa Cruz had given him a copy of *Anna Karenina*, Leo Tolstoy's great novel, when he was eighteen and made him read it to help him develop empathy, but nothing could have prepared him for the complexities of Diana's feelings. What he had desperately hoped for in a wife was someone to share the burden, give him support and love, and relieve the loneliness, which although he was surrounded by people almost all of the time was very real. But because of her difficult start in life and the illness that sprang from it, Diana could never have been that person. She didn't have it in her. She needed all her energy to take care of herself, and she could barely do that.

Their childhoods had been very different, and Charles was no victim of a broken home, but his experiences – his distant mother, his bullying father, his miserable school years – had left him just as needy in his own way as Diana. They were two very damaged people who could do nothing to help each other. Their marriage was quite simply the most terrible mismatch, one that both of them leapt into far too quickly.

Charles may have walked away from the rows and the tantrums, but he did spend hours trying to comfort her at those times when it was possible to talk to her calmly, and he certainly didn't give up on the marriage for several years. He was totally loyal to her and told no one but those very closest to him what was going on. Not even after the Queen found Diana at the bottom of the stairs after her fall, mercifully unharmed, did he take the opportunity to confide in his mother. And if ever anyone else tried to ask, he cut them off. He had convinced himself that he must be responsible in some way, that marriage to him was too awful and that he'd destroyed her by bringing her into his bizarre way of life and exposing her to the unrelenting media scrutiny.

He did what he could to try and make her better. He organised a psychiatrist – whom she swiftly stopped seeing, saying she was better. When she took against her private secretary and refused to speak to him or answer his phone calls, Charles found him a new job. When she took against members of his staff, people who had looked after him for years, he removed them. She didn't like his faithful old Labrador, Harvey, so he gave him away. And without a word of explanation, he quietly dropped almost all of his friends, because she didn't like or trust them – despite having written many of them warm and loving letters in the past.

The Romseys were among the last to go, even though the couple had stayed at their holiday home in Eleuthera when Diana was pregnant. When the Princess threw an ornament at him in the midst of yet another screaming match, the Prince finally lost his cool and said, 'I should have listened to Norton. He said I should never have married you.' Not surprisingly, Norton and his wife were never allowed in the house again. But none of it made Diana either well or happy, and the Prince grew more and more depressed and despondent.

He had been greatly excited by Prince William's birth in June 1982. Having been with Diana throughout her labour, he was completely blown away by the experience, and it did bring some temporary relief to their relationship. But Diana had endured a difficult pregnancy with a lot of morning sickness, in addition to the self-induced sickness of her bulimia, and after the initial euphoria of the birth, developed severe post-natal depression.

Harry's birth in September two years later was described by Diana as 'a miracle'. 'By then I knew he had gone back to his lady but somehow we'd managed to have Harry,' she told Andrew Morton. 'Between William and Harry being born it is total darkness. I can't remember much, I've blotted it out, it was such pain … We were very, very close to each other the six weeks before Harry was born, the closest we've ever, ever been and ever will be. Then suddenly as Harry was born it just went bang, our marriage, the whole thing went down the drain.'

16

A Plea for Help

Charles had not gone back to his lady before Harry was born. Apart from annual Christmas cards to both Camilla and Andrew, and a phone call to Camilla to tell her that Diana was pregnant before it was announced, there had been no real contact between them. They had seen one another out hunting, but because the Prince never came to the meet and always rode up front with the huntsman, such glimpses were only ever fleeting. He may have thought fondly of all their happy times together compared to the nightmare he was experiencing with Diana, but that was the extent of it.

These were not the easiest of years for Camilla, but she threw her energy into her children, her garden, her horses and her friends and family. The children were both at a little prep school called Heywood House in Corsham, a town not far from home. She diligently turned up for every event an attentive mother should, often in riding kit. She was always very casually dressed, even on speech day, with her collar not always turned down properly. But she would sit on the desks at parents' evenings and chat to everyone. She went to nativity plays, Easter bonnet parades and the harvest festival service in the village church. And in the summer term there was sports day, and no one was more ready for it than Andrew. He had been the Army sprint champion and was fiercely competitive. Some of the parents jokingly suspected he had spikes on his running shoes, and say he turned up one year to take part even though Tom was ill. Mary Howard, who ran the nursery Tom had attended when he was younger, used to say,

'When you see Andrew Parker Bowles in the running race you understand why England won the war!'

At the age of seven, in September 1982, Tom and Jake Irwin moved on to Summer Fields school in Oxford, where sports day included a family race. Again, Andrew's competitiveness made everyone laugh – he sprinted ahead ensuring that the Parker Bowles team won the relay race five years running. They were good, fun days with lots of teasing and laughter. Their friend John Irwin had to be dissuaded from taking to the track. He was a very big man and older than the others. 'For God's sake don't run in the fathers' race, John,' Camilla said one year. 'You might have a heart attack and then we'll have to run the John Irwin Memorial Stakes for ever more.' John did sadly collapse and die from a massive heart attack several years later.

Tom was a reluctant boarder and badly missed home, as so many little boys do. He is now married with two children of his own, Lola and Freddy, who go to London day schools, and on Lola's seventh birthday he reminded his mother that she had sent him away eight months after his own. 'My mother was slightly appalled, saying she'd never do it again, but it was the thing you did.' Girls were not usually sent away until they were older, but at that time amongst that milieu, most people did send their boys away at the age of seven – and plenty still do today. From the age of four, Laura, who is three years younger than Tom, was left on her own in the house, but she was a friendly, gregarious little girl, and had plenty of friends who came to stay or whose houses she would go to; Camilla drove her to and from an endless round of birthday parties.

She also began house-hunting. She and Andrew had decided that Bolehyde was too big for them and too grand, the heating antiquated and too expensive for them to replace. There had been a touch of *folie de grandeur* in living at Bolehyde and so they put it on the market with Antony Brassey, her father's friend, Hugh Brassey's son. He ran the local office of Lane Fox in Cirencester, but also hunted with Camilla, so he was a friend. Delighted as he was to get the job, however, the market was slow and it was not an easy house to sell. In the years they had been in Bolehyde, the town of Chippenham had expanded and was now so close you could see the lights at night, less than ideal for such an imposing and prestigious property. But he 'had huge cooperation from Camilla', who showed every potential buyer round the house herself and worked hard at selling it. 'She was fantastic, and very good at reporting back to me about who'd gone round and what she thought of them. Very good on communications and very calm and matter of fact about the job, which is quite stressful for people. She couldn't have been a nicer client to deal with.' They finally sold the property in 1985 for £600,000 and bought Middlewick House in Corsham, about four miles away.

Jane Irwin, who had a house-search business, found Middlewick, having looked at several houses with Camilla. She and Andrew both loved it. Being Georgian, it was a completely different style of house, much more like The Laines where Camilla grew up. With generous windows and high ceilings it was filled with light, and although it was still big, with seven bedrooms, it was more compact than Bolehyde. It was also in a much nicer position: out of the village, away from the road, and surrounded by fields, woodland and paddocks, with a rambling garden and walled vegetable garden. It had a very pretty drawing room, and a bigger kitchen than the old house, where they could feed friends informally. Middlewick was also perfect for Laura's school.

After Summer Fields, Tom and Jake both went to Eton College – along with Tom's cousin Ben Elliot – and finally to Oxford University, and when life became tough for Tom, when his mother was in the newspapers every day, during his final years at Eton, to have such friends to look out for him made all the difference. Equally, when Jake's father died so suddenly, and his mother came to the school to tell him, Tom was a tower of strength for him.

Laura also had close friends to look out for her in the bad times – and the pair's cousins, Ben, Alice and Catherine Elliot, were like siblings. One of Laura's friends was Laura Chisholm, whose mother Carlyn was another close friend of Camilla's. Carlyn, now Baroness Chisholm, also grew up in West Sussex on an old family estate at Petworth House. She was born Carlyn Wyndham – her father Lord Egremont had been private secretary to Harold Macmillan during his premiership. She is younger than Camilla, so they had not been friends as children – Camilla was better acquainted with her elder brother Max – but when Carlyn and her husband, Colin, moved to Tetbury in the mid-1980s, they hooked up with one another. Carlyn worked as a nurse but they both hunted with the Beaufort and kept their horses at livery in the same yard in Sherston. Their daughters were exactly the same age; both went to Heywood, where they were in the same class, and they spent most of their time together.

Camilla had always kept her hunter, Molly – a wonderful horse, a bay that stood about 16.3 hands high, solid and dependable, who was Camilla's for many years – at livery. But she and Andrew had other horses, mostly National Hunt horses which they bred from and brought on, and those horses lived out in the fields at home.

Despite having two parents and a grandfather who were mad about horses, the bug had curiously not bitten Tom and Laura. When Andrew was away the horses were Camilla's responsibility – as were the dogs, the chickens, the children, the garden, the vegetable garden and everything else. And the tasks involved would all be detailed on the famous Sunday night list of things to do. The dogs were Lucas terriers – a cross between a Sealyham and a Norfolk terrier – and Labradors, which were Andrew's gun dogs. The chickens were nothing special until Andrew took a shine to Jane Irwin's birds, Marans that laid chocolate-brown eggs. She had an incubator and Andrew said he would like to buy some, if ever she had too many. So she sold him a dozen chicks, eleven of which turned out to be cockerels. She's convinced to this day that Andrew thought she knew how to sex a chicken and had done it deliberately.

In the midst of all this humdrum domesticity, Camilla was approached by Emilie van Cutsem, whom she knew well through the Prince of Wales when she and Andrew had been fellow guests at parties and on the many fishing holidays and shooting weekends held over the years before his marriage. Emilie and her husband Hugh were two of Charles's friends that the Princess had not cast into the outer darkness, and they were worried about him. Emilie told Camilla she thought the Prince was having a nervous breakdown. There was a change in him. The joy and the sparkle had gone out of him. He was no longer fun to be with – he'd become serious, moody, morose and thoroughly difficult.

'Frequently I feel nowadays,' he wrote, 'that I'm in a kind of cage, pacing up and down in it and longing to be free. How awful incompatibility is, and how dreadfully destructive it can be for the players in this extraordinary drama. It has all the ingredients of a Greek tragedy … I fear I'm going to need a bit of help every now and then for which I feel rather ashamed. All I want to do is to *help* other people …'

The fleeting moments of happiness in the couple's marriage were far outweighed by the rows, the misery, and the despair that he increasingly felt. Diana had come to love the power she was able to exercise. It was intoxicating to step out of a car or a helicopter to find hundreds of people waiting for her, cheering in excitement, desperate for her to stop and touch their babies, shake their hand or say something they would treasure. Or to walk into a room and have everyone turn to admire her. She loved the effect she had on men, and maybe to compensate for her husband's indifference, she milked it. She wore eye-catching fashions and knew that with no more than a coquettish tilt of the head, a smile or a teasing laugh, she could have men eating out of her hand. My own father, Sir John Junor, a powerful newspaper editor and columnist, fell soundly in love with her, and he was not the only journalist who would have walked over hot coals for her. It was too much, too soon; she was too young to handle it, and there was no one there to steady her. No solid, dependable family to remind her who she was and to keep her feet on the ground. She was allowed to believe her own publicity, which is dangerous for any superstar. And in the absence of love in her marriage, she fed on the adulation of strangers. But ultimately it was no substitute.

For most of the 1980s, the Prince had been desperately trying to find a role for himself and to address some of the ills and injustices he saw around him. But he was feeling horribly frustrated. Time and again Diana had unwittingly stolen his thunder – a new hairstyle seeming more newsworthy to the newspapers than an important speech he'd spent days honing. She slavishly read everything that was written about her – but it was not all to her liking. The Palace was like a leaky sieve and stories seeped out about the staff who had been sacked, the changes she'd made to the Prince's routine. She'd insisted, for instance, that he be in the nursery at the beginning and end of the day to see the children, which ate into his working day. Other stories – that she had turned him into a vegetarian, for example, or stopped him hunting and shooting – were made up. When she liked what she read she was elated; when she didn't, she was hurt and inconsolable. One by one the couple invited the newspaper editors to intimate lunches with them both at Kensington Palace, in the hope that if they heard at first hand what the Prince was attempting in the inner cities, they might be persuaded to explain it to their readers and stop printing trivia and lies about the Princess. But all in vain. It was the Princess, and not the Prince's worthy work, that sold newspapers.

Emilie van Cutsem was not the only one who contacted Camilla in the hope that she might be able to talk to the Prince. Lady Susan Hussey was another. She had known Charles since he was twelve years old, when she became a lady-in-waiting to the Queen, and had been a friend, a confidante, a shoulder to cry on and a tower of strength to him for many years. She had a very soft spot for him and there was scarcely a secret he hadn't shared with her. She was also an old friend of the Spencer family and had been a welcoming and familiar face when Diana first arrived at Buckingham Palace after the engagement. She had known of his misgivings, witnessed the change in Diana; on the night before the wedding, when neither of them was able to sleep, they had stood together in Lady Susan's sitting room, in their night clothes, looking down the Mall at all the people and the excitement going on below, both with tears streaming down their faces.

Lady Susan was one of the few people Charles had spoken to about Diana, and she was sick with worry. She thought he was cracking up and she knew there was just one person who could save him: Camilla. And so Camilla phoned him.

17

For King and Country

I interviewed the Prince of Wales for *Charles*, my first biography of him, towards the end of 1986. I now realise it must have been just then that Camilla made that first phone call. I didn't know that at the time, obviously, but I did know all was not well. But even if I had not heard from the people I had interviewed that his marriage was in trouble, I would have known it from the hour and a half I spent talking to him that day. As I wrote at the time:

> Never have I met anyone who has done so much – largely unrecognised and unrewarded – and yet who feels he has contributed so little. He is one of the saddest men I have ever encountered. His entire life has been sacrificed to duty. He has been criticised, he has been hounded, he has been ridiculed and still he battles on carrying his bruised and fragile ego into another minefield of controversy. He lives well and has a number of good friends, yet he is lonely as only one other person on earth is lonely: the Queen.

The Prince of Wales is a talented amateur artist and is drawn to sketch scenes of lonely moorland, seascapes and buildings that take his fancy. Given his time again, I suspect he might wistfully imagine himself an artist or a gentleman farmer, maybe even an entrepreneur, but there is no doubt that there are certain aspects of being HRH The Prince of Wales that he enjoys, and the notion of following the Swedes and becoming a bicycling monarchy appals him. He likes the formality and he enjoys his luxury.

He takes after his grandmother in that respect, and not his parents. They may live in castles and palaces and have the staff to run them, but they are essentially modest and frugal in their lifestyle. Charles isn't. When the 11th Duke of Devonshire was alive, the Prince used to be a regular visitor to Chatsworth. As well as his personal protection officer he would take two valets, one helicopter and enough luggage to fill a medium-sized living room. He would be staying for two days – and Chatsworth was one of the last remaining grand houses in England to have enough valets for twenty guests. At home he has a full complement of staff to look after him, and he expects high standards. He is a perfectionist, and while he may be charming and self-deprecating, forget to call him 'Sir' if you are one of his farm workers and you will know all about it. However, if that same farm worker fell ill, the Prince would personally ensure that he was well looked after, if necessary for the rest of his life – and he would visit him personally.

When I asked him about such matters, he insisted the trappings are important. If you are going to have a monarchy, you need to do it properly. Do away with the trappings and you destroy the mystique, and then you discover, as Frederick the Great of Prussia observed, that 'a crown is just like a hat that lets the rain in'. It is partly because of his exalted position that he has been able to achieve as much as he has. One of his great talents is bringing people together to solve problems. In 1990, for example, he dreamt up a programme called Seeing is Believing, which has been hugely success- ful. His thought was that instead of simply telling chief executives about the problems of poor housing, drugs, crime and racism, if you could let them see for themselves what was going on in run-down parts of the country and meet some of the people who lived there, they would be more inclined to help. Since then over nine thousand business leaders have trudged round inner cities, community projects, prisons, housing estates – and at the end of it they've been asked to write reports for the Prince on what they've seen and, over lunch at either Highgrove or St James's Palace, discuss with him what they might be able to contribute. Many of them have been shocked to discover so much deprivation on their own doorsteps that they were obliv- ious to and they have been galvanised into action. The Prince knows that if he was plain Mr Charles Windsor, who wore jeans, drove around in a Ford

Escort and lived at 5 Acacia Avenue, people at the top of their fields of expertise would not be so quick to clear their diaries for him.

Back in the autumn of 1986, he was still young, thirty-eight, and he didn't yet have that level of success to bolster him. What little confidence he'd had before he met Diana had been shattered by the violence of their life together. He had changed in the last few years, he admitted, and become more philosophical, more intuitive; he was in what Jung would have called 'the middle period', he said. What others might call a mid-life crisis. While his contemporaries were settled in their careers, he was still desperately trying to carve out something worthwhile for himself, something that might please his father, aware that it could be decades before he took up the job he'd been born for. He was utterly charming, but there was none of the sparkle or the humour that he has today. He looked depressed, demoralised, frustrated and trapped, and I felt an urge to mother him. Had his own mother, whose portrait he'd hung so loyally over his desk, not noticed that he was in need of help?

Camilla was flattered, as anyone would be, to be told that she was the only person who might be able to lift his spirits, but it was true. What he needed was someone who was on his side, who understood him, liked him, loved him even, who wouldn't make demands or be moody or temperamental, who was kind and warm, who would make him feel safe, boost his morale, restore his confidence and make him laugh again. Camilla was all of those things, and because she'd had the solid start in life that Diana had been denied, she *could* address the Prince's needs. Emilie van Cutsem and Lady Susan had not exaggerated his state of mind. He was exhausted from five years of trying to handle Diana's distress, saddened beyond belief that he should have failed so spectacularly, and dangerously depressed. 'I never thought it would end up like this,' he wrote. 'How *could* I have got it all so wrong.' And in another letter, 'I am beginning to experience that kind of confusion and rundown of confidence which makes me feel temporarily miserable ... I can't see a light at the end of a rather appalling tunnel at the moment.'

I spoke about the difficulties in my book, *Charles*, that was published in 1987, and thereafter it was as if open season had been declared on the Waleses' marriage. Any scrap of evidence that suggested it was in trouble provoked a media feeding frenzy. Everyone was after photographs that would confirm the endless rumours; the paparazzi were everywhere. The tabloids worked out that in that summer, the couple had spent one day together in six weeks; they noticed that Diana stayed away from Balmoral, they spotted her with friends like James Gilbey, Philip Dunne and David Waterhouse, they insinuated that Charles was having an affair with Sarah Keswick, who was in Scotland as usual with her husband, they suggested he had rekindled his affair with Dale Tryon.

Diana had begun seeing James Hewitt the year before. He was not the first man she had gone in search of love from, but their relationship lasted longer than her other affairs and she appeared to be happy until she abruptly dumped him. He was a good-looking major in the Life Guards who gave her horse-riding lessons, and was a regular visitor to Kensington Palace and Highgrove, where she would entertain occasionally when Charles was away. William and Harry came to know him well.*

Initially, no one seemed to suspect Camilla. The one man who probably came closest was Stuart Higgins, who since 1979 had been a local reporter for the *Sun* in the West Country, covering both Wiltshire and Gloucestershire. He had spent a lot of time in cars chasing after the Prince of Wales before his marriage, trying to work out which girlfriend he had hidden in the boot of his Aston Martin, and he knew Camilla had always been there in the background as a friend and confidante. He suspected an affair but had nothing to go on, but he did think it was very cosy and unusual that she and Andrew and Charles were all so close, given the history. It wasn't how the average man in the street behaved.

Camilla tells the story about how she found Stuart in her kitchen at Middlewick one morning, making himself a cup of coffee. He says she must have a very strange memory – who would do that? – but this is the man who was arrested in 1982 for 'testing security' at Gatcombe. Whether it was over coffee or not, he became friendly with Camilla and phoned her regularly to check whether stories he'd heard about Charles and Diana were

---

* There have been endless rumours that he is Harry's biological father because they both have red hair, but this is complete fiction. Harry was already born by the time Diana and Hewitt met, as both Hewitt himself and everybody who was around Diana at the time have said. Harry's colouring comes from the Spencer family, which is peppered with redheads. What's more, the *News of the World*, which specialised in celebrity exposés until it was closed down in 2011 after the phone-hacking inquiry, had some of Harry's hair DNA tested. If he'd been Hewitt's child, the whole world would have known about it.

true. She never volunteered anything and never made any calls herself, but she gave him a steer, and was always fiercely protective of the Prince. Stuart knew he was verging on becoming a phone pest, but the *Sun* was clamouring for stories and she was always so obliging – and as a result, the *Sun* had some of the most accurate stories of all the newspapers. In 1994 they made him editor – the year he won Scoop of the Year for all his insights. In retrospect, he reckons *she* was using *him* to find out what the press knew.

The person who put Camilla's name out into the public arena was Diana. Revelations from an ex-valet had branded Diana a tyrant with a heated temper who had swept into the Prince's life and, like a spoilt child, banished trusted staff and old friends and even stopped the Prince from hunting and shooting. Journalists 'in the know' said Charles was being 'pussy whipped' by a petulant and jealous wife. Diana was nobody's fool, and soon realised that she could feed stories to the newspapers herself and use them as a way of punishing her husband, while controlling what they said about her. She set out to woo selected journalists at a series of one-to-one lunches set up by the press secretary at the time, Geoff Crawford.

Stuart Higgins was among those journalists. 'Ah, Mr Higgins,' she said, looking about six feet seven inches tall, and stunning in a herringbone suit. 'The man who knows me so well. You're the chap who's very close to Camilla, aren't you?' At the end of lunch she walked him to his car with a box under her arm. It was full of photographs of William and Harry which she laid out on the bonnet; she wanted him to choose the best picture for their Christmas card – very flattering.

From time to time she would ring Higgins, usually to complain about a story. But the person to whom she fed most information, and with whom she developed a closer relationship than any, was Richard Kay, the *Daily Mail*'s royal correspondent. It may have been his boyish good looks, or it may have been that Diana knew the *Mail* and its sister paper the *Mail on Sunday* had a higher circulation amongst middle- and upper-class readers than any other tabloid, and were therefore the most influential. They also had a high proportion of female readers. She'd given Sir David English, who ran both titles, the one-to-one lunch treatment. He'd been duly charmed, but he also knew that taking Diana's side in the war with her husband would be good for business.

Over the years too many people have been ready to believe Charles was a bad man. He wasn't. He was an honourable man who was dealt an unplayable hand of cards. Who knows whether anyone else – a different man, from a different family, in a different job – might have coped better, but he was who he is, and by 1986 he was sinking fast. Camilla brought him back from the brink and gave him the strength to face the world, but only after Emilie van Cutsem and Susan Hussey asked her to. She was not in the picture before that. There were no dastardly plans for her to become his mistress. That happened because the need to feel loved was mutual, and in the way of these things, what started out as friendship and a sympathetic shoulder to cry on turned into a powerful love affair.

At first there were just phone calls. Then he started inviting her to Highgrove when he was there alone, although usually in the company of Andrew or other friends. He and the Princess by this time could hardly bear to be in the same house. Most of their engagements were solo, but when they had to appear together in public, particularly on foreign tours, they were a sensation. Diana, while looking ever more glamorous, had chosen to focus on gritty causes like drug abuse, marriage guidance and Aids, and she was quite unparalleled in her ability to charm, communicate and empathise with vulnerable people. She wasn't like any royal we had seen before; she was a beautiful angel of mercy, and the public couldn't get enough of her. So when she told them that her husband was to blame for the failure of their marriage because of his obsession with Camilla Parker Bowles, many people took what she said at face value.

She did make it all sound very plausible – and people had long wondered how Charles could have walked away from the woman that most red-blooded men lusted after. But it didn't match the facts. He is a deeply religious man, and will one day be Supreme Governor of the Church of England and Defender of Faith. Yes, he may have had misgivings when he walked down the aisle, but he took his marriage vows seriously. He never intended to rekindle his love affair with Camilla, and had those two women not contacted her, and had she not made that phone call, he may never have done so – and the monarchy today may have been facing a very different future.

18

Annus Horribilis

In July 1991, Charles and Diana celebrated ten years of marriage, and although we now know it was over in all but name, this was not common knowledge at the time. Aware that I had written what turned out to be a sensational book in 1987, I was asked by a different publisher to write a book about their marriage for the anniversary, hoping, no doubt, for wonderfully scandalous stories that would sell a million copies. Instead, in *Charles and Diana: Portrait of a Marriage* I said that as Prince and Princess they were still a formidable double act, feted abroad and earning respect for their individual work at home. I didn't retract what I had said about the marriage five years before – they had not found 'the soulmate in one another they had been looking for' – but their working partnership was so strong that I prophesied they would happily go their own ways privately, while staying together for the sake of the monarchy, the country and their children. It is, after all, what people of their class had done for generations to protect their estates.

According to Andrew Morton, whom I know a little and like, my book was the catalyst for his. Diana was so incensed that I should have suggested she was happy with the situation in her marriage that she determined to tell the world otherwise. And she chose Andrew – another man with boyish good looks – to be her conduit.

I have always believed the story that Diana told Andrew Morton about her life needed to be read with extreme caution. By 1992, eleven years into her marriage, she was very angry, very bitter and very unwell. The marriage had broken down irretrievably, they were living largely separate lives and both had lovers. The War of the Waleses was at its height, and Diana, who waged war far more effectively than her husband, was prepared to do and say anything to damage him.

'Diana driven to five suicide bids by "uncaring" Charles', ran the headline on the front page of the *Sunday Times*, which serialised the book. It went on to talk about Diana's bulimia, her husband's indifference towards her, his obsession with Camilla, his shortcomings as a father and the loneliness and isolation she had felt for so many years, trapped in a loveless marriage within a hostile court and disapproving Royal Family. It was uncomfortable and at times shocking reading.

Having written books about both Diana and Charles, I was asked by a number of broadcasters to comment. I pointed out that what seemed to me the most important revelation in the entire book was that the Princess suffered from bulimia, something I, like most people, had not known before. I didn't know about it when I wrote *Diana, Princess of Wales* in 1982 and I didn't know it when I wrote *Charles* in 1987, but having presented a couple of television programmes about eating disorders in the intervening years, I happened to know a bit about them.

Morton accurately described the disease, explaining that sufferers 'indulge in episodes of massive overeating associated with a sense of loss of control':

Between episodes of eating most sufferers fast or induce vomiting. Binges tend to be secret, sometimes pre-planned and are often followed by strong mood swings expressed as guilt, depression, self-hate and even suicidal behaviour. Sufferers usually have a normal body weight but see themselves as being fat, bloated and ugly … and commonly have a sense of failure, low self-esteem and loss of control … Unlike anorexia nervosa, bulimia survives by disguise. It is a sophisticated illness in as much as sufferers do not admit that they have a problem. They always appear to be happy and spend their lives trying to help others. Yet there is rage beneath the sunny smile, anger which sufferers are afraid to express … While the roots of both bulimia and anorexia lie in childhood and a disordered family background, uncertainty and anxiety in adult life provide the trigger for the illness.

Given the nature of Diana's illness, I said in the first radio interview I did that it sounded as though the key to this book was in the title: *Diana: Her True Story*. It was Diana's truth, which may not necessarily have been everyone else's truth – and the stories that Morton related did not sound like the Prince I knew. I had just put the phone down when it rang again and Norton Romsey was on the other end. We had met when I was writing about Charles five years earlier. He had just heard what I had said and encouraged me to keep on saying it. I immediately rang Richard Aylard, the Prince's private secretary, and asked what was going on. He said that he and the Prince and one or two others were baffled because the stories in the book were true in essence but most of them had been given a spin, which made them not quite as anyone else who had been present at the time remembered them. He cited several examples.

From the moment *Diana: Her True Story* hit the newsstands in 1992, life as they had known it was over for Diana, for Charles, for William and Harry, for Camilla and for the entire Parker Bowles family, not to mention the monarchy. And the reverberations from Diana's soul-baring were also felt far further afield. The young princes, then aged ten and eight, were attending Ludgrove, a boys' prep school in Berkshire where they boarded. However much the Barbers, the kindly people who ran it, did to keep the newspapers away from the children, there was only so much they could shield them from. Diana adored her children, but during these years she seemed to lose sight of what was best for them. She made no attempt to hide from them her mood swings or her tears, and she encouraged them to meet the men friends who came to the house. They used to have pillow fights with James Hewitt, and he took them to his barracks in Windsor so they could play on the tanks. They couldn't help but hear the rows between their parents, or notice that their father was seldom there, but they spent most of their time with nannies who did their best to distract and insulate them from what was happening.

Up to this point, the Parker Bowles children had been far less aware of trouble on the home front. Tom was seventeen and at Eton, and like most teenagers was busy with his own life. Laura was fourteen and a boarder at St Mary's, Shaftesbury, a Roman Catholic girls' school in Dorset, and was again happily absorbed with friends and in doing her own thing. If asked, they would probably have said they had a very happy home life. Both Andrew and Camilla made sure that the children came first. They had been very discreet about their extra-marital activity and because they were always so civil to one another, and the whole family made each other laugh so much, Tom and Laura were blissfully unaware that anything was amiss. The Prince of Wales – 'Sir', as they called him – was a regular visitor, but he always had been; he was Tom's godfather, so there was nothing strange about it, and they both loved seeing him. Being away at boarding school for large chunks of the year also helped, but Camilla was careful about the pair of them, and was always there for them at half term and in the holidays. Like so many children, they felt secure in believing that her world revolved around them.

So, having been an entirely private wife and mother, quietly taking her children back and forth to school, to pantomimes and parties, entertaining friends, and looking after the home, Camilla was suddenly a household name. She was painted not just as a scarlet woman but as one who had caused the Princess of Wales years of torment and pain. The press took up residence outside Middlewick. She couldn't leave her own house without being photographed and followed, and poisonous letters started to arrive.

If the Princess took any pleasure in what she had done, it was short-lived. Not long after the Morton book came out, the *Sun* published the transcript of a flirtatious thirty-minute telephone conversation between Diana and her old friend James Gilbey. It was rapidly picked up by every other newspaper and media outlet and for 36p a minute, readers could hear it for themselves on a *Sun* telephone hotline. He called her 'Darling' fourteen times and 'Squidgy' or 'Squidge' fifty-three times, which led to the scandal being dubbed 'Squidgygate' after the American Watergate scandal of the early 1970s. Between endearments, Diana talked about how her husband made her life 'real, real torture', and described a lunch at which the Queen Mother had given her a strange look. 'It's not hatred, it's sort of interest and pity … I was very bad at lunch and I nearly started blubbing. I just felt really sad and empty and thought, Bloody hell, after all I've done for this fucking family.'

On the face of it, Diana was not as bothered as she might have been. According to her PPO, she dialled the hotline herself and when he asked her if the voice she heard was hers, she said, 'Of course it is.' The recording had been made late at night on New Year's Eve in 1989 when Diana was on a landline at Sandringham and Gilbey in a car parked in Oxfordshire. A seventy-year-old radio ham in Oxford, retired bank manager Cyril Reenan, first picked it up, but where it came from initially remains a mystery.

There followed a trip to Korea. Diana tried to duck out of it but the Queen insisted she go. It was a disaster. Neither Diana nor Charles could exchange a civil look, let alone a word, and the press were onto it like a flash. Things were going downhill fast and one more domestic incident, when the Princess cancelled a shooting weekend for the boys at Sandringham with their father and a group of friends, including the Parker Bowleses, was the last straw. It happened every year at half term and they'd been looking forward to it for months. The Prince flipped. The farce had to end.

Thus, on the afternoon of 9 December 1992, Prime Minister John Major stood at the dispatch box in the House of Commons and read to a packed and silent house an announcement from Buckingham Palace that the Prince and Princess of Wales had decided to separate but had no plans to divorce. This was the culmination of a terrible year that caused the Queen to declare 1992 an 'annus horribilis'.

The horrors weren't confined to that year. Less than a month into 1993, the *Daily Mirror* published the transcript of another tape recording that was immediately dubbed 'Camillagate'. It was another late-night telephone conversation, also recorded in 1989, this time between Charles and Camilla; the sort of conversation that should never be overheard. It lasted for eleven minutes and was undeniably genuine, but the recording wasn't of one single conversation; it included bits of several, conducted on different nights and spliced together. Charles would often phone Camilla late at night – no matter where he was in the world, he felt better if he could hear her reassuring voice before he went to sleep – and on this occasion they were evidently both very sleepy. One of the conversations took place on the eve of Tom's fifteenth birthday, so the date was 17 December. They were trying to work out when they might be able to see each other again before Christmas. It is clear that several friends were happy to make their houses available to them as meeting places. Charles was staying in Cheshire with his old friend Anne, Duchess of Westminster, and said he had longed to ask her whether he could bring Camilla but hadn't dared, afraid she would tell people. He had had an exhausting week that culminated in a tour of North Wales, just over the border from Chester. Camilla was at Middlewick with the children, who were home for the Christmas holidays. Andrew was in

London, on standby in case the Army were needed during an ambulance strike.

The part of the tape that everyone remembers was embarrassing beyond words. He was saying he couldn't bear being without her. 'Oh God, I'll just live inside your trousers or something. It would be much easier!'

'What are you going to turn into?' she said with a laugh. 'A pair of knickers?' They both laughed. 'Oh, you're going to come back as a pair of knickers.'

'Oh, God forbid, a Tampax,' he laughed. 'Just my luck.'

'You're a complete idiot!' she said, and laughed some more. 'Oh, what a wonderful idea!'

What was scarcely mentioned, in the media outrage that followed, was that the conversation revealed so much about their relationship. It wasn't just a tawdry affair. It was sweet and touching and about so much more than sex. These people had a proper, loving, supportive and happy relationship, the sort that both lacked in their marriages. Camilla spent most of the conversation boosting Charles's confidence, telling him he was underestimating himself as usual, showing an interest in his work and making him feel good about himself, which no one else did. And in return, he was tender and loving and passionate, telling her how proud of her he was and how her great achievement had been to love him.

He had just made a speech and would be working on another one the next day. 'A rather important one for Wednesday.'

'Well, at least I'll be behind you,' she said, then asked for a copy. And they reverted to the subject of when they would see one another again. I think it bears repeating:

CAMILLA: 'It would be so wonderful to have just one night to set us on our way, wouldn't it?'

CHARLES: 'Wouldn't it? To wish you a happy Christmas.'

CAMILLA: (*indistinct*) 'Happy. Oh, don't let's think about Christmas! I can't bear it. (*pause*) Going to go to sleep? I think you'd better, don't you, darling?'

CHARLES: (*sleepy*) 'Yes, darling?'

CAMILLA: 'I think you've exhausted yourself by all that hard work. You must go to sleep now, darling.'

CHARLES: (*sleepy*) 'Yes, darling?'

CAMILLA: 'Will you ring me when you wake up?'

CHARLES: 'Yes I will.'

CAMILLA: 'Before I have these rampaging children around. It's Tom's birthday, tomorrow. (*pause*) You all right?'

CHARLES: 'Mmm. I'm all right.'

CAMILLA: 'Can I talk to you, I hope, before those rampaging children …?'

CHARLES: 'What time do they come in?'

CAMILLA: 'Well, usually Tom never wakes up at all, but as it's his birthday tomorrow, he might just stagger out of bed. It won't be before half past eight. (*pause*) Night night, my darling.'

CHARLES: 'Darling …'

CAMILLA: 'I do love you.'

CHARLES: (*sleepily*) 'Before …'

CAMILLA: 'Before half past eight.'

CHARLES: 'Try and ring?'

CAMILLA: 'Yeah, if you can. Love you, darling.'

CHARLES: 'Night, darling.'

CAMILLA: 'I love you.'

CHARLES: 'I love you too. I don't want to say goodbye.'

CAMILLA: 'Well done, for doing that. You're a clever old thing. An awfully good brain lurking there, isn't there? Oh, darling, I think you ought to give the brain a rest now. Night night.'

CHARLES: 'Night darling, God bless.'

CAMILLA: 'I do love you, and I'm so proud of you.'

CHARLES: 'Oh, I'm so proud of you.'

CAMILLA: 'Don't be silly. I've never achieved anything.'

CHARLES: 'Yes, you have.'

CAMILLA: 'No, I haven't.'

CHARLES: 'Your greatest achievement is to love me.'

CAMILLA: 'Oh darling, easier than falling off a chair.'

CHARLES: 'You suffer all these indignities and tortures and calumnies!'

CAMILLA: 'Oh darling, don't be so silly. I'd suffer anything for you. That's love. It's the strength of love. Night night.'

CHARLES: 'Night, darling. Sounds if you're dragging an enormous piece of string behind you, with hundreds of tin pots and cans attached to it. Night night, before the battery goes. (*blows kiss*) Night.'

CAMILLA: 'Love you.'

CHARLES: 'Don't *want* to say goodbye.'

CAMILLA: 'Neither do I, but you must get some sleep, Bye.'

CHARLES: 'Bye, darling.'

CAMILLA: 'Love you.'

CHARLES: 'Bye.'

CAMILLA: 'Hopefully talk to you in the morning.'

CHARLES: '*Please!*'

CAMILLA: 'Bye, I *do* love you.'

CHARLES: 'Night.'

CAMILLA: 'Night.'

CHARLES: 'Night.'

CAMILLA: 'Love you forever.'

CHARLES: 'Night.'

CAMILLA: 'G'bye. Bye, my darling.'

CHARLES: 'Night.'

CAMILLA: 'Night night.'

CHARLES: 'Night.'

CAMILLA: 'Bye bye.'

CHARLES: 'Going.'

CAMILLA: 'Gone.'

CHARLES: 'Going.'

CAMILLA: 'Gone.'

CHARLES: 'Night.'

CAMILLA: 'Bye, press the button.'

CHARLES: 'Going to press the tit.'

CAMILLA: 'All right darling; God – I wish you were pressing mine.'

CHARLES: 'God, I wish I was! Harder and harder!'

CAMILLA: 'Oh, darling!'

CHARLES: 'Night.'

CAMILLA: 'Night.'

CHARLES: 'Love you.'

CAMILLA: (*yawning*) 'Love you. Press the tit.'

CHARLES: 'Adore you. Night.'

CAMILLA: 'Night.'

CHARLES: 'Night.'

CAMILLA: (*blows a kiss*)

CHARLES: 'Night.'
CAMILLA: 'G'night my darling, Love you.'

Diana: Her True Story had put Camilla's name into the public arena. The tape recording, the transcription of which was printed in newspapers all over the world, confirmed that she was sleeping with the Prince of Wales. She was branded a whore, a marriage wrecker, an adulterer, and Andrew found himself in the curious position of being the wronged husband. The harassment intensified. No bunch of angry women shoppers actually pelted her with bread rolls outside a Chippenham supermarket – that was a newspaper stunt – but if she had been able to do her own shopping, they might have done. She became the butt of lewd jokes, crude cartoons, lurid headlines; she had disturbing phone calls at all hours of the day and night, received abusive letters, and became a virtual prisoner, alone for a lot of the time, in a big house in the country with no security. She couldn't even go into her garden without there being long lenses in the bushes, and if she left the house, a posse of photographers gave chase in cars and on motorbikes. Life became horrendous, not just for Camilla herself but for all her immediate family. They were all now of interest to the tabloid press, and photographs snatched of any one of them sold well.

How anyone comes back from that sort of public humiliation is unimaginable, and I suspect most people would have been crushed by it. Camilla internalised the pain and presented a brave face. She has a wonderful ability for self-preservation, to put her head in the sand and not think about things that are too difficult. She also, of course, has an unerring ability to laugh even in the most terrible of situations, and her family are the same. They closed ranks, rallied round and kept her spirits up. Rosalind was not well by this time. Her osteoporosis was quietly killing her; she was in a wheelchair, and in such pain and on so many painkillers to ease it by 1993 that she was not fully aware of what was going on, which was a blessing. Bruce was a tower of strength and Camilla's greatest support throughout all these years, right up until her eventual marriage to the Prince twelve years later. Her friends were also fiercely loyal, sticking by her and forming a protective ring around her. No one judged, no one spoke to the press; John Irwin did her shopping for her in Sainsbury's.

Camilla's main concern was for her children. Tom was at Oxford by then, which was a harsher environment than Eton had been; Laura was seventeen and still at school. But they both had friends who were there for them and kept any excessive sniggering at bay. Tom later said of the whole period that 'friends and family were everything. At home there wasn't a newspaper. At school, I've been lucky in having two or three friends – including my cousin Ben Elliot – who've been with me all the way through. By the time you are in your final year at Eton' – when the gossip started in earnest – 'no little bugger is going to talk and if they do, friends would jump in. That gives you a security that runs deeper than anything. Of course Oxford is a much more open society than Eton: there are people who might not agree with toffs or monarchy or whatever. Fine.'

And of the tape itself, 'I sort of remember not looking at the paper. Because, you know, Jesus, the things that we've all said to people that we love … that you wouldn't want the world reading. I just felt pissed off. I wasn't going to read that sort of stuff about my mother, just as much as she wouldn't want to read it about me. My kids certainly wouldn't want to read it about me.

'When it first started we thought it was entirely normal growing up to have five or six paparazzi hanging around – we would go up there with binoculars and say, "Oh look Mummy, there's five today." It was entirely normal to be chased at high speed by these people on motorbikes or cars.

'They're bullies, half of these people, and they made you very angry. When you were fifteen or sixteen and you're coming out of an airport and they were really winding you up, all I wanted to do was smack them in the face and beat the hell out of them. But you couldn't do that.'

To this day no one knows how either recording came to be made. The *Sun* had had the Squidgygate tape for several months before publishing. Stuart Higgins, then deputy editor, and reporter John Askill had met Cyril Reenan in a layby in Didcot. They had played the tape on a car cassette player, feigning mild interest while knowing that what they had was dynamite. They knew it was the real thing when they confronted James Gilbey and he turned white. But the wife of the newspaper's owner, Rupert Murdoch, didn't believe the recordings were genuine, so they kept them until the *National Enquirer*, the American supermarket tabloid, published them. As Stuart Higgins says, 'The world we live in now doesn't have many mysteries left but nobody has ever nailed Squidgygate or Camillagate; they're one of the great unsolved stories. Somebody must know how they ever came to be. How much listening do you do to get juicy stuff like that and then hit the jackpot? How does a Berkshire banker stumble across it? Before I go to my grave I would like to know.'

The original notion that the conversations were picked up by radio buffs was quickly dismissed, and a government inquiry into the intelligence agencies dismissed their involvement too. The Princess had long suspected her phone was bugged, which at the time everyone had put down to paranoia, but when the widespread hacking of mobile phones came to light twenty years later, it no longer sounded so fanciful. She had installed some sophisticated equipment at Kensington Palace, and was one of very few people who had the Prince's mobile phone number.

Diana was not well during those years from the late 1980s to the mid-1990s. She saw conspiracies everywhere – she dropped friends, family and people who worked for her like hot bricks, and was convinced that the Prince's office was trying to discredit her. She left disturbing messages on people's answering machines and pagers. 'We know where you are and so does your wife. I know you're being disloyal to me,' was the sort of message she left for her private secretary, Patrick Jephson. The Prince's private secretary, Richard Aylard, received similar communications. When one of her men friends, Oliver Hoare, tried to cool their relationship, she bombarded his wife with silent phone calls. And Camilla received a number of threatening and unnerving phone calls in the middle of the night. Diana didn't say who she was but would typically say, 'I've sent someone to kill you. They're outside in the garden. Look out of the window; can you see them?'

It serves no purpose to catalogue more of Diana's antics, because so much of it was attributable to her illness. Suffice it to say, many of the people around her walked on eggshells, not knowing what she might do from hour to hour. And with her access to the media, she was like an unguided missile. As one of their friends says, 'I don't think the Prince has ever wanted anyone to hear the whole truth [about the things Diana did] for the [sake of the] children because it's terrible to hear things about their mother. She was their mother and they loved her. Diana didn't just think of herself as a victim, she cultivated it and she played every trick, poor thing. I stopped feeling sorry for her because I resented what she was doing. But then she couldn't have done better – she didn't have it in her.'

Camilla had also been sympathetic towards Diana at first, but she too had stopped feeling sorry for her. She couldn't forgive the things Diana deliberately did and said to damage Charles, or the way she used their children as a weapon against him. Diana made sure the cameras were watching when she was giving them big loving hugs, treating them to a McDonald's or whizzing down a ride at a theme park, because she rang the papers and told them where she'd be – while he was only seen with them on formal royal occasions, like family outings to church. With her they were in jeans and baseball caps, with him they'd be in suits and ties. *Ergo*, she was the fun parent, he was a cold, uncaring father.

One of Camilla's greatest qualities is her utter loyalty to the people she loves, particularly if they are under attack, and she was unwavering in her support for Charles in his struggles with Diana, unashamedly taking his side about everything. Her instincts are good, but she takes a black and white view of life, and is not especially curious about human nature or spirituality, or even about the world. Of all the Shand siblings she is the least imaginative. She and the Prince are very different in this respect – he has huge imagination and curiosity about everything, which is perhaps why they are such a good match for one another. And after all he had been through, to have someone so firmly and fiercely on his side was balm to his battered soul.

19

The Final Salvos

As the twenty-fifth anniversary, in 1994, of Charles's investiture as Prince of Wales approached, Jonathan Dimbleby, the respected writer and broadcaster, was invited by Richard Aylard, Charles's private secretary, to make a documentary and write an accompanying book on the Prince's life. He was given unprecedented access to the Prince himself and to the thousands of private letters that he had written since childhood, and to all his journals and diaries. He was let loose in the archives, invited to speak to past and present members of the royal household, and 'at his behest' to friends and relatives, who 'talked about him openly at length, almost all of them for the first time'.

It had begun as such a well-intentioned exercise, but the consequences were unimaginable and the deal that Aylard struck with Dimbleby, without consulting anyone in the household, had left the Prince very exposed. *Charles: The Private Man, the Public Role*, which ran for two and a half hours and was seen by fourteen million viewers, was directly responsible for Andrew divorcing Camilla, for Diana's devastating *Panorama* interview – watched by twenty-three million viewers – and for her divorce from the Prince of Wales.

Because in just three minutes out of that two and a half hours of good works, the Prince admitted his adultery. 'Were you …' asked Dimbleby, 'did you try to be faithful and honourable to your wife when you took on the vow of marriage?'

'Yes,' said the Prince, and after a brief and anguished pause, 'until it became irretrievably broken down, us both having tried.'

Earlier in the film he had described Camilla in the following terms: 'Mrs Parker Bowles is a great friend of mine … a friend for a very long time. She will continue to be a friend for a very long time.' At a press conference the next day Aylard confirmed that the adultery to which the Prince had confessed was indeed with Mrs Parker Bowles. It was official. And it was a disaster.

Andrew's hand was forced. He had stayed with Camilla for the last five years – the time she and the Prince had been seeing each other – for the sake of the children. At the same time he had been involved for some years with Rosemary Pitman, whose husband Hugh was a friend; they played in the same polo team. The two couples had known each other for many years, but Rose finally got fed up with her husband's roving eye and, knowing there was a vacancy, fell into Andrew's arms. Camilla was well aware of it and liked Rose, they were friends. Life had been quite normal in some ways. They'd see family, go to dinner parties, be at home together with the children and their friends – while Andrew saw Rose, and Camilla the Prince, when the opportunities arose. In some ways it was a perfect arrangement and Camilla was happy with the way things were, but the Prince of Wales forced Andrew's hand. He had certainly not planned to leave Camilla until he had left the Army, Tom had gone to Oxford and Laura had left school, but his position as her husband was now untenable.

As the author of it all, Aylard was convinced the Prince had done the right thing. After the Morton book, the Squidgygate and Camillagate tapes, and reams of newsprint on the subject, it was certainly a question that had to be asked. The Prince's inclination was to tell the truth and Aylard encouraged him. Richard was young and loyal and would have laid down his life for the Prince, but like most of Charles's private secretaries, he was not strong enough to disagree with him – and there was no longer anyone around who was. As Aylard saw it, there were three options: the truth, a lie or evasion. If the Prince lied he would be caught out sooner or later. Some photographer would get a grainy shot of the couple together, or a disgruntled servant would sell their story. If he batted the question away on the grounds that it was a personal matter, the paparazzi that watched them day and night would never go away until they had the proof they were waiting for. And since most people believed they were lovers anyway after Camillagate, why not be honest with the British public and admit the truth?

What Aylard should have foreseen, even if the Prince didn't, was that the great British public was more interested in Diana's truth. They didn't even hear his qualification about 'the marriage having irretrievably broken down'. They heard 'Yes'. He had committed adultery with Camilla, whom according to Diana he had never stopped seeing.

Sir John Riddell, who had been private secretary when I had interviewed the Prince, had a wry view of what went wrong. 'They released Jonathan Dimbleby and the Prince of Wales onto the Scottish moor together at 9.30 and they came back breathless and excited at 4.30; and when you go for a very exhausting walk with anybody – if you went with Goebbels – after a time the blood circulates, the joints ease up, the breath gets short – you'd pour out your heart to anyone, even Goebbels. Jonathan Dimbleby's charms are huge so the Prince of Wales gave him all that stuff about how unhappy he was when he was a boy – the Queen never spoke to him, the Duke of Edinburgh was beastly to him – and it very much upsets them.

'Everyone was told this book would finally show what a marvellous person he was. And people were bored out of their wits by Business in the Community and the Prince's Trust; they wanted to know about their private life. We're interested in who they're going to bed with, except we got rather bored by that because we couldn't keep up with it.'

The 620-page tome that followed, simply called *The Prince of Wales: A Biography*, which went into Charles's feelings for Mrs Parker Bowles in greater detail, probably did more damage than the film. The Prince's difficult relationship with his parents might have been deeply illuminating in terms of understanding the man but it was not helpful for maintaining family relationships. And those friends and relations who had spoken out so honestly to help the Prince were mortified to discover that their words had helped create nothing but unhappiness. A poll in the *Guardian* newspaper showed that 49 per cent of the British public believed they would see the end of the monarchy in their lifetime. After conducting another poll, *Today* newspaper said, 'An astonishing 84 per cent of people think that Charles has damaged the image of the Royal Family by confessing his affair with Camilla Parker Bowles.'

Friends at the time said Camilla had begged the Prince not to speak to Dimbleby, but this was not true – although it is true to say that she was annoyed with him. But the person she reserved her real fury for was Richard Aylard. And from that moment on, Aylard's days were numbered. Friends leapt to her defence. 'Frankly,' said one, 'Charles has behaved like an absolute pig and landed Camilla right in it. She has done absolutely nothing to deserve this after all the support she has given him over the years through difficult times.' Andrew's brother, Simon Parker Bowles, said on behalf of the family: 'Prince Charles does not have our sympathy at the moment. You can't go back and blame your upbringing, or your parents, as he has done. That is wrong and very hurtful. Even if you feel like it, you don't go around talking about it, particularly if you're a member of the Royal Family.'

20

Dark Days

Camilla was shocked when Andrew told her he was going to divorce her. In her usual way, she hadn't wanted to think about the future; the whole thing was too difficult to contemplate. And after five years, others probably imagined things might never change. But it was unrealistic and unfair. Andrew's position had been completely undermined by the Prince's confession. It was one thing for their friends and families to know about his wife's love affair, quite another for the entire world to know.

Besides, he knew that this wasn't just a harmless affair. This was for real. There had been an occasion, a Sunday night some years before, when Andrew had come back to the flat he shared with Nic in London utterly crestfallen. Nic had never seen his brother-in-law upset like this in all the years he had known him. He was shattered. He had found letters at Bolehyde over the weekend that indicated his wife's affair was not the harmless fling he thought it was. It was the real thing. She was in love.

Andrew, now Brigadier Parker Bowles and director of the Royal Army Veterinary Corps, was now Britain's most famous cuckold; the *Sun* called him 'discreet, deceived, destroyed'. He wasn't, of course. Discreet maybe, but certainly not deceived or destroyed. But now that he had been bounced into it, he wanted to marry his girlfriend Rose Pitman, who was now divorced herself and free to marry him. The children were less surprised. They were grown up by now and well aware of what was what, and they coped with the split remarkably well because it was so very amicable.

The Dimbleby broadcast had coincided with the death of Camilla's mother at the age of seventy-two in July 1994 at The Laines. Her world seemed to be imploding. The whole extended Shand family was distraught, not least Bruce, to whom his wife had meant everything. Rosalind had been the linchpin for them all, adored by them all, especially her five grandchildren, who had known her almost as well as they'd known their own mothers but with that extra-special something that's the exclusive preserve of grandmothers. For them she had always been warm, funny and wonderful. They remember pouring her large glasses of gin and Dubonnet. She would always ask for two fingers of gin, which was quite a small measure when they were small, but as they grew older and their fingers larger, she never changed her instructions, the gins simply grew stronger. But it was a very unhappy time for Camilla. In her last few years Rosalind had been a shadow of her former self: she was shrunken, hunched over and in terrible pain; it had been heartbreaking to watch the slow deterioration. She had been suffering from osteoporosis for decades, but in her final three years, her lungs became so bad that she lived on painkillers and alcohol and retreated into a world of her own; mercifully, she was not fully aware of what Camilla was going through or what the press were saying about her daughter.

Rosalind had been appalled when her daughter's name first started to be mentioned after the publication of the Morton book. When the tapes were published, no one talked to her about it; they tiptoed around the subject, thinking that secretly she was choosing to block it out. And although they lost her long before they should have done, everyone in the family agrees that it was a blessing that Rosalind didn't live to see everything that followed. She was suffering already from the osteoporosis that would kill her.

What is so devastating about osteoporosis is that initially there is no pain and the first indication of a problem is when a bone fractures – although even then it's not always picked up – or height is lost or the classic widow's hump develops. Until not so long ago, most doctors thought those changes were a natural part of the ageing process – something that happened to little old ladies. But it's not – the fractures occur and the spine collapses because disease has weakened the bones; bones that should be strong and solid develop the consistency of a fragile honeycomb, leaving the skeleton so weak that the simplest knock or fall can snap a bone, particularly in the wrist, spine and hip.

Like most people at that time, the Shand family knew nothing about osteoporosis when it struck Rosalind, as it had Sonia Keppel before her. As Camilla has since said, 'My mother's GP was kind and sympathetic but he was able to do little to alleviate the terrible pain she was in. We watched in horror as she quite literally shrunk before our eyes. She lost eight inches in height and became so bent, she could not digest her food.'

After Rosalind's funeral, Bruce, Camilla, Annabel, Simon, Nic Paravicini and his second wife Sukie all went away together to a house they rented in Portugal, inland, high up and away from the tourist spots. It was in such an elevated position that when they woke up the first morning they thought it was a foggy day. The house was actually shrouded in cloud; down in the valley there was blazing sunshine. All they wanted from the holiday was a rest, a little peace and quiet away from the beastly photographers that followed Camilla everywhere. After the sadness of the last few weeks they needed some respite. Yet they had scarcely been there five minutes when in the midst of a game of tennis Camilla suddenly said, 'We've got to stop; they've found me.' She had developed almost a sixth sense by this time and had spotted the glint of a lens high up in the hills above them. The English girl they'd taken on to do the catering – who was a terrible cook – had tipped off the *News of the World*, so everywhere they went there was now a camera lens hiding in the bushes. The holiday was wrecked.

Camilla spent a lot of this unhappy time after the Dimbleby revelations and their mother's death with Annabel, hidden away at her large family house at Stourpaine in Dorset. Annabel and Simon had lived there since their marriage in 1972, and it was where he grew up. A successful business-man and property developer, Simon is steady and straightforward, and when the axis shifted from The Laines to Stourpaine after Rosalind's death he took over the role of family patriarch; he's the dependable one they all go to when any of them is in trouble and he sorts it out.

Despite their closeness, Annabel and Camilla have always been very different people, with their own aspirations. Annabel was a reluctant debu-tante; she had travelled, she'd studied art in Florence, she'd stayed with her great-aunt, Violet Trefusis. She'd had an Italian boyfriend for a long time, to her sister's bemusement, and had been a bit of a hippy. She is strong, steely and determined, like her sister, and has all Camilla's warmth and charm, but is more of an introvert than her sister. She was not conventional in any way; she had no interest in the London social circuit, the sporting season or smart parties – and she and Camilla share very few of the same friends. 'They are very direct, there's no bullshit with these ladies,' says one of the men in the family. 'They are not people who are shy about saying what they think and are very candid if they dislike someone.'

Annabel runs a very successful business from home. She started out with antiques – buying, selling, turning things into other things; it was something she'd loved doing since the late 1960s. She's now expanded into interior design, and at Camilla's suggestion has done a great deal of work for the Prince of Wales, renovating and furnishing Duchy properties. The appearance of her name in the Duchy's annual accounts regularly causes a flurry of indignation in the press. In 2016 they showed that she had been paid £1.5 million in the eleven years since her sister's marriage in 2005 'for goods and design services', but as Annabel has been heard to say, 'For that amount I've done up forty houses and bought every stick of furniture – and get a pretty tiny fee. Working for the Royal Family doesn't keep the wolf from the door. Of course it gives you a profile, but financially, forget it.' Her largest commission was decorating and furnishing the 26-bedroom Duchess of Cornwall pub/hotel in Poundbury, which the Queen and the Duke of Edinburgh visited that day at the end of 2016. And while he may not be the best payer, she does love her brother-in-law dearly.

Mark was even less conventional than Annabel. He and Camilla were chalk and cheese. They loved each other fiercely as brother and sister – and all three siblings just had to catch each other's eye to become helpless giggling wrecks – but otherwise the eldest and the youngest had little common ground apart from their family ties. Annabel was the bridge between the two of them, but was more akin to Mark than Camilla was – and always more likely to confide in him than her, because she was a terrible gossip and couldn't keep secrets. Annabel was the only one of the three with a business brain.

Having not made the grade for Eton, Mark was sent to Milton Abbey School. Having been expelled at sixteen for smoking dope, he was sent to work on a sheep farm in Australia by his father, who thought 'it might put some spine in the little bugger'. He travelled with his friend William Waldorf Astor III, and a stopover in India for a few days turned into a month. 'I immediately felt at home,' he said. 'I had lived there in another life, at another time. It was that smell – the smell of incense, cow-dung, smoke, shit, sweat, burning fires, Chamoli and Champa blossoms, sandalwood, disinfectant, frying curry leaves, chilli, chai and moth balls. It is a fragrance so heady that I've always thought if a great perfumer could bottle it, the scent would be the most intoxicating in the world.'

Mark got into some terrible scrapes in his crazy, wild life before it was cut short tragically in 2014. He was a mad adventurer, best defined by his first book, *Travels on my Elephant*, in which he described the 600-mile journey he made across India with an elephant called Tara that he fell spectacularly in love with. In a recent reprint of the book, he wrote, 'How did a posh, privileged, fat, little boy with a fiendish temper end up one steamy, Indian monsoon night, deep in the jungles of Orissa, buying an elephant? It was a circuitous 35-year route, detouring through the respectable and the disreputable, the fast, the furious and the far reaches of adventurousness.'

Part of the journey involved a lifelong friendship and one-time business partnership with Harry Fane, second son of the 15th Earl of Westmorland. They founded Obsidian in New York, specialising in objets d'art and Art Deco jewellery, much of it by Cartier:

> Like posh swagmen in linen suits, with sacks of beautiful booty over our shoulders, we hit the rich and famous, the old and new wealth in the money-drenched capitals of the Americas: Caracas, New York, Dallas, Houston, Los Angeles, Palm Beach and Miami. In the mid '70s, New York became the party capital of the world with the advent of the infamous nightclub, Studio 54. It was hedonistic, decadent, glamorous and fuelled by the drug of the moment – cocaine. Although this period remains a complete haze I made many good friends.

For respite, the two of them escaped to the island of Bali every year, where a friend built them a beautiful Robinson Crusoe house on a surfers' beach. They 'lived a bohemian life, chilled-out and very anti-social'; a notice on the door said, 'If you are a friend of a friend fuck off.' Just as the business became successful, opening in Jermyn Street in London, and he found himself in a suit going to work every day, Mark quit. He sold his flat, persuaded his doting grandmother, Sonia Keppel, to persuade his parents to release the last funds he possessed in the world, bought an old 28ft, eight-tonne yacht in Thailand, restored it and set off to write the story of a man he'd heard about late at night in a bar in Bangkok called Sexy Tyler, who lived with many wives in paradise on an island called Rennell. It was hurricane season in the Pacific, his travelling companion forgot to buy a sextant, the first leg of the journey took fourteen days instead of four and they ran out of food and water, nearly dying in the process. They were hit by a hurricane off the Solomon Islands and, having been thrown around the cockpit like matchsticks, were rescued from the 'massive pounding surf' by locals, who patched them up and saved their lives. The yacht was less fortunate. 'I burst into tears and cried all night,' he wrote, 'as I watched my beloved boat fighting for her life, illuminated by the headlights of the many vehicles lining the shore ... in the morning, I saw her rise up once more, topple backwards and snap in two like a matchstick. I was numb. My dream had ended. I had lost everything.'

After several months sitting in a heap in Bali, Mark received what he described as 'one of my father's very special letters – which read: "I think it's about time you stopped feeling sorry for yourself, contemplating your navel under the bodhi tree, and got back home."'

Uncle Mark was a hero to his nephews, Tom and Ben. Tom later wrote of 'the way his face creased with glee and his shoulders clenched together as tears began to roll down his cheeks'.

He was a master of church mischief. All he needed to do was catch the eye of my mother or aunt and that was it. They were off, consumed by helpless hysteria. And the more inappropriate the occasion, the better.

It didn't always amuse my grandfather, who would turn around with a furious glare. But Mark made church fun. Whoopee cushions under our great-uncle's chair. Wind-up mice let off down the aisle. Stink bombs rolled under pews. The moment his tricks were discovered, he'd wink at us then put on a very serious face and blame us. God, we loved him. While he was adored by our sisters, my cousin Ben and I worshipped the man. We'd do anything for him.

He could swim three lengths of our grandparents' pool underwater, throw a cricket ball over the house and deep into the downs. He'd buy us cigarettes and booze and take us to the pub at 14. What other uncle would arrive back for Christmas with supermodel girlfriends – supermodel girlfriends who would come down to breakfast in tight silk negligees? My mother and aunt were less than impressed.

The glamorous girlfriends came and went until the age of forty, when Mark married the actress Clio Goldsmith, daughter of conservationist Edward Goldsmith and niece of the financier Sir James Goldsmith. Sir James's second wife, Lady Annabel, was an old and close friend of Simon and Annabel Elliot. And it was in the Goldsmiths' beautiful Queen Anne house near Richmond, in 1989, that Diana confronted Camilla for the first and only time about her affair with her husband. It was Annabel Elliot's fortieth birthday party, which Annabel Goldsmith had offered to host for her. Charles and Diana were amongst the guests and Diana used the occasion to have it out with Camilla, who was also there with Andrew. As the Princess described it to Andrew Morton, she found Camilla talking to Charles and another man, both of whom made their excuses, when she joined them and left. She invited her rival to sit down, then said, 'Camilla, I would just like you to know that I know exactly what is going on between you and Charles, I wasn't born yesterday.' Camilla was furious that Diana should have made such a public scene.

Mark and Clio had a big family wedding at The Laines in 1990, although the Shands were convinced that their new in-law thought them the family from hell and hated them all, especially Camilla. Clio had been married before, to the Pirelli heir, Carlo Puri Negrib, with whom she had a twelve-year-old daughter called Talitha. Rosalind adored Mark – he was her out-and-out favourite – but alas she didn't live to meet the daughter he was so proud of, Ayesha, who was born in 1995.

After Mark's sudden death, falling on a New York pavement, Annabel spoke to the writer Bob Colacello about their mother for the American magazine *Vanity Fair*. 'Camilla and I were having lunch with her. And she said, "Darlings, I've always been completely fair between the three of you, haven't I?" Camilla's and my jaws dropped. Because that was *not* the way it was. Literally, Mark could do no wrong. There's the theme that should run through your whole story: Mark, having been worshipped by my mother, was spoiled by women his whole life.'

They didn't love him any the less but because he was so often off doing his own thing he was less aware than other members of the family when his eldest sister's life started to implode.

21

Divorce

In December 1994, Andrew and Camilla jointly filed for divorce on the grounds that they had been living apart for more than two years. The plea was heard in the High Court Family Division on 19 January 1995, and took seventy-five seconds. The plan was for Camilla's lawyer, Hilary Browne-Wilkinson, to issue the following statement to the Press Association, and for Simon Elliot to handle all enquiries:

> The decision to seek an end to our marriage was taken jointly and is a private matter, but as we have no expectation that our privacy will be respected, we issue this statement in the hope that it will ensure that our family and friends are saved from harassment.
>
> Most especially we ask that our children, who remain our principal concern and responsibility, are left alone to pursue their studies at what is clearly a difficult time for them.
>
> Throughout our marriage we have always tended to follow rather different interests, but in recent years we have led completely separate lives. We have grown apart to such an extent that, with the exception of our children and a lasting friendship, there is little of common interest between us, and we have therefore decided to seek divorce.

The plan had come out of a meeting of rather unlikely participants, including Patty and Charlie Palmer-Tomkinson, at whose house in Hampshire they all met. Also present were Camilla, the Prince of Wales, Jonathan Dimbleby, Annabel and Simon Elliot, Richard Aylard and Alan Kilkenny, a public relations wizard who had helped the Prince with various enterprises over the years.

The day before the announcement, Andrew went to see the housekeeper at Middlewick, Margaret Giles, who lived in a tied cottage at the end of the drive, to warn her there might be a deluge of press on the doorstep. She tipped off the South West News Agency – Stuart Higgins' old employer – and within minutes Higgins was on the phone to Simon saying he'd heard the Parker Bowleses were about to divorce. It was impossible to deny the story, which was all over the *Sun* the next day, accompanied by a number of personal photographs. Some came from a family album which had been kept in the house; others – including one of Camilla's four-poster bed – were taken by someone who had access to the house. It didn't take Sherlock Holmes to work out who the culprit was. Mrs Giles, who had a set of keys to the house, had been offered £25,000 for the photos, although the money was never paid. Andrew and Camilla sued the *Sun* and the tabloid settled out of court, agreeing to pay £25,000, which went to charity.

The ink was scarcely dry on their statement when the *News of the World* ran a photo of the Prince of Wales's bed at Highgrove, alongside a story with the headline: 'Charles Bedded Camilla As Diana Slept Upstairs'. One of his valets, Ken Stronach, who'd been with him for fifteen years, was tricked into selling his story and taking the photograph.

Camilla felt very vulnerable after the divorce. All the old certainties were slipping away. She no longer had the protection of her marriage and once Middlewick was sold, she didn't even have the house. It was bought in May by Nick Mason, the Pink Floyd drummer, and his actress wife, Annette Lynton. Camilla had lost everything: her mother, her husband and her home. She'd had no thought about the future, no thought that her divorce, or the Prince's, might mean that she and he might one day be together. The future she feared was alone, alarming and uncertain. But her father and her family closed ranks around her as they always had done and kept the world at bay. They had spent one last Christmas together as a family, the first one without Rosalind, but as always with Bruce and the Elliots and all the cousins. Before Rosalind became so unwell, The Laines had always been the house the family went to for get-togethers, weddings, birthdays, Christmases, Easters and holidays in general. Everyone adored The Laines, it was heaven – and even as the grandchildren grew older they still loved going there and being with their grandparents. But now Stourpaine took over.

As they suspected, the harassment didn't go away, it only intensified after the divorce. But what they hadn't expected was the impact of Camilla's infamy on their children. Tom was arrested in a nightclub at Oxford for possession of cannabis and ecstasy, something that happens at universities every second week. Most twenty-year-olds get a fright, are given a caution and it's forgotten. Not Tom. He was indeed cautioned, but because of his mother, his offence was front-page national news. Difficult for Tom, it was devastating for Camilla. It violated all the natural laws of motherhood.

Again family bolstered her, along with a circle of local and loyal friends, several of whom felt she'd been let down by Charles; people like Fiona Shelburne, Patty Palmer-Tomkinson, Carlyn Chisholm, Amanda Hornby, Carolyn Benson, Candida Lycett-Green (Sir John Betjeman's daughter) and Amanda Ward, who was married to Gerald Ward, a very old friend of both the Prince and Andrew Parker Bowles. It was with Gerald Ward that Camilla had caught her first salmon years ago. His uncle owned Kinnaird, an estate in Perthshire with one of the best salmon-fishing beats on the River Tay, and Camilla triumphantly caught two fish, one weighing 18lb and the other 15lb. But it was Charlie and Fiona, the Earl and Countess of Shelburne, now known as the Marquess and Marchioness of Lansdowne at Bowood, their stately home near Calne, who put a roof over her head after Middlewick was sold and took in her dogs – Freddie and Tosca – as well.

She and Amanda Ward, along with another friend, Sarah Troughton, went to painting classes together every week for four or five years in the village of Sherston. Sarah is now Lord Lieutenant of Wiltshire – her husband Peter is an old university friend of the Prince – and she was known by the other two as 'teacher's pet'. Their teacher was Neil Forster, a local artist and friend of the Prince. 'I did take it slightly more seriously than they did possibly,' she admits, 'but it sort of fizzled out as these things do. We were doing still lifes – lifes you say, not lives – and landscapes and occasionally portraits. We used to paint each other or get some hapless model in to paint. Just the three of us. It was great fun and then we had lunch in the Angel pub in Sherston. It kept us human.' Neil, who sadly died in 2016, had taught the Prince on and off and would go on painting holidays with him. His animal portraits are astonishing.

Camilla soon found Ray Mill, a Regency house near the village of Lacock, outside Chippenham, which was under an hour and a half from Stourpaine, and less than half an hour from Highgrove. Lacock is one of the prettiest villages for miles around; there's an historic abbey, founded in 1229, with cloisters and twisted chimneys, honey-coloured houses with undulating stone roofs, also dating back to the thirteenth century, and very little sign of modern life. The River Avon meanders nearby. It is owned by the National Trust and is often used as the setting for television series and films. The BBC production of *Pride and Prejudice* was shot there, as was *Downton Abbey*, and many of the classrooms and corridors at Hogwarts in the Harry Potter films are found in Lacock Abbey. It attracts thousands of tourists – but none of them could get a glimpse of Ray Mill.

A friend knew the owners, the Gilsons, were downsizing and so the house, with a swimming pool, stables and seventeen acres of land, never came onto the open market. Camilla bought it quickly, paying £850,000. It was perfect and the situation, well hidden away at the end of a long drive, just fifty yards from the river with an old mill, was delightful. It has six bedrooms, a big kitchen at the heart of the house with a blue Aga keeping it warm, a sitting room with a large open fireplace, floor-to-ceiling bow windows and double doors leading into the garden, a smaller, cosier sitting room that she calls the 'snug', again with a big fireplace and oak panelling, and a big dining room. There was already a productive vegetable garden, a greenhouse with grape vines, and fruit trees including a fig. And mature trees all round. Particularly appealing is an area the Gilsons had preserved as a wildlife sanctuary for swans, geese and river birds.

Worthy Gilson was an art historian who stored his priceless objets d'art and antiques in a rather ugly modern red-brick barn. As a result, the property had already been turned into a fortress with eight-foot walls, high hedges, metal electric gates, security cameras and alarms. And because he didn't have room for all his treasures in the house he was planning to move to, Camilla agreed to a delayed completion to give him time for Sotheby's to conduct a house sale in the autumn. So she, Tom and Laura and their livestock moved in in time for Christmas 1995.

Her hope was to convert the barn into a cottage for her father to live in. She hastily submitted a planning application, but it was doomed to failure.

The house was in a conservation area and the Wiltshire District Council planners are notoriously awkward. To her great disappointment, it wasn't possible for Bruce to live with her; instead he went to stay with Annabel in Dorset, where he very happily spent the rest of his days living in a little cottage across the courtyard from the main house.

Although it was a lonely time for Camilla – perhaps it even came as a surprise to her not to get what she wanted – it was probably for the best that Bruce went to Stourpaine. Her siblings definitely thought so. They didn't want him pulled into all the media nonsense at his age. They thought he needed a more peaceful existence than he would have had at Ray Mill; as it turned out, his daughter would seldom have been there and he would have been the lonely one. He wasn't lonely at Stourpaine, although he became a bit forgetful in his last couple of years – if a pretty girl from the *Daily Express* walked in, he would be quite likely to say, 'Come and have a glass of champagne, my dear.'

Shortly before Camilla moved into Ray Mill, and just as things seemed to be calming down, Diana released one final salvo. By then her halo was beginning to slip. She had been seeing Will Carling, the England rugby captain, whose wife Julia took a dim view of events and sued him for divorce. Carling never admitted adultery but the public, who had followed the story closely in the tabloids, were left in no doubt that Diana had been instrumental in what became a very acrimonious and public break-up. Having nurtured her role as victim, it was uncomfortable for her to feel the chill wind of disapproval.

But it wasn't for long. Ever resourceful, she secretly invited the television journalist Martin Bashir into Kensington Palace, where he interviewed her for the BBC flagship current affairs programme *Panorama*. Looking pale and vulnerable, with heavy black kohl lining her eyes, head to one side and slightly tilted down, brushing away the odd tear that threatened, she talked about her feelings of isolation and emptiness in her marriage, of being a strong woman, a free spirit. She talked about her bulimia, her self-harming, her cries for help. She talked about the Prince's friends who waged a war in the media against her, indicating that she was 'unstable, sick and should be put in a home'. She talked about his obsession with Camilla, and 'the enemy' that tried to undermine her – her 'husband's department', jealous that her work got more publicity than his. She talked about the men in her life and admitted she had been in love with James Hewitt and unfaithful to her husband with him. And she talked about being so distressed when James told his story that William had produced a box of chocolates and said, 'Mummy, I think you've been hurt. These are to make you smile again.'

The most memorable moment of the broadcast was when she explained why her marriage had failed. 'There were three of us in this marriage,' she said, 'so it was a bit crowded.'

As a parting shot, when asked whether he would ever be King or would wish to be, she said, 'Being Prince of Wales produces more freedom now, and being King would be a little bit more suffocating. And because I know the character, I would think that the top job, as I call it, would bring enormous limitations to him and I don't know whether he could adapt to that.' And when William came of age, would she wish to see him instead of his father succeed the Queen? 'My wish,' she said, 'is that my husband finds peace of mind, and from that follows other things, yes.'

It was a superb performance, worthy of an Oscar, and shrouded in such secrecy that not even the governors of the BBC had an inkling. Charles didn't watch the programme himself but was soon told about it. Camilla watched it at home with her family and laughed at the sheer theatricality of it, as did many people who knew the Princess. She had manipulated Bashir just as she had Andrew Morton, turning her private battle with the Prince into a public execution without a thought for her children. Shortly before it went out, she'd told her private secretary she'd done an interview but refused to tell him what it was about. 'It's terribly moving,' was all she'd say. 'Some of the men who watched were moved to tears. Don't worry, everything will be all right.'

That's where she was wrong. Things were by no means all right. The Queen finally lost her patience. This public mud-slinging wasn't just harming the monarchy, it was damaging for the young princes. After consulting with the Prime Minister and the Archbishop of Canterbury, she wrote formally and privately to her son and daughter-in-law asking them to put the country out of its uncertainty and to divorce as early as practicable.

22

Blackadder

The Prince's divorce could not have been more acrimonious. Richard Aylard, who handled it for him, spent several hours almost every day for several months closeted with lawyers. Charles was represented by Fiona Shackleton from the royal solicitors, Farrer and Co., while the Princess had engaged Anthony Julius, a high-profile divorce lawyer from the well-established firm Mishcon de Reya.

By July 1996 they had reached a settlement thought to be worth more than £17 million, although both parties signed a confidentiality agreement about it and the precise deal was never known. They retained equal access to William and Harry and equal responsibility for their upbringing. The Princess was to continue to live at Kensington Palace, but her office would be there too and not at St James's Palace as she would have liked. The only contentious issue was what she would be called. She was stripped of the title Her Royal Highness. This was not what the Prince wanted, but it was not in his gift; it was a decision for the Queen. It made little practical difference but in public relations terms it was a blunder. When she asked Prince William if he minded her losing her royal status, he replied, 'I don't mind what you're called – you're Mummy.'

On Richard Aylard's advice, St James's Palace issued a statement saying that the Prince of Wales had 'no intention of remarrying'. It was a gesture to bridge the divide between the two Palaces, a peace offering to the Queen, to the public and to the Anglican Church, but from Camilla's perspective it was a giant snub.

She felt as though she was being publicly consigned to the box labelled 'mistress' – and that may well have been the final stiletto in Aylard's coffin.

As anyone who has been through a divorce will know, divorce lawyers are a breed apart, but Camilla's was an exception to that rule. Hilary Browne-Wilkinson, who worked for the law firm Charles Russell and was married to Law Lord Nico Browne-Wilkinson, became a good friend and ally. Antipodean by birth and typically forthright, she agreed that Richard Aylard had given the Prince of Wales bad advice over Jonathan Dimbleby, and was one of a growing band of people at court who thought it was time for Aylard to go. It was not just the admission of adultery; it was the lack of control over the whole project, the lack of consultation with colleagues, and the decision to let Dimbleby into the inner sanctum to plunder letters and journals with such devastating results.

She had a suggestion about who might replace him. Over dinner with Charles and Camilla and another couple one night at St James's Palace, when Aylard was present, her husband waited until coffee was served, then cleared his throat and launched into a fearsome attack on the way the Prince's staff had handled the media. He said it was the collective view of the legal profession that the situation could not be worse, or more damaging for the monarchy.

'Have you come across a man called Mark Bolland?' Hilary asked the Prince. 'He works for the Press Complaints Commission,' on the board of which she sat. She described this Canadian-born, comprehensive-school educated, clever, entertaining, powerful, tough, irreverent, well-connected thirty-year-old who had been director of the PCC for the last five years. 'You should hire him,' she said, 'and see if he can do anything to help.'

Bolland was taken on at a lowly level as a press officer in July 1996, with the promise of good things to come. The press office at that time was run by Allan Percival and his deputy Sandy Henney, two former civil servants, and without reference to either of them, Bolland was appointed Sandy's assistant. Within months he was deputy private secretary, Percival had jumped ship and Aylard was gone. The Prince, as always, had given in to pressure – a certain amount of which was coming from Mrs Parker Bowles. He was deeply fond of Aylard and knew it wasn't fair to blame him for everything. Aylard had loved him and served him loyally for seven years, working long hours, over weekends – at the cost of his own marriage; he was always at the end of a phone, always ready to drop everything when the

Prince needed him. He had been there through many difficult years and had sorted out Charles's impenetrable divorce for him. But he had alienated some powerful people, and that was his mistake. As one observer said philosophically, 'Richard is a classic case of that S-level cliché: "The victims always get a bad press because the victors write the history books."'

Overnight, Bolland became the Prince's golden boy. He is gay, tall, good-looking, direct and very persuasive. He had taken on the position telling Charles that he could not only 'bear' to do the job – the Prince's word – but that he intended to have some fun doing it. 'If you don't have fun in a job,' he said, 'there's no point in it. It doesn't all need to be so terrible. Things can get better.'

'If you say so,' the Prince had said.

'Well, I do, actually.'

Bolland's upbeat nature and his attitude to the job, to life, the universe and everything appealed to the Prince. They struck up an instant rapport and very soon Bolland had leapfrogged into a position of power. He was indispensable, the man the Prince trusted above all others. William and Harry nicknamed him 'Lord Blackadder' after the scheming comic character in the TV series of the same name, played by Rowan Atkinson. His task was to rescue the Prince's reputation and make Camilla acceptable to the British public. He went about it with gusto, by whatever means it took.

Julia Cleverdon, who then ran Business in the Community and has worked with the Prince for more than thirty years, was once in a meeting with Bolland and Stephen Lamport, who succeeded Aylard as private secretary, discussing some arcane subject, and the following morning the entire conversation apppeared on the front page of the *Daily Mail*. 'I said to Stephen Lamport – I was slightly nervous because I was a relatively new chief exec – "I only talk to those that I'm given permission to talk to and only on the basis that it will be helpful, but I certainly haven't said anything to the *Daily Mail*" and he was absolute classic Foreign Office – hear no evil, see no evil. "Yes, there was something but I don't think we're going to make too much fuss about that, Julia." I thought, you're the leader and you're not going to make a fuss about it, in which case I take it this is either authorised or you're not prepared to face him down.

'And in a way, looking back on it, his task was to get them married, bring Camilla out of the shadows, and he did exactly that. I don't expect the entire household was privy to what the plan was, but that was the plan.'

Bolland rather liked the Princess. Despite her divorce she still took a lively interest in her ex-husband's office and lost no time in inviting Bolland to tea at Kensington Palace to see whether he might be an ally. She rang him regularly to complain if she wasn't happy about something. 'Mark, I'm very cross,' she would say, 'I don't know what's going on.' One of the things that made her blood pressure soar was the lavish fiftieth birthday party that Charles hosted for Camilla at Highgrove in July 1997. It wasn't the party that worried her. It was the *Daily Mail*'s report of the evening, which began, 'She was the first to arrive, sweeping into Highgrove last night with all the confidence of a queen.' Normally, Camilla came to Highgrove secretly by a little-known back drive that was unmarked and off a completely different road. She thereby avoided any photographers who might be lurking by the main entrance. But on this occasion, at Bolland's suggestion, the press had been told about the party and were out in force, and when Camilla's chauffeur-driven Ford Mondeo arrived at the gate, it slowed right down to let the photographers get a good shot of her. She looked wonderful in a figure-hugging black dress with a diamond and pearl necklace round her neck, her birthday present from the Prince, and she was smiling.

When Sir Robert Fellowes, Diana's brother-in-law and private secretary to the Queen, had heard about plans for the party, he was furious; he said that if it went ahead he would have to advise Her Majesty to tell the Prince that he must give up Camilla for good. His colleagues, Robin Janvrin and Mary Francis, deputy and assistant private secretaries, were dismayed by his attitude and told him that if he advised the Queen as he threatened, they would have to offer different advice.

By this time Diana was quite relaxed about the Prince's relationship with Camilla. She was forging a new life for herself; she'd become a crusader for land-mine clearance and made much-publicised visits to Angola with the HALO Trust, and she had new romances of her own. For two years she'd been seeing a Pakistani heart surgeon, Hasnat Khan, and was said to have been very much in love and considering converting to Islam so they could marry. What agitated her about the glitzy party was the prospect of Camilla becoming a public figure. But Camilla had no such ambitions. She was more than happy to remain in the background, a private person, seeing the Prince for occasional nights and weekends – whenever his busy schedule allowed it – and taking holidays together. And in-between times, having the habitual long late-night telephone conversations when they were apart.

The joy for them now they were both divorced was that they could legitimately go away together, and they could stay with friends, some of whom – like Nic and Sukie Paravicini – hadn't welcomed them together until they were divorced. The Paravicinis had a beautiful home at Glyn Celyn House near Brecon in Wales, and it was there in July 1996 that the paparazzi snapped a grainy photograph of Charles and Camilla together. However secretly they tried to move around, the Prince of Wales can go nowhere without a performance. His PPOs have to check out in advance anywhere he is planning to stay, the sniffer dogs are brought in, the local police are involved and often news leaks out via one means or another. On this occasion, the *News of the World*, which broke the story, claimed they'd had an anonymous tip-off from 'a well-spoken woman'. Some time after they'd arrived, Nic was walking his dogs down a line of beech trees in the grounds of the house when the dogs shot off into the bushes and flushed out two photographers, who legged it. He ran after them, shouting and waving his stick. The police caught them and made a show of taking their cameras, but no real crime had been committed and they were released. But by then the *News of the World* had its front page – a totally innocuous photograph of the two couples walking along the terrace, with an ill-fitting headline to go with it: 'Camilla And Charles In Love Show. Mysterious caller brings illicit affair into open.'

One of the few members of the Prince's staff who was taken to meet Camilla at that time was Sandy Henney, who was still number two in the press office. Richard Aylard introduced them and told Henney to let no one know, not even her boss, Allan Percival. The only other person present was Colin Trimming, one of the Prince's PPOs. Her first thought was 'Blimey, why am I getting involved in this?' but secretly she felt quite privileged. 'And then, of course, you meet her and you think, Ah, now I see what he sees in her, you really do. The press were always publishing pictures of her that made her look unattractive, but when you actually meet her, she's incredibly attractive, and she's got a kind of smokey voice, and she's got that look in her eye, and I thought, Yep. I understand now. She has a great sense of humour and though she was extraordinary, she was actually ordinary. She sometimes would invite a few of HRH's team to her home at Ray Mill and cook us lunch. There was a homeliness about the place, it was lovely – I want to say it was organised chaos. There was a huge table in the middle of her kitchen and she would get up and be fussing around and bringing stuff to the table and saying, "No, no, I'll do it." She was just totally hostess at home with lots of people. And laughter, just laughter, sometimes at his expense as well, which was good! And there was no "Mrs Parker Bowles". She said, "My name's Camilla, so please call me Camilla." I was ill at one point and the next thing I knew the doorbell rang and she'd sent flowers and a note saying "Get well soon." At Christmas there'd be presents. She didn't have to do that. It wasn't currying favour, she just wanted to do it.'

Every year during the summer months, the Prince of Wales and his court spend a week in Scotland at the palace of Holyroodhouse in Edinburgh, a week in Wales and a week in Cornwall, visiting local businesses and projects, meeting people and giving a nod to his various titles: Duke of Rothesay, Prince of Wales, Duke of Cornwall. His staff always used to joke that he had shares in Eddie Stobart, the haulage company, because it takes one – some say two – large articulated lorries to move him. Not much more than the kitchen sink remains at Highgrove, and it is all set up at the other end just how he likes it. He now has a property in Wales, but for several years he used to stay at an apartment at Powis Castle near Welshpool, not far from the Paravicinis. It is always a very intense week, when a lot is crammed into a few days.

One year, as the sun was setting in a pink sky, the royal helicopter touched down at the castle at the end of a very long day. Sandy knew her boss was exhausted and desperately in need of a restorative martini but as they walked into the private wing of the building, there was a reception party waiting to greet them, amongst them Andy Crichton, a member of the Prince's staff. Camilla was also there – she was staying at the castle, as she often did, beneath the radar. Sandy noticed she was beckoning her over. '"There's going to be an almighty explosion," she said conspiratorially. "I thought you might like to hide around the corner with me." Andy was there to tell the Prince that some foreign dignitary had died and he would have to go to the funeral. He was knackered, he'd had hours of talking to people, it was the height of the season, he's had full-on exhausting days and just when he wants to put his feet up he has to travel thousands of miles to a funeral. And she absolutely read his mind. All hell broke loose and I just said to her, "Thank you!" She got me out of the way of the explosion and I loved her to bits for that.'

Andy had been with the Prince for years, originally as a PPO. After he retired from the Metropolitan Police, he became an extra equerry in the office, and then a chauffeur. He also looked after Camilla for the Prince from time to time, accompanying her on the foreign holidays that she took with her sister or girlfriends, and on flights if she was on her own – anywhere he thought there might be a question mark about her safety. Her face was now well known, and thanks to all the books and tapes and television programmes, she was one of the most hated women in Britain. And yet as a private individual she took regular flights, sat in airport lounges, walked the streets and had no protection.

The only organisation Camilla had become involved with was the National Osteoporosis Society (NOS), and she did so on the strict understanding that there would be no publicity. Not long after her mother's death, Linda Edwards, then director of the NOS – a remarkable woman and brilliant campaigner, who sadly died of cancer some years later – wrote to Camilla. She had read an article that mentioned Rosalind's osteoporosis and enclosed some literature which she thought might help, inviting her to get in touch if she wanted further information. Camilla replied to say that sadly her mother had died since the article was published, but she wished she had known about the society earlier. Could she please come and see them? In due course she went to meet Linda at the NOS's research centre near Bath, and after looking round and hearing about their work said she would like to do something to help prevent others suffering the way her mother – and, by association, every other member of the family – had.

What the charity needed most at that time was money, and with Camilla's contacts, she knew she could help. And so it was that a year later, in September 1995, she raised £10,000 hosting a soiree at Bowood House, which was where I first met her. Alan Kilkenny, who is a friend, had helped organise the evening and knowing I wanted to meet Camilla had put my name on the guest list. Years before, when I wrote my book about Charles, I had stupidly muddled Camilla Parker Bowles with another pretty blonde, Camilla Fane, with whom he had been photographed at polo matches. I said, 'The Prince fell deeply in love with Camilla, more, some friends say, than he has ever been again.' Both Camillas took legal action and I paid dearly for my mistake.

Eager for a bit of sport that night, Alan introduced me to Camilla with the words, 'Penny tells me you sued her.'

'It wasn't me, it was my ex-husband,' she said, with a mischievous twinkle in her eye. 'Let me find him for you.' With that she clasped my hand and we wove our way across a marquee full of chattering people until we found Andrew. Andrew is a charming and delightful man, also something of a hero. As commander of the Knightsbridge barracks when an IRA bomb killed four soldiers and seven horses, wounding many more, in Hyde Park in 1982, he was first on the scene and responsible for saving Sefton, the black gelding who was so badly injured but became a symbol of defiance against terrorism. Camilla, nevertheless, took great delight in embarrassing him. But it was a measure of just how civilised and amicable their divorce had been that he was there that night.

It was a beautiful evening in a beautiful setting. There was champagne, music, sculpture, theatre and short speeches. Linda talked about the charity and in front of two hundred illustrious guests, despite crippling nerves, Camilla spoke about her mother's illness, Tom recording her words on video. It was the first time she had spoken in public and it was profoundly moving. Laura was also there, as were the rest of her family: Bruce, Simon and Annabel – who's also become very involved in the NOS – Mark and Clio, and even Nic and Sukie Paravicini. Camilla also quietly donated to the charity her half of the £25,000 settlement she and Andrew got from the *Sun*.

A few months after the soiree, Linda wrote to Camilla inviting her to become a patron of the NOS. 'Do you really think I will do you any good?' was her immediate response. She knew just how unpopular she was and thought any formal association with the charity could be positively harmful. Linda was adamant.

'Look,' she said, 'your mother died of osteoporosis; your grandmother, you now realise, died of osteoporosis. You have spoken from time to time about the devastating effect it had on your family, so you are very aware of how osteoporosis can destroy someone's quality of life. You've learnt that at first hand. Inevitably, people want to read about you and if at the same time they are reading about osteoporosis and putting osteoporosis on the map, then you are helping an awful lot of people. We can make it a household word and give it the recognition it needs to get something done about it.'

And so Camilla agreed. A photograph was released, taken by society photographer Sir Geoffrey Shakerley, a friend, which for the first time gave the public an image of Camilla that was not snatched by a paparazzo, and allowed people to see what the woman there'd been all the fuss about really looked like. The *Daily Mirror* devoted a full-page spread to the photograph, with a team of experts analysing Camilla's hair, make-up and clothes, the image, the smile, and what the picture was saying. 'A new chapter has opened in Camilla Parker Bowles' life. And this is the picture that proves it ... Now she is rid of the role of furtive mistress,' it concluded, 'she can look into the camera with confidence instead of fear ... Most people found it difficult to see why Prince Charles divorced stunning Diana to spend his time with Camilla. But now we can see for ourselves a little of the magic that he fell in love with.'

Following on from the success of the soiree, Camilla and Annabel decided to host a fundraising extravaganza at Talisman Antiques, Annabel's business in Dorset that was housed in a former brewery. The date was set for 13 September 1997, the invitations promised 'an evening of enchantment, fascination and the unexpected'. Tickets were £100 each and while they aimed for an attendance of 500, there were so many applications they didn't stop till 700 had been sold. The acts were booked, the ticket money was in, donations had flowed in, the cheques had been banked, the catering organised, and as the excitement of the day grew nearer there was mounting speculation in the press that the Prince of Wales would attend. If so, it would be another step in the direction of making Camilla a legitimate part of his life.

All was to change, when in the early hours of Sunday 31 August 1997, Diana was killed in a devastating car crash in a tunnel under the River Seine in Paris. She was in the back seat of a powerful Mercedes with her lover, Dodi Fayed, by her side. The French driver was trying to outrun a posse of paparazzi that was chasing them on motorbikes. He had been drinking, he lost control at high speed and ploughed into a pillar. He, Dodi and Diana all lost their lives. There was only one survivor: a bodyguard, sitting in the front passenger seat – the only one wearing a seatbelt – who was seriously injured.

William and Harry, mercifully, were with their father and the rest of the Royal Family at Balmoral, as they were every August. Earlier in the holidays, they had been to the South of France and stayed with their mother and Dodi on the Fayed yacht, but had returned in time for the family migration north. They were due to fly to London the next day to spend a few last days with their mother before the start of the school term.

23

Week of Waiting

The first call alerting the family to the accident came through to Robin Janvrin, the Queen's deputy private secretary, at one o'clock in the morning while he was asleep in his house on the Balmoral estate. It was from the British ambassador in Paris, who had only sketchy news. The Princess had been injured but no one knew how badly. Janvrin immediately telephoned the Queen and the Prince of Wales in their rooms at the castle, and put together a team of people to set up an operations room and man phones throughout the night. Meanwhile in London, the Prince's team – Mark Bolland, Sandy Henney and Stephen Lamport – were being woken and told the news, ironically, by the tabloid press. Their information, which came directly from the emergency services, was therefore more up to date than the ambassador's, and for once they were a great help to the Prince's staff. Dodi they knew was dead; the Princess was injured but alive.

Never was the relationship between the Prince and his mother more starkly demonstrated than that night. They were just feet away from one another in their separate rooms, divided by paper-thin walls, but they didn't go to one another, either for comfort or to discuss logistics. It was left to Camilla, five hundred miles away at Ray Mill, and other friends the Prince rang, to do the comforting through what remained of the night, and to his staff to debate how the Prince should get to Paris to visit his ex-wife in hospital. Mark Bolland played a pivotal role that night. The most obvious answer was to use an aeroplane of the Queen's Flight, but that required Her

Majesty's specific permission and Janvrin was doubtful it would be forthcoming.

At a quarter to four the debate became academic. A call came through from the embassy in Paris to say that Diana was dead. She had lost consciousness very quickly after the impact and had been treated for an hour at the scene by the emergency services, who then took her to the Pitié-Salpêtrière hospital. Surgeons there had battled for a further two hours but had been unable to save her.

Camilla had at first thought that Diana's injuries were not much more than a broken arm – which is what the Prince had been told. So when he rang at 3.45 with the news that Diana had just died on the operating table, she was as shocked as he was. They spent a long time on the phone for what remained of the night. She was terrified for him. He didn't know what to do about the children, whether to wake them and tell them straight away or let them sleep until the morning and tell them then. He was absolutely dreading it. The Queen said they should be left to sleep. Charles knew immediately what the public reaction would be; they would blame him. The world would go mad and it could destroy the monarchy. He'd said as much to Bolland, who had known, as Camilla knew, that he was absolutely right.

I was woken by the telephone at five o'clock that Sunday morning. As I dragged myself to consciousness, a voice at the end of the phone said, 'This is ITN News, we are getting reports from Paris that the Princess of Wales has been killed in a car crash. We are live. Can you comment?' I was as shocked and speechless as everyone else. It was the first of about fifty such phone calls from all over the world – and that day, as fate would have it, I was giving a big lunch party in the garden of my house in Wiltshire. Dozens of people stayed away but as the first dazed souls arrived, there was an apocalyptic crack of thunder and the heavens opened. It was a very surreal day, I think for most people old enough to remember it. ITN were persistent and I agreed to appear on *News at Ten*. They sent a car for me and as we reached central London the streets were eerily full for a Sunday night. Thousands of people had come out to line the fourteen-mile route between RAF Northolt, where the plane with its sad cargo landed, and the Chapel Royal at St James's Palace, where Charles insisted the Princess be taken. Not knowing what else to do, the public had taken to the streets to watch and weep. They were on the roadsides and bridges, the embankments, the roads and pavements, and they were still there long after the hearse had passed.

The Prince had taken Diana's two sisters with him to Paris. It had been a gruelling mission for them all and while Jane and Sarah went home to their families, Charles got into the plane again and flew straight back to Scotland to be with his sons.

There followed the most extraordinary and dangerous week for the Royal Family. They remained in the Highlands while the rest of the country went crazy. Their reasoning couldn't have been better – and in the long run, I think, was right. They felt that the two young grief-stricken Princes, then just fifteen and twelve, were the priority. The funeral would be on Saturday and they needed some time to adjust before they were confronted with the public outpouring of grief. Meanwhile the country bayed for their monarch to show her face in London. Diana's death was a national tragedy and at times of national disaster, the Queen, or a senior member of the Royal Family, is usually one of the first to visit, to express sadness and commiseration, to spearhead the national sentiment – to represent the nation to itself. It's one of the functions of monarchy. But the Queen and other senior royals stayed at Balmoral, while in London mountains of flowers piled up outside Kensington Palace and to a lesser extent Buckingham Palace, and the headlines screamed at them. 'Show us you care'. 'Your subjects are suffering, speak to us Ma'am'. 'Where is our Queen: Where is her flag?'

The Royal Standard only ever flies when the monarch is in residence, and it never flies at half mast because technically the country is never without a monarch – a fact expressed in the age-old saying, 'The King is dead, long live the King'. Therefore, while every other flag in Britain was lowered, there was no flag flying at Buckingham Palace. It seemed symbolic of everything that was wrong with the monarchy – stiff, hidebound and out of touch – compared with everything that was so perfect about Diana, who was warm, compassionate and loving. Prime Minister Tony Blair got it right. That Sunday morning when Charles had the painful task of collecting her broken body, Blair paid a moving tribute to the Princess. His voice cracking with emotion, he said, 'I feel like everyone else in this country. I am utterly devastated. We are a nation in a state of shock, in mourning, in grief. It is so deeply painful for us. She was a wonderful and a warm human being. Though her own life was often sadly touched by tragedy, she touched the lives of so many others in Britain and throughout the world with joy and with comfort. She was the people's Princess and that is how she will remain in our hearts and memories for ever.'

In the most brazen display of hypocrisy, the newspapers picked up the theme. Just four days before Diana died, Lynda Lee-Potter, then the doyenne of women columnists, had written in the *Daily Mail*, 'the sight of a paunchy playboy groping a scantily-dressed Diana must appal and humiliate Prince William … As the mother of two young sons she ought to have more decorum and sense.' Her sentiments were echoed elsewhere.

Did they ever make the wrong call. By the time their words were published Diana had found beatification. And her brother had the press in his sights. From his home in South Africa he said, 'I always believed the press would kill her in the end,' adding that the editors and proprietors of every newspaper which had paid money for intrusive pictures of his sister had 'blood on their hands'.

'Born a Lady, Became our Princess, Died a Saint' ran one headline. 'Magic Touch of a Goddess' said another. 'She was the butterfly who shone with the light of glamour which illuminated all our lives,' wrote Ross Benson in the *Daily Express*; 'A beacon of light has been extinguished,' said Lady Thatcher; 'A comet streaked across the sky of public life and entranced the world,' wrote Simon Jenkins in *The Times*; and Paul Johnson in the *Daily Mail* called her 'A gem of purest ray serene'. 'Goodnight, Sweet Princess,' said the *Sun*, which sold an extra million copies that day. 'She was Royal but she was Special – because she was one of us. Around the world, the words "Lady Di" brought a smile to the lips of the needy, the sick, the dying and those in despair. They probably didn't know what the words meant – only that they made them feel better … The World will never Forget Diana.' And Dodi had turned from a 'paunchy playboy' into 'true love at last'.

The media were saturated with tributes, photographs, stories, eulogies, supplements. Other news scarcely got a look-in. The death in Calcutta five days later of Mother Teresa, who subsequently *was* beatified by the Roman Catholic Church, passed virtually unnoticed. And meanwhile from Scotland there was no word, no tribute, just the news that the boys had gone to church with the family on the morning their mother died – business as usual. The press were even critical of that.

The family was not unaware of what was going on south of Aberdeen – plenty of people were telling them – but the Prince of Wales knew better than to say anything. The bulk of the blame was directed at him. Not at Dodi, nor even at his father, who supplied the car and the driver, who hurtled through Paris at dangerous speed, or the bodyguard, for failing to stop him. The paparazzi were obviously the immediate cause of the accident, so the common narrative ran, but the real villain was Charles. If he had loved Diana as he should have done, if he had honoured his marriage vows and not committed adultery with Camilla Parker Bowles, then the Princess would never have been racing through the streets of Paris without proper police protection.

The *Daily Mail* that Tuesday ran a front-page photograph of the Prince out walking by himself, looking rapt in thought, with the headline 'Charles Weeps Bitter Tears of Guilt'. They omitted to say that the photograph had been taken some months earlier. The paper described how he had gone, 'bleary-eyed', walking across the moors in the early morning, 'asking, why, why, why? He had stayed up into the early hours drinking stiff gin-based martinis and making telephone call after call to friends, most of whom had long gone to bed. By now the tears that had coursed down his ever-sun-tanned cheeks had gone ... The question is: What made Charles weep such bitter tears? Sorrow, naturally ... Shock and nostalgia also at what he had seen, standing there beside an electric fan which made a breeze that lifted the fringe of the dead Princess's hair. And guilt ... No one has ever seen him racked with such a sense of frustration and confusion as yesterday. He was distraught, and entirely drained, seeking answers to the unanswerable.'

The first sign of life from Balmoral came on the Thursday, the day the *Daily Mirror* shouted, 'Your People are Suffering. Speak to us Ma'am'. That day the Union flag was hoisted to half mast over Buckingham Palace – for the first time ever – and the family emerged from the gates of Balmoral to view the messages and floral tributes that had been left there. The children had said they would like to go to church again, so Charles took the opportunity to give them a taste of what awaited. The Queen, the Duke of Edinburgh, the Prince of Wales, William, Harry and their cousin Peter Phillips all got out of their cars to look at the flowers and tributes. About sixty members of the public were there, as were some photographers, and apart from the sound of their camera shutters clicking there was not a sound to be heard apart from the voices of the royal party. It was a touching scene and they were visibly moved by what they saw.

'Look at this one, Papa,' said Harry, grabbing hold of his father's hand and pulling him down. 'Read this one.'

This was not the cold, uncaring Prince whom Diana had described, and that gesture alone spoke volumes. Of all the accusations Diana threw at

Charles during their bitter war of words, the charge that he was a bad father was the one that hurt the most. It was demonstrably untrue, as anyone who has seen Charles with his children knows very well. Diana knew it too and she later regretted her words.

The next day, in the nick of time, the Queen made a surprising live television broadcast and saved the day. In forty-five years she had only once before broadcast to the nation other than at Christmas, and that was during the first Gulf War.

'Since last Sunday's dreadful news we have seen, throughout Britain and around the world, an overwhelming expression of sadness at Diana's death.

'We have all been trying in our different ways to cope. It is not easy to express a sense of loss, since the initial shock is often succeeded by a mixture of other feelings: disbelief, incomprehension, anger – and concern for all who remain. We have all felt those emotions in these last few days. So what I say to you now, as your Queen and as a grandmother, I say from my heart.

'First, I want to pay tribute to Diana myself. She was an exceptional and gifted human being. In good times and bad, she never lost her capacity to smile and laugh, nor to inspire others with her warmth and kindness. I admired and respected her – for her energy and commitment to others, and especially for her devotion to her two boys. This week at Balmoral, we have all been trying to help William and Harry come to terms with the devastating loss that they and the rest of us have suffered.

'No one who knew Diana will ever forget her. Millions of others who never met her, but felt they knew her, will remember her. I for one believe that there are lessons to be drawn from the extraordinary and moving reaction to her death.'

After a heated debate, the Prince's wish that Diana be given a full state funeral in Westminster Abbey prevailed, and he, the Duke of Edinburgh, William and Harry all joined Charles Spencer in walking behind the cortege as it progressed from St James's Palace to the Abbey. There were stories that the boys had been forced to participate in order to protect their father from abuse from the crowds, but it was nonsense. They walked because they chose to.

Thousands of people had flocked to the capital, and some of them camped on the pavements and in the parks, but many of them walked the streets. United in their grief, there was a camaraderie amongst them. Most had candles, some of them cried, many of them sang, but overall the mood was good-humoured. Earlier in the week it had been menacing.

The funeral was immensely moving, a perfect mix of ceremonial pageantry with informality. Tony Blair read 1 Corinthians 13 and Elton John sang a specially rewritten version of 'Candle in the Wind', which left not a dry eye. But the denouement of the service was Earl Spencer's tribute to his sister.

'Diana was the very essence of compassion, of duty, of style, of beauty. All over the world she was the standard bearer for the rights of the truly downtrodden, a very British girl who transcended nationality ... she needed no royal title to continue to generate her particular brand of magic ... Diana explained to me once that it was her innermost feelings of suffering that made it possible for her to connect with her constituency of the rejected.' He went on to talk about her insecurity, her deep feelings of unworthiness, of which her eating disorders were merely a symptom. Her bafflement that the media seemed intent on bringing her down, and the irony that she shared a name with the ancient goddess of hunting but was 'in the end the most hunted person of the modern age'.

But it was his pledge for her sons that offended. 'She would want us today to pledge ourselves to protecting her beloved boys William and Harry from a similar fate, and I do this here, Diana on your behalf. We will not allow them to suffer the anguish that used regularly to drive you to tearful despair.

'And beyond that, on behalf of your mother and sisters, I pledge that we, your blood family, will do all we can to continue the imaginative way in which you were steering these two exceptional young men so that their souls are not simply immersed by duty and tradition but can sing openly as you planned.'

24

A Low Profile

The Prince of Wales did indeed cry as he strode over the Scottish heather in those days after Diana's death. He's a deeply emotional man and he cries very easily, as does Camilla. On this occasion the tears flowed, but they weren't tears of guilt – unless it was for the sense of relief he felt that all the pain and the suffering was now over. In many ways Diana had been the ex from hell. She had spied on him, made it difficult for him to see his sons, upstaged him, embarrassed him, leaked stories to the press; had been all in all deeply infuriating. But a part of him loved her – she was the mother of his sons, and he loved her for that if for nothing else.

He wept bitterly at the sheer tragedy of it all, that their life together, which they had both so wanted to work, should have ended in such acrimony and anger, and he wept for William and Harry. For all the confusion and distress they sometimes felt around their mother, they adored her and she adored them, and that unique bond could never be replaced. They would never feel her comforting arms around them again, never hear her infectious laughter, and they would carry that loss for the rest of their lives. And he wept for his failure to help Diana. He knew he had done his best – no guilt there – but she'd been beyond any help that he was able to provide. It was a bruising and difficult time for him – and he worried about Camilla and what he had done to her too.

'That must have been an appalling period for her and I thought she was courageous and humble and decent,' says Julia Cleverdon. 'He was in agony about it, he really, really was, and the fact that she was prepared to go through all this for him I think illustrates what an incredibly strong relationship and partnership they've had. Knowing a bit about it at that time, when we ever talked about it, he was in genuine agony about what she was putting up with – and that does of course then mean, "It's all the bloody press, the beastly journalists, it's Murdoch, it's all of them." That's an entirely understandable and natural default mode.'

Camilla went to ground. Charles needed to devote his energy to his sons and to rehabilitating himself, and for the time being, as far as the public was concerned, she needed to vanish. They were back to cloak-and-dagger antics – and long telephone conversations. It was a few weeks before he summoned the courage to face the public and he knew it would be a long time before his name could be linked to Camilla's again – longer still before they could be seen together. They had been so close but were now so far apart. But he had already made it perfectly clear to anyone who would listen that Camilla was a non-negotiable part of his life. The Queen had wanted her gone before Diana's death and felt no differently after it. It was nothing personal. She had been very fond of Camilla in all the years she had been married to Andrew, but it was Camilla who had been responsible, wittingly or not, for all the disasters that had befallen the Prince since his marriage.

Her stance was one of monarch not mother, and therein was the problem. Her son badly needed support and this woman had given it to him. She had rescued him from the depths of depression, had shown him love and comfort, approval, tenderness that had been so woefully lacking from any other quarter.

Amid conflicting advice, the Prince got back on the road at the end of September. He was encouraged to do so by Julia Cleverdon, the extraordinarily charismatic, inspiring and lovely woman who has been his special adviser on his Prince's Charities. The two have had a very close and fond working relationship for years and Julia was one of the first people he introduced to Camilla. It was 1996 and they were preparing to go to a Tesco golf tournament to collect a cheque for £250,000, a donation to the Prince's Trust. The Prince was complaining bitterly, which is his standard practice, almost as if it's a mechanism for combating his natural shyness or summoning his adrenalin. 'Yes, I do agree,' said Camilla sarcastically. 'Sunningdale is a very long way from Highgrove' – in fact it's eighty-three miles, a quick hop down the M4 – 'but you're only going to be there for fourteen minutes.

Let's divide fourteen into a quarter of a million. It's probably a rather higher rate than the Spice Girls earn.' And as usual he giggled and his temper was restored.

Julia had stayed at Highgrove overnight and on their way there, the Prince had said, 'Julia, I've got a very good friend coming to dinner tonight.' She quickly said she would leave him to it and have an early night.

'No, I'd very much like you to meet her. It's Mrs Parker Bowles.'

There followed a very jolly evening. To her delight, she found that Mrs PB, as everyone in the office had taken to calling her, was someone who makes life fun – she's a great giggler – and has a capacity to make Charles talk and laugh about what has happened during the day while making it quite clear that doing what he may not always enjoy is his duty. It was obvious she was interested in him as a campaigner and that she cared about the causes he cared about. Above all, she was funny, and a good raconteur, and she lifted the mood. It was a common observation. Often friends invited to Highgrove for dinner would try to find out whether Camilla would be there beforehand. The Prince was always so much more fun and the evening so much more relaxed if she was.

Julia's advice about resuming his public appearances in September was 'It's always better to get out there and be seen rather than to stay hidden behind closed doors.' It was advice drawn from painful experience. By an extraordinary coincidence, her husband had died very suddenly and unexpectedly on a family holiday in Greece, two weeks before the Princess died. She had made her way back home with their children, in a state of great distress, to be met by her mother who said, 'I've had the Prince on the phone four times, he says he must be the first person to speak to you as you come in through the door.' At that moment the phone rang again and it was Charles.

His support since then had been unstinting. So although Julia had planned to take two months off, she went to Manchester to offer her own support. As did Tom Shebbeare – who at the time ran the Prince's Trust – Mark Bolland and Sandy Henney. The Prince was terrified – they all were; Diana had been dead for less than three weeks, Manchester can be a tough city, and none of them knew what sort of reception he might get. As the plane landed, he straightened his tie in front of the mirror for a second or two longer than usual, took a deep breath and stepped out to face the cameras.

He abandoned the speech they had all helped him prepare, and at his first port of call, a Salvation Army centre, spoke movingly from the heart, thanking the public for their kindness in what had been an unbelievably difficult time, and paying tribute to the courage of his sons.

After the separation back in 1992, the Prince had brought in Alexandra Legge-Bourke, known as Tiggy, to keep an eye on William and Harry when they were with him rather than their mother. The 28-year-old daughter of a family friend was a delightful, bouncy nursery school teacher, who was like a big sister to the boys. They adored her and she them, which the Princess had found very hard to take, but by good fortune she was at Balmoral the day Diana died, and her presence there during that week was a godsend. Once they returned to Highgrove after the funeral, she was there too, as impulsive as ever.

On the Monday, she took them, on foot, to the meet of the Beaufort Hunt. They were going to follow the action by car, as many people do. Seeing them arrive, Captain Ian Farquhar, the Master, went over and, speaking on behalf of the entire meet, said very simply, 'It's good to see you, sirs. I just want you to know that we are all very, very sorry about your mother. You have our deepest sympathy and we were all incredibly proud of you on Saturday. That's all I'm going to say and now we're going to get on with the day.'

'Thank you,' said William. 'Yes, you're right. We all need to get on with the day.'

Diana was worried that her boys loved Tiggy more than they loved her – she had sacked a nanny when they were small for exactly the same reason – but she never had any worries about Camilla on that score. Since their separation, the Prince made certain that Camilla was never in the house when the children were present. He had once broached the subject of Camilla with them. It was two months before their mother died, during the summer he threw the party for Camilla's fiftieth, and he was hoping to gradually ease her into his life. He sat them down together and tried to explain the situation, but both boys went very quiet. He sensed that William in particular didn't want to know, and so he left it.

By that summer the press had turned their attention to Diana's land mines and her love life, and Camilla could once more come and go from Ray Mill without automatically being followed. She still had no protection and no driver – until one evening in June, when she had an accident and everything changed. She had been humming along the lanes between Ray Mill and Highgrove in her Ford Mondeo – owned by the Prince – on her way to have dinner, when she met a woman in a Volvo coming the other way. The winding roads are single-track in places, with numerous dips and crests, but she knew the route well. She was momentarily distracted, and with a terrible banging and crashing of glass and metal, the two cars collided. The Volvo ended up on its side in the ditch, while the Mondeo lost a wheel. The other driver was trapped inside because her skirt was shut in the door, but apart from being very badly shaken and bruised, neither woman was seriously injured.

Camilla's first reaction was to ring the Prince, who immediately sent a car to the rescue, with a couple of protection officers, while someone at Highgrove rang the local police. They found her sitting by the side of her car in the road crying. She had gone over to the Volvo, looked in through the window, screamed loudly, panicked and run off. The driver said Camilla's car had 'appeared like a missile' and complained that she'd left the scene, but didn't press charges.

It was only then that the Prince realised how very vulnerable Camilla was. She had always been resistant to the idea of protection, even when things were at their worst, but now he insisted upon it and she was persuaded. The idea of being driven everywhere, being shielded from the media and having someone to arrange her life for her did have its appeal – so, as well as a car and a driver, he provided a part-time personal assistant. From that day onwards Camilla was taken under the protective umbrella of St James's Palace. She was becoming a visible and acknowledged part of the Prince's life.

25

Raw Recruit

Amanda MacManus is still with Camilla today, still part time – a private secretary, a trusted aide, a touchstone and a vital part of the Duchess's operation. Like everyone who works for Camilla, she is good fun, refreshingly normal and friendly and untouched by the red-carpet fever that affects so many courtiers.

It was Hilary Browne-Wilkinson, Camilla's divorce lawyer, who suggested Amanda for the job. They had known one another when Hilary was married to Barry Tuckwell, the professional horn player. Amanda had lived in their house and organised his concerts. She was then in her early twenties; her parents had both died young, after which she had cared for her younger brothers, fallen in love with a Frenchman and missed the university boat. Domestically proficient but with no formal qualifications, she organised Barry's life for him, though she had never worked in an office environment.

Hilary thought Amanda would be perfect for the job and took her down to Ray Mill to meet Camilla. They liked each other immediately, but the pair were equally inexperienced. By now Amanda was married with young children and was living in Dulwich in south London. The deal was that she would drive down to Ray Mill once a week to meet Camilla, go through her correspondence – file the hate mail – send autographs to those that wanted them, and deal with anything else she wanted help with. For the other couple of days she would work from home.

On rare occasions she went into the Prince's office at St James's Palace. One of those occasions was shortly before the big birthday party when she was asked for help with the guest list, and shown to a desk and a computer. On screen was a detailed spreadsheet with the names of those who'd been invited, when they'd replied, the drivers' details, when they were coming and where they were staying.

'When I got the job, no one had asked me if I'd ever worked on a computer before,' she says, gaily, 'and I hadn't. Somehow I got this list up in front of me and it said, "Do you want to save?" and I thought no, so I pressed "Don't save" and these pages flew off the screen. I tried to get it back and I thought, Ooh that's strange. I literally knew how to press a button to turn the thing on but nothing else. At some stage this guy came along to see me and I said, "I think I've lost the guest list, do you think you could help me?" And that was *the* guest list, the *only* guest list. So he said, "I don't know what you've done but you've done it very effectively, you've wiped the entire thing." God was on my side and I found one hard copy but there was general hysteria – and everybody worked out that I'd never used a computer before.

'And then the Duchess rang – literally twenty minutes later – and said, "I hear you've wiped my guest list," and I said, "Yes I have, and I think I'm going to take a one-way ticket to Argentina." She said, "I don't think you need to do that." Nothing really fazes her, she always sees the funny side of things. And we did have some very funny times.'

One night they were driving up to London to an art exhibition to which Camilla had been invited. As they walked into the gallery Amanda was aware that people were looking at them and saying to one another in surprise, 'That's Mrs Parker Bowles.' She began to feel slightly uneasy and then it dawned on her they were looking at oil paintings, while the invitation was to an exhibition of watercolours. 'I said, "Listen, we're in the wrong exhibition."

'"What do you mean, we're in the wrong exhibition?"

'"I've brought you to the wrong exhibition."

'"So what are we going to do?"

'"We're just going to put our drinks down and potter off to the right one."

'So we went round the corner into the next gallery where her sister and family were and, of course, it was hysterical. "You'll never guess what Mandy's just done – taken me to the wrong exhibition!" I didn't live that down for a long while.'

A less amusing incident, in July 1998, lost Amanda her job briefly. Prince Charles's fiftieth birthday was looming in November 1998, and William and Harry had decided to give him a surprise party, initially to be attended by his godchildren and their parents, which would take place at Highgrove on 31 July. They'd seen Tom Parker Bowles, who was of course the Prince's godchild, and Laura at Easter. Charles had wanted them all to get together – they hadn't seen each other properly since they were children – and so he invited them to stay at Birkhall, the Queen Mother's former residence at Balmoral. Despite the age difference, the four had got on well. William told his father he would now like to meet their mother.

One day William rang from school to say he was coming to London for the weekend. It caught everyone on the hop. At the time they were living at York House, next to St James's Palace, and since neither of the boys were expected, Camilla was there. She immediately said she would leave. The Prince said, 'No, stay. This is ridiculous.' He then rang William and told him Mrs Parker Bowles was in the house, would that be a problem. To which William had answered, 'No.'

They were expecting William at seven that evening, but he turned up at half past three and went straight up to his apartment at the top of the house. Camilla was with Amanda and feeling decidedly anxious, as they all were. The Prince of Wales came and found her. 'He's here,' he said. 'Let's just get on with it. I'm going to take you to meet him now.' He took her upstairs, introduced her to his son and left them alone to talk. About half an hour later, Camilla came out saying, 'I need a gin and tonic!'

She was joking. It had gone well. William was friendly and Camilla was sensitive enough to know things had to go at William's pace. She was a mother, after all, and well understood how conflicting and difficult this would be for him, particularly now his mother was no longer alive. A few days later they met for lunch, and then she started spending the odd night in the house when he was there. But she never stayed at Highgrove when either of the boys was home. There were no memories for them of their mother at York House, but Highgrove was a different matter. It had been Diana's house.

Shortly afterwards, Rebekah Wade, then deputy editor of the *Sun*, and a close friend of Mark Bolland, rang Sandy Henney to say she'd heard there had been a meeting. Sandy was furious. She obviously couldn't deny it but knew it would undermine all the work the communications team had done to reassure William the press had a place. Furthermore, he didn't trust his father's office and would think someone was spying on him. She asked Rebekah for 24 hours to give her time to speak to William.

An internal inquiry was immediately launched and days later Amanda MacManus fell on her sword. She had gone home that night and told her husband, a *Times* newspaper executive, about the meeting and he had mentioned it to someone else who had told the *Sun*. She was devastated, but surprised and touched, by how upset Camilla was to see her go. As they said goodbye at the door of Ray Mill for the last time, and Amanda headed home to Dulwich, they were both in tears.

A few days later Camilla rang her and asked her to come back. She has been with the Duchess ever since. And when Amanda's had crises in her life, when she's been going through personal difficulties, Camilla has been there for her. 'She would never get involved, never ask but always be quite supportive. She'd never say "You need to do this," or "Why don't you do that?" She would never offer advice unless she was asked for it. I rather like that. Staggering loyalty, and she expects loyalty in return.'

So the routine of a day a week in Wiltshire continued, working either in the little study or at the kitchen table, breaking for coffee and for lunch, when they would put together something simple from the fridge. The children were both away – Tom was working and Laura at university; and a cleaning lady/housekeeper came in for a few hours every day. Otherwise it was just the pair of them. It was a comfortable, lived-in family home, with lots of pretty pictures on the walls, and dogs on the furniture. And as time went by and Camilla's life became busier, Amanda became more involved in her domestic life as well, arranging for things to be delivered, for appliances to be fixed or serviced, and sometimes they would go shopping together. Whatever Camilla wanted help with, Amanda would do it.

Another story that wasn't reported from the day Camilla met William was that Charles, feeling buoyed by how well the meeting had gone, thought he would introduce her to his mother's deputy private secretary, Sir Robin Janvrin, as he now was. Janvrin had been in the building that afternoon for a meeting, so Charles asked Stephen Lamport to tell him that the Prince of Wales wanted him to meet Mrs Parker Bowles.

'I can't possibly do that,' said Janvrin. 'I couldn't do it without asking the Queen's permission and making sure it was the right thing to do.' He was not to be budged.

When Lamport reported back, the Prince's language was unrepeatable. 'In my house ... How dare he be so rude in my house?'

Whether or not it was because they knew Camilla would be there, Charles's parents stayed away from William and Harry's surprise party for their father in July, although his siblings all went, including Princess Anne – who, not without reason, Camilla found terrifying. The party was not such a surprise after one of the guests inadvertently blew the gaff and the *Sunday Mirror* published details the week before. It was a huge success, nevertheless, and the Prince was enormously touched by the trouble they had gone to and the fact that they had invited Camilla and put her in pride of place.

The day after the boys went back to school, that September, Charles and Camilla flew to Greece for their first ever holiday together. They almost called it off at the last minute because just the week before Camilla had been in Corfu with Candida Lycett-Green, staying with Jacob Rothschild, and the paparazzi had been a menace. But they kept their nerve and with a touch of subterfuge remained undetected. Charles flew from London to Balmoral to lay a false trail, then to RAF Lyneham in Wiltshire to collect Camilla, and on to Greece in a friend's private plane. Another friend had lent them a small but powerful boat and for five days they cruised around the Greek islands, dodging bad weather. It was a very happy time, not just a chance to be away together but knowing they were there with William and Harry's blessing.

The Queen gave an official fiftieth birthday party for Charles at Buckingham Palace on 13 November to celebrate his public work. It was attended by a thousand people; quite rightly, Camilla wasn't invited. It was one of the rare occasions when the Prince's mother has praised him in public – for his 'diligence, compassion and leadership' – and he, in thanking her, delighted everyone by calling her 'Mummy'. The public display of warmth between them that night belied the real situation. The Prince was infuriated by his mother's continued hostility towards the woman he loved.

But there was another big party on his actual birthday, 14 November, organised for him by Camilla and the Shelburnes at Highgrove. It was an extravagant event with 350 glittering guests, but although foreign royals came, politicians, actors, artists, comedians – even Andrew Parker Bowles and their children – the two people the Prince really wanted to be there stayed away. His parents turned down the invitation, as did all three of his siblings. It was a watershed in his relationship with his mother. Her presence at the party would have indicated, if not approval, a tacit acknowledgement of the woman who had meant so much to him for so long. But it was not to be. Not yet.

The relationship between Buckingham Palace and St James's Palace – mother and son, and their all-important courtiers, through whom they speak – could not have been worse. The Queen wanted Camilla out of Charles's life, and her private secretary, Sir Robert Fellowes, strongly reinforced her view. Prince Charles insisted that Camilla was not going anywhere and that Mark Bolland's job was to make the public accept her. The two Palaces had reached an impasse.

So when Janvrin took over from Fellowes in February 1999, there was a sigh of relief at St James's Palace. He was a much younger and more amenable character, and although he had snubbed the Prince over meeting Camilla at York House that day, he did have an amicable meeting with her on another occasion when he had warned the Queen in advance. He is a nice man and he was sympathetic to their situation. He hadn't intended to be rude, but he knew that what the Queen hated above all things were surprises, and that if he had agreed to that earlier meeting, the news would have quickly found its way across the park. If warned in advance the Queen is always 100 per cent supportive, even if things go wrong.

Bypassing Fellowes and going directly to his deputy a year earlier had enabled Camilla to spend her first weekend party as a divorced woman with the Prince at Sandringham. She was fed up with being marginalised and Mark Bolland, unafraid to rattle cages or poke bears, told the Prince he should invite her. 'It will be a two-day wonder in the press and then it will go away. It won't be a problem.' That was the phrase he most commonly used in talking to the Prince, and it was one of the characteristics that most endeared him to his boss. Charles loves can-do people and hates being told why something can't be done. Traditionally, senior courtiers were in the latter category; cautious, conservative, hunting, shooting and fishing types, often ex-military or Foreign Office, members of gentlemen's clubs and often rather unimaginative and dull. Bolland was none of those and he had no patience with that kind of logic.

He rang Janvrin to let him know about the plan for the weekend, knowing that if he'd informed Fellowes and it had been he who had spoken to the Queen about it there would have been a row. Bolland said there would be a story in the newspapers (leaked, inevitably, by an unnamed source within the royal household) which would beg the question of whether the Queen had given her permission for Camilla to be invited to Sandringham. And on Janvrin's advice the Queen's reaction was that it was a private party, it was up to the Prince to invite whomsoever he wished and she would not have expected to be consulted.

Bolland managed news – whether good or bad – with immense skill. He shamelessly had favourites in the newspaper world and he used those favourites to plant stories, trade stories and manage stories. He didn't issue formal statements as his predecessors had done, and as his successors would do; instead he gave non-attributable briefings to editors and journalists. William and Harry have a lot to thank him for in suppressing negative stories about them in their teenage years that would have embarrassed them. As often as not this was done by giving the newspaper an even juicer story instead. Bolland made friends and enemies in equal measure, but he got the job done, and had fun while doing it.

26

Rebecca

'Last night I dreamt I went to Manderley again' must be one of the best-known lines in modern English literature. It is the opening sentence of Daphne du Maurier's haunting novel, *Rebecca*, which Camilla knows well and has long felt mirrors aspects of her situation with Charles.

The narrator, whose name we never learn, is a shy, penniless young girl whose family are dead. She meets Maxim de Winter, a wealthy English widower, in a hotel in Monte Carlo. She is there working as a paid companion to a ghastly American woman, Mrs Van Hopper. He owns the legendary house Manderley. 'I never knew her,' says Mrs Van Hopper of the dead wife, Rebecca, 'but I believe she was very lovely. Exquisitely turned out, and brilliant in every way. They used to give tremendous parties at Manderley. It was all very sudden and tragic, and I believe he adored her.'

While Mrs Van Hopper takes to her bed with influenza, Maxim, who is twice the narrator's age, takes her to lunch.

They marry within just a few weeks of meeting and, filled with insecurity, she returns with him to Manderley, as the second Mrs de Winter. There she meets the sinister, evil Mrs Danvers, the housekeeper, who has kept the house as a shrine to the dead Rebecca and does everything in her power to unnerve her usurper. The second Mrs de Winter becomes obsessed with her predecessor, smells her perfume on the staircase, hears her voice. She imagines Rebecca to have been an icon of womanhood, everything she herself is not: she was a perfect hostess, a perfect sexual partner, a perfect chatelaine and a perfect wife; and as Frank, Maxim's agent, says, 'Yes, she was the most beautiful creature I have ever seen.' She begins to doubt Maxim's affections for her. How could he have ever fallen in love with someone as plain and gauche as her? They are persuaded to revive the fancy dress ball that the de Winters used to host every summer and Mrs Danvers tricks the new Mrs de Winter into wearing the same costume Rebecca wore before her death. Mrs de Winter can't wait to surprise her husband with her dress but when he sees it, he is furious and orders her to take it off at once. She's distraught. Mrs Danvers later corners her, pushes her towards an open window and tells her to jump. 'Why don't you go. We none of us want you here. He doesn't want you. He never did. He can't forget her. He wants to be alone again in the house, with her.'

Later that stormy night, the remains of Rebecca's body are discovered at sea, and the narrator discovers the truth. Her predecessor didn't drown in a boating accident. Maxim confesses that he shot her and dumped her body at sea. She'd had more and more brazen affairs, and the night he killed her, she'd taunted him. She'd told him she was pregnant with another man's child that she intended to pass off as his, and when he was dead that child would inherit his beloved Manderley.

An investigation into Rebecca's death reveals that she was not pregnant, she'd been suffering from cancer and had goaded Maxim into killing her. A verdict of suicide is recorded, and Maxim and the heroine walk away from Manderley as it burns (the fire is started by Mrs Danvers) and spend the rest of their lives living in second-rate hotels all over Europe.

Rebecca has never been out of print since it was first published in 1938 and there have been numerous film, theatre and TV adaptations – so it is not surprising that Camilla should be familiar with the story. But the eerie similarities between the protagonists in the book and the personalities in their real-life drama are not lost on her and she has occasionally mused on it in heart-to-hearts with others. This was life imitating art. There were obviously similarities between the Princess and Rebecca: she was the picture of beauty, the epitome of womanhood, the elegant dresser, the sexual adventurer, who met a tragic end but who transcended death to haunt the husband who spurned her. "'Rebecca has won," he said ... "Her shadow between us all the time."'

Charles and Maxim share some of the same emotions. Trapped in a love-less marriage that everyone envies him for, but which is a sham, holding it together for the sake of the house, or the country. Maxim had even married Rebecca on the advice of his grandmother. 'Even Gran, the most difficult person to please in those days, adored her from the first. "She's got the three things that matter in a wife," she told me: "breeding, brains and beauty."' And from the start there had been a seed of doubt at the back of his mind. Camilla is like the narrator, the less beautiful woman, unkempt, uninterested in fashion, who is brought to the house as the new Mrs de Winter. And, at the risk of treason, one could suggest the Queen would be Mrs Danvers, urging the newcomer towards the open window.

But the insecurity that du Maurier ascribes to the narrator, her certainty that Maxim is in love with his dead wife and not with her, which eats away at their marriage and their chance of happiness, are uncannily similar to Diana's conviction that Charles was still in touch with Camilla in the early years of their marriage.

Rebecca only had Mrs Danvers to keep her spirit alive. The Princess of Wales had the media and the public to keep her memory fresh. On the first anniversary of her death William and Harry had had more than enough. They refused to go to church with their father unless Sandy Henney issued a statement on their behalf: 'They have asked me to say that they believe their mother would want people now to move on – because she would have known that constant reminders of her death can create nothing but pain to those she left behind ...'

But it didn't happen. Their mother had been elevated to superhuman status and she is still selling newspapers and television documentaries from beyond the grave.

The twentieth anniversary of her death in August 2017 was an excuse for more – there is, and perhaps always will be, an element that there are still three people in the marriage – and there had been a faint chill running through the corridors of Clarence House in anticipation. There is still an awkwardness between the Prince and his sons over the subject of their mother. William and Harry organised no public event this time, as they did for the tenth anniversary – instead they announced plans for a statue of Diana to stand in Kensington Gardens as a perpetual memorial. Their father offered to help find a sculptor. And they courageously spoke publicly for the first time about the emotional impact of her death. She would have been proud of them. And, of course, she lives on through them.

27

Coming Out

As the last year of the century began, there was one big hurdle still to jump. The public had now seen photographs of Camilla on her own, as well as a couple of poor-quality shots of her with Charles taken from the bushes, but there had been no decent picture of the two of them together. For the paparazzi this had become the Holy Grail. Charles was determined to thwart them, and the couple were both sick of being unable to go anywhere together because of it. And so Mark Bolland devised a plan.

Annabel's fiftieth birthday was coming up, and she was having a party at the Ritz on the evening of Thursday, 28 January 1999 to which Charles and Camilla were both invited. Originally, the plan had been for them to be seen together at the NOS extravaganza in September 1997, but that was stopped in its tracks by Diana's death. Linda Edwards had telephoned Camilla the moment she heard about the accident to say they ought not to go ahead. She found her patron in a state of shock – desperately worried for the Prince and his two sons – and Camilla agreed: the evening couldn't just be postponed, out of respect to the Princess it had to be cancelled. Camilla's concern was that the charity wouldn't get its money. But although they offered refunds to all 700 people who had bought tickets, very few asked for their money back and many more sent in additional donations. They raised £80,000 in all, but there was no party.

So, a few days before Annabel's birthday, Mark made some judicial phone calls to alert the media to a photo opportunity. Word quickly spread;

they came from far and wide to park their satellite trucks, put up their ladders and stake their positions, three deep, across the road from the side entrance to the Ritz. By Thursday well over a hundred photographers and film crews were there. American networks began running hourly bulletins from Wednesday afternoon, alongside their European, Canadian and Australian counterparts, immaculate-looking presenters gesticulating at their cameras, excitedly filling in viewers with the back story.

At half past seven guests started to arrive. In went Charles; in, separately, went Camilla. The shot they were waiting for – the first of the two of them together since Diana's death – finally came at the end of the evening. It was quick. They emerged through the doors and stood together briefly while a bank of cameras flashed, whirred, clicked and rolled. Then Charles put a guiding hand on Camilla's back to steer her to the waiting car and they were gone.

In those few well-orchestrated seconds, every media outlet in the world had the photographs that confirmed the Prince of Wales and Mrs Parker Bowles were a couple. All that remained was to see how the news was interpreted. The *Sun*'s headline 'Meet the Mistress' went on in a softer tone, 'She'll never replace Diana. But many will think better of Camilla having seen her courage last night.' The *Mirror* devoted six pages to it with the headline 'At Last'. The *Mail*'s was 'Together'; it was 'the culmination of a carefully-laid strategy that completes Camilla's coming out and anoints her officially as Charles's escort'. The weightier publications were left to consider the impact on the clergy and the unforgiving Diana supporters, but most of the latter are so firmly entrenched in their views that they will never entertain forgiveness.

There had been great nervousness about that night. Many people in the Prince's office thought it had been too early for them to be seen together, as one of them says: 'But that was Mark, he was always pushing things on because he wanted to get there, he wanted to achieve the goal of getting them married.' And just six years later they were married – something no sane person would have put money on. Mark was gone by then, eased out without ceremony, but had it not been for him and the ground work he did between 1998 and 2002, that marriage might never have been possible. He turned round public opinion. A book I wrote in 1998, called *Charles: Victim or Villain?*, about the three of them in the marriage, had caused outrage and I had briefly felt like the most hated woman in Britain, but compared with

Camilla I was a rank amateur. Bolland moved mountains. He caused a lot of collateral damage in the process and he was not a popular man in either Palace, but he did pave the way.

Camilla was very fond of him. He looked after her, they lunched together, gossiped and laughed together, had long conversations on the phone; he was a good friend to her at a time when friends were thin on the ground both at St James's Palace and across the park. She wasn't popular in the Prince's office in those early days. Many of the Prince's staff had known and liked the Princess, and had been greatly distressed by the break-up and everything that followed. 'Camilla wasn't around much,' says someone who came into the press office after Diana's death, 'so she was unpopular as a name rather than as a person. Just like any marital dispute, people took sides, and she was the other woman, and they thought that if it wasn't for her everything would have been fine and the beautiful Diana would not have been so miserable and got herself into awkward situations. I could see there was real divided loyalty.

'People were very suspicious of Mark, not really sure what he was up to, confused about his role and what was going on, and what she was doing on the sidelines. She was seen as hindering the Prince's progress. We needed a strategy that promoted the Prince and got her out of the limelight but Mark's strategy was to get the public to accept her.'

In September 1999, Mark took Camilla to New York on a private four-day visit to test the water on the other side of the pond, where Diana had been so immensely popular. Accompanying them was Michael Fawcett, the Prince's former valet, who had become an *éminence grise* and one of the most controversial people in his employ. Mark masterminded the trip, in conjunction with his friend Peter Brown, founder of Brown Lloyd James, a PR firm based in New York that specialises in reputation management. According to a report in the *New York Times*, guests curious as to why 'the Prince of Wales's longtime paramour' was thirty minutes late for a cocktail party in Manhattan were told by Brown, 'There was a call from a certain gentleman in London, so of course she was late.'

An unlikely explanation. Camilla, like Charles, is a fanatical timekeeper. She hates being late herself and doesn't appreciate others being late. What is possible is that she was suffering from acute nerves. Diana had taken the city by storm on her first solo visit in 1989. Dressed in the most fabulous, sequin-encrusted evening gown, she'd attended a gala charity dinner for a thousand of New York's richest and most illustrious party-goers – and at the other end of the spectrum, she'd visited children with Aids in a hospital in Harlem. Her last visit had been shortly before her death in 1997. A collection of her most iconic dresses were auctioned at Christie's in Manhattan and raised $3.25 million for cancer and Aids charities; she had flown to New York specially for a private viewing of them. For Camilla to launch herself into a gathering at which, however carefully handpicked, people would be making comparisons with the Princess, was daunting.

A *Mirror* headline that week was 'Camilla's A Di Copycat', while *New York* magazine described her as a 'horsey royal heart-throb'. They stayed at the Carlyle Hotel and over the four days, she visited friends in East Hampton, saw a production of *Cabaret*, wandered through SoHo galleries and attended a luncheon given by 97-year-old Brooke Astor, the New York socialite and philanthropist, who was a friend of the Prince. Astor turned to Camilla during the meal and said 'Your grandmother would be proud of you. You're keeping this mistress business in the family.'

Slowly Camilla was being brought out. Without telling anyone, she would turn up at public engagements, dinners and events where a couple of media representatives would be present. 'It was quite hard on her, people pointing and whispering, but she coped really, really well. What I noticed quite early on was the effect she had on the room. You'd have a load of guests standing around drinking and then Camilla would come in and she really has whatever it is that men go for. The press all criticised her looks and called her horrible names, but when you see her in person she does have that *je ne sais quoi*, and they were like bees to a honeypot. She'd suddenly be surrounded by this gaggle of men. I think she was quite nervous of doing things – because she was absolutely hated, and I think she went through some really gruesome times, a lot of pain and hurt – but the great thing was I can't remember anybody ever being disappointed or rude about her once they'd met her.'

What amused the team in the office was that in the early days, 'Camilla would open her diary and and say, "Well, I've got hair on Monday, I've got to go to see an exhibition because it's a friend on Tuesday" and point to some other trivial thing on Wednesday "and I don't know if I'd be able to fit anything else in". And I thought, you're hardly doing anything. It was a bit like that at the beginning, she just wasn't used to working.'

But it wasn't long before Camilla turned the office around. Once she started appearing in person, they couldn't help liking her. They liked that she was so normal and down to earth – 'a bit kick your shoes off, have a fag, let's talk about *Coronation Street*' – and they realised she had a very calming effect on the Prince of Wales that they came to appreciate. She became their secret weapon. 'Mark started to invite her to the diary meetings, which were always a painful process. It was always freezing cold because the Prince is always hot, so the windows are flung open and it's snowing outside and everyone's sitting there shivering. She would be sitting at the table listening to him behave badly and all she would have to do is look at him and the whole atmosphere would change. She made our lives a lot easier – including getting the window shut! We could see how she was on our side a lot of the time, she was there to help us achieve what we wanted. So she became a friend to the office. Very clever. So when the other private secretaries and people around wanted things, they knew who to talk to, they knew who could help you to get what you wanted. It did make him behave a little bit better, because when she wasn't there, boy could he kick off! But when she was there, it was a bit calmer, a bit warmer, a bit more civilised.'

Those who had been there in Diana's day saw a massive difference. She and the Prince had started off having joint diary meetings, but they became so acrimonious they were abandoned. When they set up separate offices the acrimony only increased. 'I think people could see that actually Camilla was not going to be demanding and difficult. She was always very supportive. She never came with her own agenda or things she wanted you to do for her, she was always there to help you. I think she is genuinely a nice person. And in that role she was just herself, easy-going, tries to keep the peace, wants to see the best in everybody.'

There were occasions when the press office did use their clout to protect Tom and Laura. Their attitude was that, like William and Harry, the pair were innocent children who didn't deserve to be targeted by the press just because of what their parents had done. Mark would lean on the editors but he couldn't stop every story getting into the newspapers. To Tom's great embarrassment, a full-length photograph of him in a state of dishevelment appeared on the front page of the *News of the World* in May 1999 under the headline, 'This Is Camilla's Son High On Coke'. Tom was the victim of a classic honey trap. Along with a high proportion of people of his age – he was twenty-four – he drank too much, and he took recreational drugs from time to time, more as a rite of passage than anything more worrying. But someone he knew had made money out of him. The paper had dispatched a pretty young female reporter undercover to the Cannes film festival – a place, no doubt, awash with cocaine – where Tom was working as a publicist. She said she was a friend of his cousin Emma Parker Bowles, and asked him if he knew where she could get some coke. Tom is an encyclopaedic film buff and the saddest part of the story is that he had to give up a job he was really enjoying. He is philosophical about it now – in an interview with the *Daily Telegraph* he said, 'If you get caught you can't blame anyone apart from yourself. You just put your hands up and say you are young and stupid' – but at the time he was very upset, mostly about embarrassing his mother and godfather. The Prince's reaction was to telephone him and say, 'You've been a bloody fool. Pull yourself together.' The newspaper's justification, inevitably, was that William and Harry's closeness to Tom was putting the young Princes in danger.

A rather bizarre outcome of all this was a rift between the Prince of Wales and his oldest friends the van Cutsems, who thoroughly disapproved of Mark Bolland's influence and were not enamoured by Camilla. The feeling was entirely mutual. They had once enjoyed a position of great power with the Prince – he had leant on them heavily when his marriage had been failing, and after Diana's death, their house became a second home for William and Harry, who were like brothers to the van Cutsems' four boys. But since Camilla had become an acknowledged and permanent fixture in the Prince's life, that influence had waned.

It was a classic case of old friends feeling miffed at being marginalised by a new partner – and they weren't the only ones whose noses were put out of joint. The van Cutsems took their frustration out on Mark Bolland, whose style was anathema to such conservative and traditional people. Hugh fired off a legal letter to Bolland accusing him, after the drug story, of making 'highly damaging' remarks about his sons to deflect onto the van Cutsems criticism about Tom's influence over William and Harry. It was not a clever move to take on the master of spin.

Even more foolish was their behaviour when their son, Edward, married Lady Tamara Grosvenor, the Duke of Westminster's daughter, in November 2004 at Chester Cathedral. Charles and Camilla were both invited, as was the Queen. By this time, the Queen had met Camilla and her antagonism towards their relationship had dissipated. However, both the bride's and the groom's families felt that because Charles and Camilla were not married, according to protocol they should not sit together for the ceremony. Had this been a formal occasion, that would have been correct. Indeed, at the two concerts for the Queen's Golden Jubilee at Buckingham Palace in July 2002 – one pop, one classical – Camilla was in the royal box with the family, but two rows behind. The wedding, though, was a private occasion and the plan to seat Camilla several rows behind Charles was a snub. She was also expected to arrive at the cathedral separately and travel in a separate car to the reception. The Prince was furious and boycotted the wedding entirely. He went instead to Warminster in Wiltshire, as Colonel-in-Chief of the Black Watch regiment, to meet the wives and families of soldiers deployed in Iraq. Camilla spent the day at home.

She and the Queen had finally met in the summer of 2000 when the Prince threw a sixtieth birthday party at Highgrove for his cousin, the exiled King Constantine of Greece. His mother attended knowing full well the implications. It was the first time the two women had met in more than a decade. They shook hands, smiled at one another, Camilla curtseyed and they had a moment or two of small talk before going to different tables for lunch. But it was highly significant.

The next crucial step was for Camilla to be seen in public with Prince William. The perfect opportunity arose in February 2001, when she, Charles and William attended a party at Somerset House to mark the tenth anniversary of the Press Complaints Commission, by then run by Mark's partner, Guy Black. It was billed as William's first public engagement and an opportunity for him to thank the newspaper editors for allowing him to complete his education unmolested by press intrusion. They arrived and left separately, but they were there right under the noses of every editor in Fleet Street.

'Part of the thinking was that in order for the public to approve of Camilla she had to be seen with the boys or it wouldn't work,' says one of those involved. 'I think the relationship between them all is warm now but if I'm honest, it wasn't then. I think they found it hard when they were little. I remember Harry being uncomfortable and saying something awkward. It was difficult for them; it was a natural thing. You want your mum, you don't want her, and she had her own family. To be fair to Camilla, she never tried to be Mummy, but she was the "other woman" and she was there and taking Daddy's time. It wasn't all happy families for quite a long time, but William was happy to see his father happy.'

The boys' feelings were a major consideration, but Mark's principal task was to bring the public around. And so Camilla was back at Somerset House two months later, when another significant milestone was captured on film – this time an evening drinks party to mark the fifteenth anniversary of the National Osteoporosis Society. It was held on the forecourt, where five hundred guests – a mixture of family, friends and celebrities – drank champagne and mingled against the backdrop of jazz and splashing fountains. Camilla was nominal host, along with her sister Annabel, and they were there early to meet and greet. Her children were with her, as was their father Andrew, by now happily married to his girlfriend Rosemary. When the Prince of Wales arrived, accompanied by Queen Rania of Jordan, he clasped Camilla warmly and said 'Hello, you'; they smiled, giggled, and kissed each other on both cheeks. It was another major step, engineered by Mark, to soften up the public. The Prince left ahead of Camilla but she joined him later for a private dinner at St James's Palace, with Rania and her husband, King Abdullah.

Just as important as winning acceptance from the Queen was winning round the fourth estate. Although most of the papers had delighted at casting her in the worst possible light, Camilla had earned a great deal of respect from photographers and journalists alike. In all the years she had been in the limelight, despite all the provocation, all the slurs, all the falsehoods, all the damage to her family, she had never reacted, never retaliated, never attempted to set the record straight or to defend herself, even when her precious son was in the spotlight. She had kept her own counsel, she had not allowed friends or relatives to speak on her behalf and when she was out and about, if a photographer approached her, she would simply smile and say nothing, no matter how much they goaded her or called her names in the hope of a reaction. They often lay in wait for her when she was hunting, or simply out for a ride with a friend. She would come round a corner and meet a car full of photographers, or men would suddenly appear out of the bushes, giving her and her horse a terrible fright. Carlyn Chisholm, who often used to ride with her, would lose her temper with them – apart from anything else it was dangerous, they had flighty horses and could have been thrown off. But Camilla never did. 'She would say things like "If you take a picture now, will you leave us alone?" and they'd say "Yes" and then half an hour later they'd all be there again. But I never, ever saw her get cross with them.'

28

A Little Local Difficulty

Camilla's once empty diary was filling up, the hair appointments becoming ever more frequent. She needed to look good when she was on show, so she started adding designer outfits to the wardrobe that she'd never paid much attention to and getting professional help with her make-up. Laura was helpful and so was Tom's girlfriend Sara Buys, who is now her daughter-in-law and the mother of two of her grandchildren. Sara, a fashion journalist, was able to suggest some designers. Anna Valentine became a firm favourite but there were others. Sara had started as the self-confessed 'worst PA in the world' to Alexandra Shulman, then editor at *Vogue*, but she was swiftly moved to features, and from *Vogue* went to *Harpers Bazaar*, where she became associate editor. Laura by this time had been travelling, been to Oxford Brookes to read History of Art and was working in a gallery; Tom had a job on the *Daily Mail*, writing about food.

With the diary filling up – there were NOS dates as well as the events she attended with the Prince of Wales – and the higher profile resulting in an ever-larger mailbag, Camilla also needed more help in the office, which was still the kitchen table at Ray Mill. So Amanda MacManus asked a friend in Dulwich, Joy Camm – a fellow mum from school – if she knew anyone locally who might want to work with her three days a week. Joy had been a nursing sister at a London teaching hospital, where she'd met and married her physician husband, but had taken a break to have children. 'It took me about forty-eight hours to realise why would I give that to somebody else?'

she says. So, after an interview with Camilla at York House, she joined forces with Amanda in 2000. She retired in the summer of 2017, having believed, like her friend, that she had the best job in the world. They did seem to have a lot of fun at it, complementing each other perfectly. Amanda is slightly flyaway and brimming with ideas and creativity; Joy, having organised surgeons all her working life, is neat, meticulous and methodical. 'The Prince never lets me forget I was a sister,' says Joy. 'He'll say, "What does Nurse think about this?"' Belinda Kim has replaced her.

Joy's first impression of Camilla was how small she was. 'That was the big surprise to me, having only ever seen photographs. In came this petite, pretty, lovely woman – beautiful, actually, beautiful eyes, laughing eyes.' The routine of working two days at Amanda's house in Dulwich and driving down to Wiltshire on a Wednesday worked well. 'It was very informal. We had a working laptop and we'd sit and chat. Of course we would talk to Mrs PB every day anyway – the visits to the house were to do the practicalities because she wasn't up in London that often and it was good to see her, catch up with what she wanted us to do, and bring stuff back. We'd have lunch and before you knew it the day was over and we'd be driving back to London. But a lot of work was done.'

Camilla was more comfortable in the country than in London, as she always had been, and has always been very happy with her own company. She was still getting abusive letters but she also had fans – including a man in Germany who wrote regularly to offer his support. She was very sanguine about it all. The letters and the unkind things written about her in the newspapers never outwardly upset her. In all the years Joy has been with her, the times she has seen her most upset have been while listening to other people's misfortunes.

When she did go to London, for whatever reason, either Amanda or Joy would accompany her. 'It's always fun walking behind her,' says Joy, 'because people look at her – and the British are so proper – they kind of look and see that it's her and once she's gone past they turn. We were doing some Christmas shopping in M&S and there was a husband sitting in the shoe department, thinking he wished his wife would choose these shoes. He happened to look up and she walked past and he looked at her – she was Mrs PB then – and she said, "Hello." He went "Hello" and she smiled and walked away. I was just behind her, close enough to see him nudge his wife and say "You'll never guess who I've just seen, I've seen Camilla Parker

Bowles." The wife said, "Don't be ridiculous, don't you like these shoes?" And he said, "No I really have seen her." They were still chatting – and it was almost as if Camilla had known, but she couldn't have heard – when she walked past again. "Hello again," she said. "See! It is her." It couldn't have been better timing.

'You get to know somebody very well when you're in their home, and we hit it off, absolutely. She was very intuitive, she knows, she catches the nuance of everybody very quickly. I really trust her in that, she is invariably right. A very good judge of character.'

The only snag about using Amanda's home as an office was that it wasn't always easy to keep work and family apart. 'I had quite young children,' she says, 'and I will never forget my son picking up the phone, aged about five, and saying, "Dave's on the phone."' In fact it was Sir David Frost, the veteran broadcaster. So, in 2004, they were found a space at Clarence House.

Clarence House had been the Queen Mother's home, and after her death in 2002 – another very sad time for the Prince of Wales – the house was refurbished at a cost of £4.5 million. Although they were still unmarried, he and Camilla moved in a year later. The cost had been met by the taxpayer from money set aside for the maintenance of royal palaces, but it was made very clear that the Prince had spent £1.6 million of his own money on a suite of rooms for Camilla. The designer Robert Kime, who redecorated Highgrove after the Prince's divorce, had done the work. He had kept the spirit of the place and many of the Queen Mother's paintings, but given it a more up-to-date feel.

The Prince had been skiing with his sons when the Queen Mother died. She was 101, with two new hips, but she still had a full set of marbles and a wonderful sense of humour, although she had been ailing for some time. She had made a heroic effort to attend the funeral of Princess Margaret, her troubled younger daughter, who had died after a series of strokes six weeks earlier, but it was clear she was failing. She died peacefully in her sleep on 30 March with the Queen by her side.

The Prince was 'completely devastated'. He flew straight home and gave a very personal and moving tribute on television to 'the original life enhancer – at once indomitable, somehow timeless, able to span the generations. Wise, loving, with an utterly irresistible mischievousness of spirit.' She was 'quite simply the most magical grandmother you could possibly have and I was utterly devoted to her'. There was none of the hysteria there had been over Diana's death – Diana was snatched in the prime of her life, whereas the Queen Mother had done better than most – but no one foresaw how affected the public would be. Thousands of bouquets were left on the lawns at St George's Chapel in Windsor and the queue for the lying-in-state in Westminster Hall stretched for three miles.

The house his grandmother had loved most was Birkhall on the Balmoral estate in Scotland. Charles took it over as well – and he and Camilla love it more than anywhere else. He had stayed there often when his grandmother was alive and he'd always loved it. It had tartan walls and carpets, while the dining room held a collection of eleven grandfather clocks – the family used to delight in watching newcomers jump with fright when they all started chiming, never quite in sync.

Charles and Camilla now go there several times a year and it is the one place where they are almost entirely alone, or in the company only of family and guests. It doesn't double up as an office and courtiers are not normally in attendance; it's their home together, and it's the place where they are happiest and most relaxed. That is not to say they answer the door themselves and go and make a cup of tea when visitors arrive. Bernie and Tony, the butlers, are there to look after them and run the house, which suits Camilla down to the ground – she loves having people to do things for her. Those who visit regularly to fish, stalk and walk say that it has the feel of a normal house rather than a royal residence. It's comfortable and cosy with big open fires, but it is a bit of a shrine to the Queen Mother. Her hat and coat hang in the hallway, and the clocks chime on, still leading first-timers to jump on the hour.

That year had begun with a bizarre story about the Prince of Wales and Harry that caused a lot of grief. Mark Bolland had given the *News of the World* an exclusive account of how, after Harry confessed he'd been smoking cannabis, Charles had taken his younger son to a drug rehabilitation centre for a short sharp shock. What no one knew at the time was that Mark had done some nifty horse-trading – but that it was to be the last time he did it at St James's Palace. He and his team had been working for months to protect William and Harry from damaging stories – some of them true, some fabricated – but this was one that they recognised they couldn't fight. The *News of the World* had a dossier of damning evidence about the sixteen-year-old. They'd discovered he had been drinking under age and after hours and smoking cannabis at the local pub, The Rattlebone in Sherston; they'd then dug deeper and discovered more serious misdemeanours. Mark did a deal with Rebekah Wade, now editor, to save Harry's skin and gave her the story about the visit to rehab. He turned a negative report into a heart-warming one, thereby ensuring that the Prince of Wales won high praise for his sensitive, responsible handling of a situation which so many parents face, and for setting such a good example.

Harry had in fact once visited a rehab centre, but not with his father – and not because his father was worried about him. Charles had no idea of what either of his sons got up to, and Harry bitterly resented being made to look bad so his father could look good. Worse, he was furious that the blame for leading him astray should have fallen on Guy Pelley, a good friend of both Princes, whose reputation was trashed.

This wasn't the first time Mark had massaged stories to make the Prince of Wales look good at the expense of others, but his days were numbered. He had made some powerful enemies amongst those who had the Prince's ear, and they were circling. He had done what he had been hired to do, but he had caused difficulties and tensions in the office, where no one quite trusted him; and he'd created a yawning chasm between the two Palaces. He thought royal courtiers snooty, grey-suited sycophants stuck in the 1950s, who needed a monumental shake-up – which many might have agreed with. But championing one member of the family in isolation from the others was not good for the institution of which they were all a part – or, as it turned out, for his career as a courtier.

At the beginning of 2002, Stephen Lamport announced his intention to leave his post as the Prince's private secretary in the summer. Bolland imagined he would get the job, but a deal had been done behind his back. The Queen was parachuting in her own man to sort out St James's Palace, to get adultery off the front pages and make sure the Prince's charitable work and more positive stories about the monarchy appeared there instead; and to get rid of Mark Bolland. That man was Sir Michael Peat, the inscrutable accountant who as Keeper of the Privy Purse had revolutionised the royal finances.

When Bolland heard that Peat was to be the Prince's private secretary – and therefore his boss – he knew it was time to go. But after all he had done for the Prince of Wales, it was a shabby way to treat him. He was hurt, and he was angry.

The person most sorry to see him go was Camilla. As Julia Cleverdon says, 'All one knew was that Mark was the only person who ever bothered to ring the Duchess and tell her what was going on. In those early days there wasn't ever a sense that there was a support structure for her. She was not part of what went on, but I remember Mark ringing her up on the way back from Manchester and the first speech which the Prince made after Diana's death. She was terribly worried about how he was, how it had gone – all the writing and the rewriting of the speech, was he going to mention the children and so on. He said "I'm just going to tell Mrs PB it's gone fine." I think they had a close relationship. And Mark was very hurt when he was then removed. He thought he was doing what he had been asked to do, and he probably was.'

Camilla and Mark were allies. They were united in their views of some of the Prince's stuffy old friends and hangers-on, who disapproved of him just as much as they did of her. And he had helped keep the tabloids away from her children; he had even helped Tom get a job in journalism. But once he knew he had been passed over, in February 2002, he didn't hang about. He left immediately and started up his own PR company, although he agreed to carry on advising both Camilla and Charles in a private capacity. The arrangement was to last no more than a year. He was trying to run a business and the money from the Prince – never a big payer – didn't begin to compensate for the hours he spent at their beck and call. And he was constantly at odds with Michael Peat, whose skills and manner were wildly different from his own. After one or two skirmishes it became apparent to everyone that the situation couldn't continue. He cut his ties with the Palace completely, although unofficially he continued to be on the end of a phone for Camilla, and a few years ago she started inviting him to occasional receptions at Clarence House.

The Prince is easily swayed. On some occasions he can be blindly loyal – as he has been to Michael Fawcett, who is disliked and feared in equal measure – and on others he can be inexplicably harsh to people who have served him equally well. Sandy Henney was a case in point: her resignation when a newspaper editor played dirty over William's eighteenth birthday photographs should never have been accepted. And Mark Bolland, who may have had unorthodox methods but was doing what he'd been asked to do, is another. He is the only member of the household who worked in a position of such seniority for so long who has never received an honour – the usual award is an LVO (Lieutenant of the Victorian Order).

Nor was he invited to Charles and Camilla's wedding – but by then he had committed the ultimate treachery, taking up a pen to vent his grievances. In one article he called the Prince a 'very, very weak man' for allowing Paul Burrell, Diana's faithful butler, to be prosecuted for theft. In another he said that only the Queen, her son and his children were important. 'The other members of the family are unpopular, irrelevant and likely to drag the institution into disrepute.'

The police had raided Burrell's home in January 2001, looking for a mahogany box containing 'sensitive' material that Diana's family, as executors, had reported missing. They found instead over three hundred items from the late Princess, squirrelled away, worth millions of pounds. The pretext for the raid had been the theft of an eighteen-inch-long jewel-encrusted model of an Arab dhow worth £500,000, that had been a wedding present to the royal couple from the Emir of Bahrain. It had been offered for sale in a London antiques shop and the man accused of stealing it was Harold Brown, another of Diana's butlers. He claimed Burrell had authorised its disposal. Burrell was tried for theft but claimed he had taken the items for safekeeping, and had told the Queen so.

She, alas, only remembered this when the trial was under way and his life had been shattered. Although the trial immediately collapsed, Burrell was aggrieved and felt he had been let down by the Royal Family. And so he sold his story to the *Mirror*, following it up with an explosive book called *A Royal Duty*. Amongst other damaging material he included was a letter written by the Duke of Edinburgh to Diana. 'We do not approve of either of you having lovers,' it said. 'Charles was silly to risk everything with Camilla for a man in his position. We never dreamed he might feel like leaving you for her. I cannot imagine anyone in their right mind leaving you for Camilla.'

It wasn't long before the mahogany box became the subject. The sensitive material concerned was a tape recording made by Diana of a conversation with George Smith, a former valet, who claimed that he had been raped by a man in the Prince's household in 1989. This was accompanied by the revelation that unwanted gifts received by the Prince and Princess of Wales were given to their staff as a perk of the job, while others were sold and the proceeds given to charity. The person who handled it all was Michael Fawcett, the Prince's former valet, who had been the subject of repeated character assassinations by the press.

One of Michael Peat's first jobs when he arrived at Clarence House in July 2002 was, with the assistance of Edmund Lawson QC, to launch an inquiry into all such matters. Whatever else, Peat was thorough. He had run an audit on Buckingham Palace in the mid-1980s and come up with 188 recommendations for change. He also found plenty of room for improvement in the Prince's household. 'Peat did a good job,' says someone who was there. 'He wanted to sort everything out because they were all up to naughty things like taking flights from dodgy people and all that. He wanted more openness and transparency and he achieved that, and that was good for the Prince.' On the day Peat's findings were announced in March 2003, Fawcett resigned. 'It was a bit naughty in a way but they needed to point a finger at somebody as they always do, and Michael Fawcett did have this image, and so the idea was to make it obvious we were starting afresh. So he's going and everything's open and honest and they'd have an annual report, you can see where the money's going, how we make the money, what we do with it, it's all clear.'

Fawcett's settlement from the Prince of Wales was reported to be £1 million. He was allowed to buy from the Duchy his grace and favour house, where he lived with his wife, son and daughter, and he was guaranteed freelance earnings from the Prince of £100,000 a year. 'It was a bad idea to try and get rid of Fawcett but it served a purpose at the time, it looked like we were having this big cleanup.'

Camilla is another explanation for the man's extraordinary sticking power. She really likes him and relies upon him. He's another Mark Bolland in some ways – tall, confident, protective and good at making things happen; and Camilla likes being looked after, and of course only ever sees the charming side of the man. One final, not insignificant fact is that Fawcett began working for the Prince as a valet in 1981, when he was not yet married to Diana, and was probably closer to him over the ensuing seventeen years than any other human being. He knows where all the bodies are buried. If he were ever to feel disaffected enough to write his memoirs, they would make Burrell's book read like Enid Blyton.

Before the entire matter was put to bed another allegation, said to have been on the missing tape, became public. Mark Bolland's column in the *News of the World*, under the by-line Blackadder, 'the man who knows the royals best', caused a great deal of mischief when he claimed one week that in a phone call Peat had asked him whether Charles was bisexual, to which he had said 'emphatically that the Prince was not gay or bisexual'.

George Smith, who had mental health problems, claimed that he had been taking breakfast to a principal member of the Royal Family in bed and witnessed an 'incident' between that person and a Palace servant. It was assumed the incident was homosexual – and the only obvious candidates were the Queen's three sons. Hence Michael Peat's question to Mark Bolland. The rumour had been circulating in Fleet Street for years but the *Mail on Sunday* had Smith on its payroll and was ready to publish names. The Palace issued an injunction which was not enforceable in Scotland. Other legal farces followed and the upshot was that Michael Peat issued a statement from Clarence House. It said everything and nothing, but did serve to take the sting out of a story that had been floating around the internet:

> In recent days, there have been media reports concerning an allega-
> tion that a former royal household employee witnessed an incident
> some years ago involving a senior member of the Royal Family.
> The speculation needs to be brought to an end.
> The allegation was that the Prince of Wales was involved in the
> incident.
> This allegation is untrue. The incident which the former employee
> claims to have witnessed did not take place.

With Mark Bolland gone, the chief firefighter throughout this period was Colleen Harris, the Prince's press secretary, who had taken over from Sandy Henney in 2000. Colleen is wry, philosophical and unsentimental. She was the first black face to hold a senior position in the Prince's household and like Sandy, she had a particularly good relationship with William and Harry. It was a terrible time. Every week seemed to bring a new scandal, every weekend was spent in the office with lawyers trying to fend off stories the tabloids were threatening to run. The technology was changing; social media was beginning and the idea of being able to control what was being said was fast receding. And every Sunday Bolland's column undermined her. They had been very close when they worked together and he had expected her to resign out of loyalty to him. She couldn't, she had children in fee-paying schools and a mortgage to pay. By 2003 she was exhausted and had had her fill.

One of the biggest problems was that although Charles and Camilla openly lived together under one roof, because the relationship was not formalised, the media were still able to refer to her as 'the mistress' or worse, she was excluded from certain events and obliged to come and go from the back entrances of others. It was a crazy situation and demeaning.

29

U-Turn

When Michael Peat arrived from Buckingham Palace to take up the job with the Prince, he came with a clear agenda. His instructions were to sever Charles's relationship with Mrs Parker Bowles because it was a mess and was detracting from his work. This is certainly how the people in St James's Palace who worked with Peat during those first months viewed the situation. Camilla had been the Prince's mistress, he'd admitted having an adulterous affair with her, and now she was sharing his bed, his house and his life. And she was being seen in public by his side, but not as his wife. For a man who would one day be Defender of Faith and Head of the Church of England, this was an awkward situation at best. She had to go.

It didn't take Peat long to realise that this was an impossible dream. The Prince would never give up Camilla, no matter what, and so Peat rapidly changed tack and, with the zeal of the freshly converted, became the loudest, fiercest advocate for their marriage. While Mark Bolland had laid the ground for it, Michael Peat was the man who made it happen. But there were obstacles to overcome first. It needed not just the Queen's permission but the agreement of the state, the church, and the great British public.

In his usual way, he was dithering. The Prince of Wales really is the most curious character. On the one hand he had stood his ground against his parents, the media and the voice of the nation in making Camilla non-negotiable. A man who for decades had dedicated himself to duty, to doing the right thing, suddenly put everything he stood for and had worked for in jeopardy because of Camilla. And yet this wasn't the first time he had needed persuading to do the right thing by her. 'I don't think the Prince was happy with the way things were,' says one of the team, 'but he couldn't see a way of making it work. He'd been through a lot of bad times with the public and I think he was probably nervous about putting himself back in a negative situation, damaging the monarchy, and he didn't know whether he could persuade the Queen to accept her. I think he thought all of these things insurmountable and he really didn't know what to do. The Prince is too diffident and nervous and I think he was scared.' Marriage was the only way their relationship and the Prince's reputation would be able to move forward.

Colleen Harris's replacement was Paddy Harverson. who arrived in February 2004 from Manchester United football club. There, as public relations officer, he had looked after millionaires and megastars like David Beckham and Rio Ferdinand, so he was not new to managing egos and fighting off scandal. In an earlier life he had been a sports journalist on the *Financial Times*. He is six foot five, bright, straightforward, fair and unflappable. I met him very soon after his arrival, when I was writing a book called *The Firm* about the monarchy, and it was very clear that he was a new broom. Scrupulous manners, straight as a die and no spin. He didn't have favourites, he was helpful to everyone – and he wasn't afraid to take the media on if he felt they were playing dirty.

One of his first tasks had been to make a formal assessment of the Prince's standing in the media, which after all the scandals had taken a nosedive. Peat had set the wheels in motion but he wanted to be sure of the facts before confronting his boss. 'As soon as I met Camilla,' he says, 'I thought she was fantastic and I saw the dynamic between the two, and this was quite important to the way the public saw the Prince of Wales and the way he was depicted in the media. It was most noticeable on overseas tours, where he looked lonely. Yet you would see them privately and they were fantastic together – funny – and she was so good for him, you could tell.'

Michael Peat went to the Prince and told him very clearly that either Mrs Parker Bowles must go or he must marry her. They could not, under any circumstances, go on as they were. And he gave Charles the confidence to believe it could be made to happen.

Someone else who was key in persuading Charles to do the right thing was Bruce Shand. He was now eighty-seven years old and although he loved the Prince dearly, he thought him weak, and was worried about how vulnerable he had made Camilla by allowing her to live in limbo. He took him aside and said, 'I want to meet my maker knowing my daughter's all right.'

Charles adored Bruce. He loved the whole extended Shand family and in turn they were very fond of him, but Bruce spoke for them all. They felt that Camilla's situation was precarious and a bit shoddy, and although she herself had never wanted marriage in the past, things were different now. She felt herself to be neither one thing nor another and was secretly grateful to her father for putting pressure on Charles.

Having been at Buckingham Palace for nearly fifteen years, where he had been close to the Queen, Michael Peat was the perfect person to pull all the essential strands together and iron out the complications. He knew Robin Janvrin well, and Janvrin, being sympathetic to the Prince, was willing to offer helpful advice to the Queen. And although Tony Blair, the Prime Minister, had been the one to christen Diana 'The People's Princess', he also admired the Prince; both men appreciated how important Camilla was to Charles. The final component was Dr Rowan Williams, Archbishop of Canterbury, who inevitably ruled out a church wedding – because the Anglican Church frowns upon second marriages if a spouse is still living. The solution was a civil ceremony with a church blessing.

In Clarence House's view, the greatest challenge was how any marriage would be received by the public. A recent Populus poll had shown 32 per cent of respondents would be in favour and 29 per cent against; 38 per cent didn't care, while 2 per cent had no opinion. As one Palace adviser put it, they knew the media would be aggressive – 'because it was like someone taking their ball away that they'd been playing around with in the back garden all that time.' Colleen Harris agrees. 'They'd all made a lot of money out of the story that Camilla was this evil, horrible person who ruined Diana's life and was ruining the children's lives and they wanted that story to continue. The more we made Camilla acceptable, the less the story had traction. The idea was to make her more human without making her more popular than him – we didn't want any of that rivalry again – but to show she was a real person with real feelings and interests.'

Charles asked Camilla to marry him at Birkhall over New Year. He had spoken to his mother, his sons, and the rest of the family when they were all together at Sandringham for Christmas, which Camilla had spent with her family. The engagement was announced shortly before half past eight on the morning of 10 February 2005 and within an hour, the world's media had set up satellite trucks and cameras at Canada Gate in the Mall, opposite Buckingham Palace. Pundits roamed from one camera to another to be asked about their particular field of expertise. Most people seemed to be pleased and thought it about time, but not everyone. One woman I met outside Clarence House was so angry she had travelled across London to protest: 'If Charles is going to marry that woman,' she said, spitting out the words, 'he should never be king.' And some of the emails viewers had sent in to BBC *Breakfast* the next morning were so terrible they couldn't be read out. 'The adulterer should not be allowed to marry his whore' was one I happened to see.

The news of the engagement was leaked by Robert Jobson in the *London Evening Standard*, but it didn't spoil a thing. Clarence House was ready to go. They had a target date, but they knew the secret was unlikely to hold and Paddy had devised a media plan covering every day for three weeks just in case. 'And bless him, Robert Jobson broke it on the one day that was the best day of the whole three weeks. There was a charity ball that night at Windsor Castle; they were both going to be dressed up in their finest. It was a complete coincidence. Perfect for us. Imagine if it had been a day when they weren't going to be out and about or seen together.'

Julia Cleverdon, the Prince's greatest and sanest supporter in all things, was uncharacteristically in bed at home with a raging temperature when Elizabeth Buchanan, one of the Prince's longest-standing private secretaries, rang and said, 'Julia, I've arranged for you to be on the other side of the Windsor doors as they come through because Mrs PB must be able to see somebody she knows in the flashing bulbs of the paparazzi.' Julia pleaded a temperature of 102. 'I don't mind if you've got a temperature of 106. Get to Windsor!' So, as Charles and Camilla came through the doors, to be blinded by flashing bulbs and requests to see the ring, Julia was behind them. 'There were very funny pictures in *Hello* magazine,' she says, 'of me scarlet in the face.' The ring, £100,000 worth of platinum and diamonds, had been a gift from the Queen. It was a 1930s Art Deco design, a central square-cut diamond with three smaller ones on either side, which had belonged to the Queen Mother and had been one of her favourites. When asked how she felt, Camilla said she was just coming down to earth, but she coyly dodged the question of whether the Prince had been down on one knee.

The Prime Minister sent congratulations on behalf of the government; the Queen and the Duke of Edinburgh were 'very happy' and had given the couple their 'warmest wishes'. The Archbishop of Canterbury was pleased they had taken 'this important step'. And William and Harry were '100 per cent' behind the couple. They were 'very happy for our father and Camilla and we wish them all the luck in the world'.

30

Final Furlong

The wedding date was set for 8 April at Windsor, and after a multitude of obstacles along the way – including a change of venue from the castle to the town hall, postponement for a day because the original date clashed with the funeral of Pope John Paul II in Rome, arguments about whether it was right or wrong for the country, good or bad for the boys, and what kind of service it should be, whether Camilla should be called HRH The Duchess of Cornwall or something more low key, and what the Princess of Wales would have thought – it finally happened. And the sky didn't fall in. They couple had a civil ceremony at the Guildhall, followed by a church blessing at St George's Chapel and a reception at the castle.

It was a nail-biting day. No one knew what the reaction of the crowd would be, what the media would say, or how the whole thing would go. There had never been a royal wedding like it, where as a divorcee a future monarch would go through a civil ceremony followed by a church service. 'It was high stakes,' admits one of the courtiers involved. 'If anything didn't go right it would have been seized upon. We'd had all that palaver about where they got married, the ceremony being moved, the Pope's funeral, the ski trip, and the famous Nick Witchell, "I can't bear that man" remark.'

Charles and his sons had been holidaying in Klosters and had posed for the annual photo-call with the media, which none of them enjoys. The Prince hadn't realised how sensitive the row of microphones in the snow in front of them were and was clearly heard saying, 'I hate doing this. I hate these people.' After the BBC's royal correspondent asked the boys for their reaction to the wedding, Charles muttered, 'Bloody people. I can't bear that man. He's so awful, he really is' – and his words were recorded for posterity.

'It was all pretty feverish stuff. And the Pope. We had to move the royal wedding back 24 hours with 800 guests, contact each one individually at five days' notice and say, "Can you come on Saturday instead of Friday?"' Friday, as it happened, was cold and blustery, and at the very time the couple's car would have pulled up outside the Guildhall, it began to hail. 'I thought, He moves in mysterious ways, Him up there,' says Paddy. 'The next day it was sunny, it was brilliant. It was a fantastic day.'

I was in Windsor that day – one of two and a half thousand accredited media from all over the world. When I arrived at half past five for my first interview, barriers were in place, but the High Street was deserted except for one brave family who had camped outside the Guildhall overnight. I couldn't help thinking about the hundreds who had camped out for days before that first royal wedding twenty-four years before. By ten o'clock there were still only a handful of people and with the ceremony at half past twelve, I began to wonder whether the public's overwhelming reaction might be indifference. Half an hour later it was a very different story. The street was suddenly a seething mass of humanity, chattering in excitement. There were a few boos to be heard when the royal car drove up, but the vast majority were there because they were delighted that Charles was finally marrying the woman they knew he had loved for over thirty years. They were not disappointed: it was the most glorious, happy day for everyone there, and the bride looked absolutely stunning. She had chosen two beautiful outfits – one for the civil ceremony, the other for the chapel – and both were sensational.

While Charles went skiing, Camilla and her sister had taken themselves off to India for some sunshine, pampering and relaxation – and developed a taste for it. She's been back several times to Soukya, Dr Isaac Mathai's International Holistic Health Centre. She has never had surgery or used Botox but she did use an organic alternative, a face mask containing bee-sting venom invented by beautician Deborah Mitchell. The novelist Kathy Lette once said of Camilla, 'She immediately endeared herself to me by revealing how many well-meaning Americans had sent her contact details of their cosmetic surgeons – which only served to give her more laughter lines. We had a good laugh that day about women on the wrong side of fifty and how the best way to avoid wrinkles is to take off your glasses.' When she took her vows that day, Camilla was fifty-seven, and whether it was the detox and mud therapy in Bangalore or the bee-stings closer to home, her skin, which had previously looked a little dry and weathered, had a new and youthful glow. And her glasses were safely inside her handbag.

Camilla was not well on the day of the wedding. All that week she had been at Ray Mill suffering from sinusitis. Several friends had come to see her and they had had girly evenings in their dressing gowns, while Lucia Santa Cruz, who had introduced her to Charles all those years ago, came to administer home-made chicken soup. 'In Chile, everything is cured by chicken soup,' she'd told her friend, and had made her eat it. She was terrified Camilla wasn't going to get to the wedding, 'she was really ill, stressed'.

On the day itself it took four people to coax Camilla out of bed. She'd spent Friday night at Clarence House with Annabel and Laura. She still wasn't feeling well, but now it was nerves more than sinusitis that kept her under the duvet. She was terrified. 'She literally couldn't get out of bed.' Camilla's dresser, Jacqui Meakin, was there alongside Annabel and Laura, as was a housemaid called Joy, but none of them could coax her. Finally her sister said, 'Okay, that's all right. I'm going to do it for you. I'm going to get into your clothes.' Only at that point did the bride-to-be get up.

She looked endearingly frightened when she stepped out of the car with Charles and waved briefly before disappearing into the Guildhall at Windsor, but it was clear the crowd was on her side. Slowly, as the day wore on, she relaxed, reassured and supported as always by having her family around her. Her father was now eighty-eight and they were aware he was not in the best of health, but it was an important day for him and he was determined to be there. He had put off going to see the doctor until after the wedding. When he finally did so, four days later, he was diagnosed with pancreatic cancer. He died fourteen months later, but he had seen his daughter married, and that was what mattered to him.

Conducted by Clair Williams, the Royal Borough of Windsor's Superintendent Registrar, it was an intimate gathering and entirely private. Just twenty-eight in all, family and very close friends, watched the couple take their vows and exchange rings made of Welsh gold. Tom Parker Bowles and Prince William were their witnesses. Andrew Parker Bowles was not present but he had rung to wish Camilla luck. The only other notable absentees were the groom's parents – according to the Queen's biographer, Robert Hardman, 'Her absence denoted her disapproval of the arrangements, not of the marriage.' I am sure that's true, but I can't help thinking it was rather sad for Charles.

Camilla was now his wife, and technically the Princess of Wales, but for obvious reasons it had been made clear that she would be known as HRH The Duchess of Cornwall – and as such, she went back to the castle with her husband for the religious ceremony in the chapel. The crowds booed in disappointment when they realised the couple were leaving without coming across and speaking to them, but she needed time to change her outfit. Amanda MacManus was one of seven people lined up waiting for them. 'It was so sweet. As they came up the stairs they were both crying and that set all of us off, so we were all sobbing. It was just so touching and I think that was the first time we said, "Hello, Your Royal Highness." It was a very powerful moment; everyone had to slightly keep it together.'

The romantic side of the day apart, their marriage heralded a complete change in Camilla's life, and true to form, head in the sand, she had not wanted to think about it too carefully. For the Prince, that day brought an end to his loneliness. Camilla already shared his private life but not all of his public life, and it was on the long, gruelling foreign tours that he missed her the most. Henceforward she would be with him to share the travel, the feting by his hosts, the wining and dining, the concerts and spectacles that were laid on for him, the beautiful views that he was always taken to see. She'd be there to laugh with him at the absurdities and mishaps along the way and to chat, have a drink and unwind at the end of each day.

She, on the other hand, was entering a whole new world. She had never been a great traveller – she can't sleep on trains and she is terrified of flying. But her future would be one of almost non-stop travel, long haul and short haul, helicopters, trains, cars. There would be state visits, receptions and formal dinners, there would be ceremonial occasions and religious ones, when she would have to be on parade with the Queen and the rest of the Royal Family, and charity work would take her all over the country. On all such occasions, she would have to dress and look and behave like a duchess – immaculate hair, immaculate make-up and nails, outfits and hats. She had already shifted up a gear in her wardrobe, and the outfits for her wedding – both by Anna Valentine – were simply beautiful. But that was just the beginning.

As she signed the register in that town hall, Camilla was signing away the rest of her life to obligation, duty and hard work. It is only when you follow a member of the family around that you realise just how hard it is to do what they do, and to keep on doing it day after day. It is like being at a wedding party that never comes to an end, where you have to smile, shake hands, remember people's names, make small talk to strangers, show an interest in widgets and whelk stalls, and stand on your feet when you are aching to sit down and your shoes are killing you. She was embarking on this at the age of fifty-seven, having done nothing much more taxing than weed a flower bed for the previous fifty-seven years.

But on that joyous day in Windsor, she was just happy to have got through it without anyone throwing an egg at her. The blessing in St George's Chapel was taken by the Archbishop of Canterbury, Dr Rowan Williams, and the Dean of Windsor, David Conner, and the congregation joined in the General Confession from the Book of Common Prayer: 'We acknowledge and bewail our manifold sins and wickedness, which we, from time to time, most grievously have committed, by thought, word and deed, against thy Divine Majesty, provoking most justly thy wrath and indignation against us.'

Afterwards, the big doors of the chapel opened and they came out into afternoon sunshine, bathed in smiles. Ian Jones, a royal photographer for the *Telegraph* who had been on many overseas trips with Charles and sensed the loneliness, was in prime position in a media pen to see them emerge. 'She was wearing this wonderful Philip Treacy hat and the two of them looked like the weight of the world had been lifted off their shoulders. She came down the steps and came up and chatted to the crowd, and she chatted to us. There was no formality. "Well done, Ma'am, congratulations." "Thanks, Ian, thank you Arthur."' (This was Arthur Edwards, the *Sun*'s veteran royal photographer.) 'We were happy for them, he was happy, he just looked relieved and content that they were together at last.'

The reception was in the state apartments, where friends mingled with British and foreign royals, politicians, Palace and household staff, actors, singers and writers – in fact the great and good in every sphere. And among them were two less well-known figures. Camilla had invited two young girls from a working-class family in Newcastle who had never been to

London, but who had written supportive letters over the years and become pen pals. Paddy Harverson remembers introducing them to Joan Rivers, while Stephen Fry, Joanna Lumley and the Archbishop were less than a foot away, all tucking into finger food and Duchy champagne. 'The mood in that room was euphoric,' he says. 'It was one of the loveliest occasions I've ever been to.'

Charles gave a touching speech in which he thanked 'my dear mama' for footing the bill and 'my darling Camilla, who has stood with me through thick and thin and whose precious optimism and humour have seen me through'. But it was his mama's speech that was so perfect and laid to rest any lingering notion that she might still disapprove. The Queen is passionate about horse racing and the date coincided with the Grand National, in which she had a horse running. She began by saying she had two important announcements to make. The first was that Hedgehunter had won the race at Aintree; the second was that, at Windsor, she was delighted to be welcoming her son and his bride to the 'winners' enclosure. 'They have overcome Becher's Brook and The Chair and all kinds of other terrible obstacles. They have come through and I'm very proud and wish them well. My son is home and dry with the woman he loves.'

William and Harry then grabbed Paddy to help. Together they dashed outside to decorate their father's waiting Bentley and tie 'Just Married' signs onto the back. The couple were off to Birkhall for their honeymoon. 'There's a lovely moment when the newlyweds are leaving by car,' says Ian, 'and William and Harry are there seeing them off. There's real engagement and real confidence between Camilla and the boys. It was transparent that William was happy for them – and Harry, but more so William. You could see that what mattered to him was the happiness of his father and how good Camilla was for him. You could see the genuine happiness of them all together.'

There was huge relief – and not a little astonishment that both the crowds and, in the main, the media had been so positive. 'I think they saw two people in their fifties getting married and why not? It's a love story,' says one of the guests.

31

It Girl

Camilla had been made acceptable enough for the British public to stomach a wedding. Most people still knew very little about her, while many clung on to the images that Diana had conjured up of Rottweilers and marriage wreckers. And the media, of course, had perpetuated such images because it sold newspapers. But marriage was a game changer for everyone. She was no longer a private individual but a public figure, the second female member of the Royal Family in seniority after the Queen – everyone else has to curtsey to her – but she is in a supporting role, she is not the main act. It was a delicate balance, one which she instinctively understood. And as she started doing public engagements, slowly at first but with a gradually increasing workload, people finally got to see her in the flesh, to hear her voice, her laughter, saw her tucking into local fare at country markets or getting the uncontrollable giggles at some strange costume or ridiculous hat – or at nothing at all. They're now able to enjoy her self-deprecating little asides, to relish being made privy to the fact that her feet are killing her or she's about to drop with exhaustion. They find her genuine, friendly and delightfully normal, and they like her.

The royal correspondents, and people like me, love her because she is so friendly and approachable to us too. She knows the names of the people who follow her regularly, she is scrupulous about saying hello and will often in the course of an engagement come across for a word or two. It may only be 'Wasn't that an amazing concert?' or 'Did you get a chance to see that sweet little girl?' but it makes me, and them, feel less reptilian and apologetic for trying to do our jobs. On long-haul flights, if there are journalists in the back of the plane, as there sometimes are, she will always go back and have a chat with them. It's always off-the-record – and in any case she is too canny to say anything she would regret – but she likes to get to know the people who are writing about her, she sees them as friends not enemies. Over the years indeed they have been friends to her; their familiar faces and greetings have been reassuring in faraway countries where she's been swamped by crowds of strangers. She'll tell them about some delicious delicacy they must try, or a wonderful new dress shop she's found that's really affordable, or swap secrets on the best shoes to wear if you're going to be on your feet all day. And if they or their children are ill or have had operations or misfortunes, she will always remember and ask the question.

When Ian Jones lost his job in January 2008, she immediately found out. He had been a freelance under contract to the *Telegraph* for eighteen years and was given just one month's pay. Like many industries, the world of freelance photography was in free fall and he had children, family and a mortgage. Two months later he was in Jamaica at the start of a tour of the Caribbean, and was invited with six or seven others in the press corps for sundowners on *Leander*, a 2,000-tonne superyacht that Charles and Camilla were hiring at a much-reduced rate to visit the five islands on the itinerary. It is owned by Sir Donald Gosling, the founder of National Car Parks, who is a big fan of the Royal Family and a friend of the Queen, and Camilla was delighted. She loves boats – and contrary to reports, she doesn't suffer from seasickness. There was no sign of Charles, only Camilla. 'She came out in a beautiful two-piece silk suit with bare feet and a drink,' says Ian. 'She came round to me and she said, "Ian, I've heard about the *Telegraph*. I think it's terrible what they've done to you. Are you looking for other things?" I said, "Well, Ma'am, I'm doing portraiture and I'll do weddings, and I'll carry on photographing the Royal Family because I have done this for twenty years and I'm not going to stop just because of this."

'She said, "That's wonderful, I really do wish you well. I was really thinking about you when someone told me about it. And you're doing portraits? Would you mind if I gave your number to some of my friends?"'

Ian has had many commissions on the back of that conversation, but one of the first, just a few months later in June, came from the Duchess herself. It was to photograph the christening of her first two grandchildren at the

Chapel Royal at St James's Palace. Tom had married Sara Buys in September 2005, and their daughter Lola was born in October two years later. His sister, Laura, married Harry Lopes, a member of the Astor family, in May 2006, and their first daughter, Eliza, was born just three months after her cousin, in January 2008. Camilla now uses Ian to do a lot of the host photography at Clarence House. 'That's the woman she is,' he says. 'Very, very loyal.'

He was there on her first official foreign tour in the autumn of 2005. It was to America – to 'Diana's heartland'. No one could have devised a more terrifying initiation. She knew the eyes of the world would be on her, and that they would be making comparisons with the Princess's first trip to America with Charles in 1985.

Diana had wowed the country. The visit, wrote the *Los Angeles Times*, 'has this officially democratic capital suddenly mad about monarchy'. Most memorable were the fifteen minutes she spent on the dance floor with John Travolta at the White House. Diana had been twenty-three, athletic, wraith-like and coy; Camilla was fifty-eight and none of those things. A banner held by a woman outside the United Nations summed it up: 'Camilla, you are not Diana'. But despite some snide reporting in the American press to begin with – and an opinion poll for *USA Today* that suggested the American public were completely indifferent to the visit – they started to warm to her and the tone changed. By the end, the eight-day tour was deemed to have been nothing short of a triumph.

Their first engagement was at Ground Zero in New York, where the Twin Towers were destroyed on September 11, 2001. She laid down flowers with a handwritten note which read, 'In enduring memory of our shared grief'. The Prince had wanted her to do it, to involve her and to show her off. At a champagne reception at the Museum of Modern Art that evening for three hundred of New York's richest and finest, he referred to her in his speech as 'my darling wife' and told Tina Brown, the British-born, New York-based magazine editor, 'Now everyone can see how wonderful she is.' Other guests included Sting, Yoko Ono, Joan Collins and Donald Trump, then newly married to Melania – and whom they are set to meet again under very different circumstances, as President, if and when his controversial on-off state visit to Britain finally happens. Elaine Stritch, the actress and comedienne, told her, 'No bullshit, you look great.' To which she replied, typically, 'You need eye-glasses.'

She had chosen to wear a simple, classic navy blue velvet cocktail dress, which next to the bling of the trophy wives caused the *New York Post* to run a picture on two-thirds of its front page with the headline 'Queen Camilla is New York's "Frump Tower"'. Inside, the paper's fashion editor, Orla Healy, wrote: 'Diana would be amused. Her former rival and successor, Camilla Parker Bowles, failed spectacularly in her attempt to wow Manhattan society with her sartorial splendor last night … the Duchess of Cornwall arrived at a chi-chi cocktail party looking more like an escapee from the choirboy pew of Westminster Abbey than the guest of honor. Despite the fact that she is travelling with an army of wardrobe consultants the Duchess of Cornwall couldn't seem to put a sartorial foot right yesterday.'

The *New York Times* said, 'She had several strings of pearls around her neck, carried a black rectangular clutch bag and – this is most important – wore black stilettos, a sign, when worn by a middle-aged woman, that she is really, really trying.' In the evening, 'The duchess wore a triple-strand pearl choker, which was appropriate, as it featured a square-cut emerald that could have choked a horse. Her calf-length gown had a lace and pearl trimmed bodice, which revealed prominent décolletage – one area in which Diana could never compete.'

'The trip to America in 2005 was the tough one,' admits one of the team. 'There were a lot of nerves around that because it was her first overseas trip but it was a triumph. "Frump Tower" was really rude and unpleasant but they would have written some of that stuff anyway, because she was not Diana and certain sections of the media couldn't understand how a wealthy royal would swap a beautiful blonde for someone less beautiful.

'Washington was a great success – and then we took an unplanned trip to New Orleans to see the damage caused by Hurricane Katrina, which had happened some months earlier but where there was still a massive amount of damage. We then flew to San Francisco and did several days in northern California. Once the American reporters on the ground started to see them in action and to hear her, they started writing more favourable stuff.'

Throughout the trip Charles was looking out for his wife, guiding her. She watched him like a hawk, taking her cue from him but making sure to stay close so that he was always in any shot of her. This wasn't going to be the Camilla show, she was there to back the Prince up, not overshadow him – and besides, she needed the moral support. After they unveiled a granite sculpture at the British Memorial Garden to commemorate the lives of sixty-seven Britons who had died on 9/11, an American journalist called out to Camilla, 'What's it like to be in New York?' She momentarily froze, unsure of whether it was permissible to answer. She glanced at the Prince, who mouthed 'Very good' in her direction. 'Very good!' she shouted back cheerfully, and the awkward silence was broken.

Like all official foreign visits, this one was undertaken at the behest of the government and in diplomatic terms, the highlight of the trip was the state dinner at the White House. George W. Bush was no great fan of late nights; this was only the sixth time he had hosted a formal dinner during his presidency, and the first time he had invited his guests to an informal lunch as well. It was significant. But before that there was the obligatory photo-call on the White House lawn, and as they stood looking into a massive bank of cameras, the President told them that he had never in his time in the White House seen so many media present. The opinion polls that indicated indifference were already seeming unreliable. When Bush abruptly brought the session to an end by turning his back on the cameras and stalking off back into the White House with his wife and the Prince, Camilla deviated from the red carpet for a heartbeat to smile and give a small wave of acknowledgement to the individuals behind those cameras. She was no doubt finding it hard to believe that not so long ago she had been hiding under blankets in the back of cars.

By New Orleans she had cracked it. They had the warmest welcome of all from both the media and the locals whose community had been devastated. The hurricane had killed about 1,200 people and left thousands more without their homes or any of their belongings. 'Camilla, we love you,' shouted out women in the crowd. Forty-seven-year-old Dee deMontluzin, a social worker evacuated from the city for five weeks, recounted her experiences to her royal visitor. She said later: 'The trouble with American politicians is they never listen. The duchess really took in it and understood what I was saying.'

Ray Nagin, the mayor, was delighted by the visit. 'It sends out a tremendous signal to the world that New Orleans is getting better. It's great for the city that they are here,' he said, commenting of the Prince that there was no world figure he would rather be there. 'Not even the late Princess of Wales?' asked one reporter mischievously. 'I will settle for the Duchess any day,' he replied.

On New Year's Day 2006, less than two months after the American trip, the *Sunday Times* ran a light-hearted feature entitled 'Camilla: The It Girl of 2006'. Their reporter had consulted futurologists about the year ahead and discovered that the 'Rottweiler' had made an astonishing turnaround. Marian Salzman, J. Walter Thompson's advertising superstar in America, was confidently predicting that 'Camilla is going to be the next great lifestyle icon. Just look at that fabulous creature,' she said, and to emphasise her point, 'Look at the young princesses today – Beatrice, Zara and whoever. No one cares. All the lights are turned on this 58-year-old woman. Camilla tells us almost everything we need to know about where society is headed. I honestly believe that we'll soon start seeing communities of older newlyweds being built because love over fifty doesn't feel stigmatised any more. Camilla makes it look wonderful.'

That, funnily enough, was the precise word that Camilla had used to a widowed friend in the mid-1990s, shortly after her divorce when she was staying in a flat at Bowood House. The friend had been alone since her husband's death and was going out with a man who was madly in love with her. The two women had been discussing him over supper together when Camilla simply declared, 'It's wonderful to be loved.'

32

Staying Sane

The late Sir James Goldsmith famously said, 'When a man marries his mistress he creates a vacancy.' That won't happen on Camilla's watch; she sees off anyone who shows the slightest designs on her husband.

Some years ago I was told by a close observer of the goings-on at court that Camilla didn't like women and was marginalising them. I don't think that is true at all. On the contrary, she is hugely supportive of women – and most of the issues and charities she has chosen to put her name to are in support of women. But she is wary of women who toady to her husband, who flatter him and laugh before he has even made a joke. Charles is very susceptible to flattery and a few such individuals have gone. 'He's a very bad judge of character and it is the siren tongues. If someone's nice to him he thinks they're wonderful, while she's very sharp on people. There's also a sense of slight unease when it's women who are prettier and cleverer and talking the same language as him, which she doesn't do. She can be quite dismissive of them, and she's quite right.'

The other truth about marrying one's mistress – or indeed a woman marrying her lover – is that the relationship changes. For all that love and support and understanding may be a part of it, affairs are about good, exhilarating sex. Marriage is about living with someone 24/7 and discovering that all the things that seemed so cute or idiosyncratic are just plain irritating if you get them at breakfast, lunch and tea. The thrill of the illicit interludes and snatched weekends morph into the reality of sharing the same space and adjusting to the other person's habits and rhythms. There is often nothing like it for killing the romance stone dead.

Someone who knows both the Prince and the Duchess well agrees. 'I'm sure there's a bit of that thing that if you have a long affair with someone and you get married you have a bit of a wake-up call. That's human nature.'

The two of them were very fixed in their ways. Diana had discovered this about Charles when she married him thirty years earlier. Now, in his late fifties, he'd become even more entrenched in the lifestyle he had created for himself. And Camilla too. Adjusting to life under one roof was difficult. Charles is obsessive about order and tidiness. Camilla has always been untidy. Her homes have always felt lived in, full of clutter, dogs and stuff that children have dumped; his are like country house hotels with not a photograph or a magazine out of place. He has never had to pick up so much as a dirty sock for himself; she has been chief cook and bottle-washer for a family of four. He has always had household staff to look after his every need; she has had no more than a cleaning lady to help. He has always had a punishing work ethic; she was new to the concept and found it hard to keep up. He likes people around him all the time and is a wonderful host; she needs a break from people and enjoys her own company – and will often announce she's off to bed. He never eats lunch; she needs to, to keep her blood sugar levels up. He can be very down in the dumps; she is almost always buoyant. He has a terrible temper and can be moody and difficult; she can get angry but she is generally very easy-going and cheerful.

One of her very old friends is married to a similar character. 'We laugh,' says the friend, 'because we both have pessimistic husbands, so I ring her up and say, "How is the glass today?" "Totally empty." "Mine is waterless." But she's strong, she makes her points and has strong views and lays them down. He takes that quite well. She's not a dormouse at all. I think it's good for him to have a counterpart. People are quite sycophantic around him.'

The other great danger in marrying Charles – or, more particularly, marrying into the Royal Family – was that she would change, and the Camilla that all her family and friends so loved would be spoilt. I have watched people around members of the Royal Family for a very long time now, and something very strange happens to them. They turn into toadies. I have seen it again and again and it is no surprise that so many of the family are selfish, petulant and demanding. At any gathering, otherwise intelligent people hang on their every word, treat the most banal of small talk like pearls of wisdom; they bob and curtsey, they laugh too loud and too long at the weakest of jokes. Meanwhile a team of people hover to rescue the royal personage, to move them on to the next eager group, to clear a pathway, to open doors, to blow their noses, to do whatever it takes to make their day go smoothly. It bears no relation to life as the rest of us know it.

One of Camilla's friends remembers fishing on the Tay years ago with Gerald Ward. She was part of a large house-party staying at Kinnaird. The Prince of Wales joined them for a few days. 'We couldn't go to bed until he did, we had to get down for dinner when he did, we always had a picnic by the bank' – rather than at the house, as they normally did – 'because that was what he liked. I thought it was completely ridiculous.' It has long been the complaint of people who have played host to Charles on overnight visits that they always have to wait up until he is ready for bed.

Perhaps the only people who get away with it are Camilla's family. They don't pander to the nonsense over bedtime or anything else. They are respectful, of course, but they are not overawed by who the Prince of Wales is, and they find the royal circus faintly ridiculous – as they do the palaver involved when he comes to stay. They treat him like any other friend of the family or brother-in-law. And he relaxes. 'I think he feels cosy with us, and I think there are few people he's ever felt cosy with,' says one of them. 'It's very sweet. There's no doubt she has absolutely transformed his life, and the way they laugh – she'll have exaggerated something beyond belief and he'll say, "Darling, don't be so ridiculous," and say to me, "Shall we cut that down by fifty-five per cent?" There's a lot of that going on, which is so nice. No doubt about it, they are happy together. He thinks she's absolutely wonderful, it makes a lot of us laugh – "Oh, Camilla's an amazing traveller!" She never used to be.'

Inevitably, eleven years as a Royal Highness has changed Camilla, but not fundamentally. Her saviours have been her family, who keep her feet on the ground, a couple of good friends, who are prepared to tell her she's talking nonsense, and the fact that she kept Ray Mill when she married Charles. She had an escape. She can forget she is a duchess. She can go and be a mum and a grandmother, a sister and an aunt, she can put on old clothes, forget the make-up, ignore the hair, potter about in the garden, watch mindless television, cook everyone some lunch, and be untidy in her own home without feeling that the Prince is itching to send in the butler to

Hunting was a useful distraction for dealing with life's disappointments.

Sir Geoffrey Shakerley's portrait, taken when she became patron of the National Osteoporosis Society in 1997, was the first image of Camilla that had not been snatched by a paparazzo.

The first photographs that told the world they were a couple, taken outside the Ritz in January 1999, had been carefully stage-managed.

The engagement that some thought could never happen was announced on the morning of 10 February 2005.

They were finally married on 8 April 2005. Bruce Shand had told the Prince, 'I want to meet my maker knowing my daughter's all right.' Clockwise from left: Prince William, Prince Charles, Camilla, Duchess of Cornwall, Tom Parker Bowles, Laura Parker Bowles, Bruce Shand, Her Majesty the Queen, the Duke of Edinburgh.

Camilla didn't just marry the man, she married the family – a large one, all of whom traditionally assemble on the balcony at Buckingham Palace to celebrate the Queen's official birthday in June.

But this select gathering during the Queen's Diamond Jubilee was a strong indicator of how a pared-down monarchy might look in the future. Camilla, Charles, the Queen, the Duke and Duchess of Cambridge and Prince Harry.

Andrew, left, at Laura's wedding with Tom and Prince William. However hard it might have been for William and Harry to accept Camilla, they have never had a problem with her children.

Camilla's first joint engagement with her mother-in-law. Once the Queen had accepted that Charles was not prepared to relinquish Camilla, she embraced her into the family.

Their first foreign tour as a married couple to America, 'Diana's heartland', was a terrifying initiation. With George W. and Laura Bush on the White House lawn. The President said he had never seen such a big media turn out.

Having a bit of fun with the media while in Uganda for the Commonwealth Heads of Government Meeting. She regards the royal correspondents and photographers as friends, not enemies, and it pays dividends.

Arriving in the Caribbean islands of Trinidad and Tobago in 2008. In every country they visit there is a red carpet and a fanfare waiting. It's not how she used to travel.

In Kosovo, 2016, Camilla was close to tears as she embraced men and women whose loved ones had vanished during the war in 1998–99.

Meeting Theresa May, then Home Secretary, on a visit to Rape Crisis South London. Rape and sexual violence has become a 'pillar of interest' for Camilla.

The annual party for children and young people with life-shortening conditions to help decorate the Christmas tree at Clarence House. It is the highlight of everyone's calendar.

Reading and promoting literacy is another of Camilla's 'pillars of interest' and greatest passions. She has always read voraciously herself.

Having spent all her life around soldiers, Camilla relishes her honorary link to the military. 4th Battalion The Rifles reckon they have 'the trendiest royal'.

Catherine Goodman's portrait of Harry Parker who, as a captain in 4th Rifles, lost both legs after being injured in Afghanistan. Camilla offered him a free course at the Royal Drawing School, which Catherine runs. It led to Harry becoming a professional artist and writer.

Not standing on ceremony: Lola Parker Bowles, Tom's daughter and Camilla's eldest grandchild, at St James's Palace.

In her element, surrounded by children and grandchildren, and her ex. Adults from left: Harry and Laura Lopes, Camilla with Andrew behind her, Sara and Tom Parker Bowles. Children from left: Gus, Eliza, Louis Lopes, Lola and Freddy Parker Bowles.

The annual grandchildren's party in the garden at Clarence House. Tom, Andrew and Peter Phillips, Princess Anne's son, lend the twins a hand in the tug of war.

Camilla has transformed the Prince and brought laughter back into his life.

One look says it all.

Mark Shand with his brother-in-law on a futile mission to see elephants in Kerala.

Mark's sudden death in 2014 devastated the entire family.

With Andrew and his second wife Rose, who sadly died in 2010. The three of them had been friends for decades – and Camilla and Andrew are still the best of friends.

Watching the tennis at Wimbledon with Lady Sarah Keswick.

Tom and Laura bring normality to the circus that is royal life.
She absolutely adores them and their children.

With Annabel Elliot, her sister, who is also key to her stability.
She is so different from Camilla, but always there for her.

Camilla has proved to
be extraordinarily good
at the job – and no one
is more surprised about
that than she is.

straighten the magazine pile or take away the empty glasses. And they appreciate her. As Tom once said in an interview with journalist Cassandra Jardine, in the *Telegraph*, 'What pisses me off most of all is when someone who doesn't know her says she's been a bad mother. A couple of times I've read how she's put her children through this hell. She's been an exemplary mother. She never judges, she's very funny, she cooks the food I like and coming home is a joy. When I go back to Wiltshire for the weekend with my mother I feel cocooned, totally happy and safe – which I do with my wife, Sara, and my father, too.'

His parents are the best of friends. They often speak on the phone and are genuinely pleased to see each other, which they do frequently. They both always go to family events and never miss Tom's book launches. Camilla was very supportive during Rose's long battle with cancer, which she lost, sadly, in January 2010, two weeks after Andrew's seventieth birthday.

The two most important women friends are Lady Fiona, Marchioness of Lansdowne and Lady Sarah Keswick. Fiona is Charlie's second wife – they married in 1987 and Fiona spent the night before her wedding with the Parker Bowleses at Middlewick. She is six years younger than Camilla. Sarah, who was Lady Sarah Ramsay, the 16th Earl of Dalhousie's daughter, is slightly older and married to Sir Chips Keswick, once chairman of Hambros Bank and current chairman of Arsenal Football Club. Sarah and Chips have known Camilla and Andrew since the Sixties – Sarah is very keen on horse racing – and like the Lansdownes, they are also very old friends of the Prince of Wales.

Camilla spends most weekends at Ray Mill, and usually Mondays too. Laura lives not far away and after her twins, Gus and Louis, were born in December 2009, just before Rose's death, giving her three children under three years of age, she was grateful for any help she could get. And Camilla loves being with them all. She will quite often have dinner with Charles at Highgrove and, if there is nothing on the next day, go home for the night afterwards. It's not so much an escape from him – the Prince sometimes goes and stays with her there – as from the baggage that comes with him. Besides, he is up working most nights until well after she'd like to be in bed and asleep.

'Anyone would change,' says someone close. 'Everyone tells her, of course, that she's the most wonderful person in the world, so she believes

she's the most wonderful person. She automatically is the centre of attention come what may. Going into a room, if Camilla's there, even my best
friend in all the world would feel they ought to go to her. For more than
eleven years now it's been "Where's my tea?" I think we'd all be affected by
it. And she has power. People will see her as ruthless; I wouldn't be surprised
about that. When she doesn't like something she's got the power to get rid
of it. Neither of them like people who disagree with them. That is the
trouble.

'Camilla is very stubborn and there are all sorts of things she doesn't
budge on, and he's probably found that quite testing. Without a doubt she's
in charge, she's a far stronger character than he is. He's very weak. Adorable.
I feel very maternal towards him. He's one of the sweetest and kindest
people in so many ways but I do fear for him. I fear for them both – but
she's got a good team around her.'

Camilla's father, who was such a linchpin in her life and who would have
provided the wisest counsel and support in the early days of marriage, was
sadly no longer alive. Once he had been given the diagnosis, having lived
long enough to see Camilla's future secured, he said he wanted no treatment. He died with all his children around him at his home with Annabel
at Stourpaine on 10 June 2006. He was eighty-nine and had had a good
innings, but he was such a very special man, with not an ounce of guile or
malice in him, that everyone, of every generation, adored him. His loss
therefore was all the more upsetting, not just to his children and grandchildren but to everyone who knew him. And it was a real blow to Camilla.

The funeral was held at the village church in Stourpaine, a short walk
from the house, and they had filled it with summer flowers and oak leaves
from the garden at Highgrove, which they had arranged themselves. The
beautiful ceremony included a poem, called 'St Valentine's Day', that might
have been written for Bruce but was in fact by the Victorian Romantic poet
Wilfrid Scawen Blunt:

To-day, all day, I rode upon the down,
With hounds and horsemen, a brave company
On this side in its glory lay the sea,
On that the Sussex weald, a sea of brown.
The wind was light, and brightly the sun shone,
And still we gallop'd on from gorse to gorse:

And once, when check'd, a thrush sang, and my horse
Prick'd his quick ears as to a sound unknown.
I knew the Spring was come. I knew it even
Better than all by this, that through my chase
In bush and stone and hill and sea and heaven
I seem'd to see and follow still your face.
Your face my quarry was. For it I rode,
My horse a thing of wings, myself a god.

Camilla and Annabel had both heard the poem for the first time at the memorial service for their old Sussex friends Lord and Lady Shawcross, held in February 2004 at St Clement Danes Church in Covent Garden. Joan had hunted with Bruce; her life had been tragically cut short in 1974 by a riding accident on the Downs when she was just fifty-six. Hartley had reached the grand age of 101 when he died in July 2003; their three children had decided to hold a joint memorial service for them. The moment Camilla and Annabel heard Joanna read the poem for her mother, they said it was so completely Bruce they would use it at his funeral.

After the service they all went back for lunch in the Elliots' garden. Bruce was cremated, as Rosalind had been, and some of their ashes were scattered in a small copse at the top of the Downs overlooking The Laines, the house where they'd all spent so many wonderfully happy years. Camilla asked permission from the landowner for them to place two stones and a small plaque there in memory of their parents; now, every year, the family all go together to clean them.

33

Pillars of Interest

Over her bowl of cure-all chicken soup at Ray Mill, two days before the wedding, Lucia Santa Cruz had suggested Camilla's life was about to change. 'Are you mad?' Camilla had said, no doubt choosing not to think about it too closely. 'Nothing will change. Everything will go on exactly the same.'

'Just you wait!' Lucia had replied with some prescience. 'She was convinced she was never going to do anything.'

Camilla was then patron of three charities. Her correspondence was taken care of by Amanda and Joy and she attended dinners and receptions with the Prince of Wales where it was appropriate. Otherwise she was a free agent. Today, she has another private secretary called Sophie Densham, who is her children's age. Sophie works full time, mixing very well with the other two, and is keeper of the diary. The Duchess has almost ninety patronages, gets thousands of letters each year – each and every one of which she reads – does two foreign tours and one to the Commonwealth a year, spends a working week each in Scotland, Wales and Cornwall, attends ceremonial events, state banquets, the state opening of Parliament and Commonwealth heads of government meetings, and works four full days a week visiting the charities she has taken under her wing. Is it any wonder she didn't want to think too closely about what she was taking on?

'I don't think she or anyone understood how demanding it was going to be when she took on the job,' says Amanda. 'I think it came as quite a surprise in the beginning. She's got extraordinary focus for someone who appears to be very relaxed, and if she's going to do something, she's going to do it well. I think the work gives her a real sense of achievement which I don't think she was expecting, and I think she's chuffed. She really enjoys the fact that her involvement will make a difference. It's getting some sort of endorsement for your work, feeling you're valued, and I think that's part of her ability to really do it well.'

'The voluntary sector was rather snotty when she first appeared,' says Julia Cleverdon. 'They said, "Oh she'll be doing a little gentle horse riding, she's rather keen on Bobby Vans [a Wiltshire charity designed to make the elderly feel secure in their homes] and there'll be something about dogs."'

The Duchess has focused on what her team call her 'pillars of interest' – and horses and dogs, and Bobby Vans, are indeed amongst them. But she has gone way beyond the safe and predictable. Illiteracy speaks for itself. It perpetuates poverty and affects the most deprived members of society, and it has never been given the prominence it merits. She has taken the issue on in a big way. She has given her name to the issues of domestic violence, rape and sexual assault – difficult subjects by any standards, and brave, I think, for someone whose own sex life was once beamed around the world. Health and well-being charities are in the mix; to the NOS she has added several hospices and other specialists. Food is another enthusiasm; not just the eating of it – although she does love food and tucks into it enthusiastically whenever a produce market is on the itinerary – but everything from the growing of it, the rearing of livestock, to marketing and even cooking, and to encouraging a healthy diet. Alexia Robinson, founder of British Food Fortnight, an event the Duchess supports, says, 'If we don't teach the next generation about the wonderful produce available in this country, there simply won't be a market for fresh produce or raw meats in the future, because the British public won't know how to cook it.' At the Queen's Diamond Jubilee, Camilla came up with the idea of a competition for schoolchildren to create from the best of British produce a new dish to rival Coronation Chicken, which was invented sixty years earlier. The winning schools would see the royal chef turn their creations into canapés which would then be served at a reception attended by the Queen and the Duchess.

And there's wine. Her father was a wine merchant; the Duchess loves it, she knows about it, she was brought up in the French style, drinking wine and water from an early age. And the United Kingdom Vineyards Association needs all the help it can get. At a reception held at Clarence House in January 2017 to celebrate the association's fiftieth anniversary, she caused a flurry of excitement in the press. Royal correspondents who had gone to the event expecting nothing more than a cheering glass of wine were suddenly jolted into consciousness when the president appeared to be applauding global warming – one of her husband's greatest bugbears. 'We don't exactly have the climate, or we didn't then,' she said, 'but I expect with global warming it's going to get better and better, we're going to get better and better wine.'

In addition to the charities, like every member of the Royal Family the Duchess has an honorary link to the armed forces. She is Royal Colonel of the 4th Battalion The Rifles, a relatively new regiment formed in 2007 by the merger of a number of other regiments. Its base is now at Aldershot in Hampshire, but was originally at Bulford in Wiltshire. Having spent all her life around soldiers – her father, Andrew, the Prince and so many of their friends and friends' children, including William and Harry – she takes her role very seriously, she cares about them all and relishes the connection. She visits military bases – she'll climb gamely into a tank or an armoured vehicle for a drive around Salisbury Plain – she presents medals and turns up for parades, at Christmas time she sends biscuits, if a baby's born she sends flowers and cards, when troops are deployed she sends parcels of goodies. And when there are casualties, she visits the wounded. 'As a battalion, we felt we had the trendiest royal,' says one of them. 'She was good fun.' 'The military is more than a pillar of interest,' says Joy. 'She's passionate about it.'

34

A Good Read

Literacy was a natural fit, and another passion. The National Literacy Trust claims that 5.2 million people in England, 16 per cent of the adult population, are 'functionally illiterate', which means their skills are at or below the level of those expected of an eleven-year-old. And that, of course, has further terrible consequences. Many jobs are out of the reach of such people; they may not be able to read to their children, help with their homework or perform everyday tasks, and the potential for a child born into such a family is severely limited. Camilla became patron in 2010 and since then other charities have followed – BookTrust, First Story, the Wicked Young Writers' Award, Beanstalk. As Julia Cleverdon says, tongue in cheek, 'She's done all that without saying phonics are the only answer, or it is appalling the way in which libraries are being shut, or any of the things which her other half would have been tempted to say with possibly challenging consequences. Very clever.'

The Duchess has presented the Man Booker Prize for fiction for several years. It's one of the highlights of the literary year – and of her diary. The Man Booker Foundation puts money into literacy projects including prisons. The chairman is Baroness Helena Kennedy QC, the Labour peer and human rights lawyer, a campaigner on every important issue you can think of – a remarkable human being who discovered very soon after meeting Camilla in the summer of 2004 that they were both bookworms.

Kennedy had known Prince Charles for some years in her capacity as chair of the British Council, and she and her surgeon husband, Iain Hutchison, were invited to spend the weekend with Charles and Camilla at Sandringham. Amongst their fellow guests were Jeremy Irons and Sinead Cusack, Jools and Cristabel Holland, Mario Testino, and Richard E. Grant and his wife Joan. 'It was a really terrific weekend,' says Helena. 'We drank, we laughed, we had fun together. For a socialist peer it was very entertaining.' The weekend was a mixture of formality and informality, with black tie dinners each night, where they swapped seats so they were able to sit next to different people. In the daytime, there were picnics on Holkham beach, long walks, bicycle rides, tea with the neighbours – the Lord Chamberlain, who had Stephen Fry staying – and church on Sunday. After dinner each night some sort of entertainment was laid on. On the first evening they sat in the ballroom and watched *Gosford Park*, the murder mystery set in a grand country house in the 1930s, written by the creator of *Downton Abbey*, Julian Fellowes. Apart from the murder, it might have been a parody of their weekend – and every time Richard E. Grant appeared on screen as George, first footman, there was caterwauling from the stalls. The Saturday night was a grander gathering. The Russian conductor Valery Gergiev came with members of his orchestra and some opera singers, who were sensational; and on the Sunday night after dinner Jools Holland sat at the piano and they all stood around him singing along.

Helena had been warned that her suitcase would be unpacked for her, but she hadn't bargained on her wash-bag being unpacked too. 'I think most women would take fright at that,' she says. But worse still was the embarrassment when she and her husband got into their car to leave on Monday morning and discovered that someone had cleaned it, inside and out. Their Renault Espace not only ferried children and a dog around but also medical detritus.

Helena has been one strand of the literacy pillar. Another was Michael Morpurgo, the children's author and creator of *War Horse* – which Camilla, like the Queen, loved and has seen in its stage adaptation many times. She and Charles met him very soon after their marriage. He was then Children's Laureate – a post that he and his friend, Ted Hughes, had dreamt up between them a few years previously, over a glass of wine or two, to try and persuade people to take children's literature seriously.

Charles had known Ted Hughes well – the poet had been at Birkhall that

Easter when Tom and Laura went to stay, and he used to read to William and Harry when they were younger. 'When we met up,' says Morpurgo, 'it became clear that Camilla was actually quite passionate about the whole world of children's literature and literacy, and it was very evident that she wanted to engage with this side of the nation's life. I think she was looking for a way to make that connection. I felt she meant it, it wasn't just a PR thing; she wanted to make a serious contribution – and she could see that there was a real job to be done. There's a slice of us that are literate, highly literate and highly educated, but far too many of us are leaving school without reading and almost worse, without enjoying books. I was very keen to point out that the contribution somebody in her position could make was very important.

'We looked each other in the eye, and I stopped thinking of her – if I ever did – as some kind of duchess or princess. I just realised this was a person who was finding a role for herself. I thought that was a good idea, and I liked the fact that she had chosen a field which I was very enthusiastic about.

'By and large, I think over the centuries the Royal Family has been more interested in horses than in books. And she is putting her mark, her stamp, her support on the literature of this country, particularly for young people. I don't think any member of the Royal Family since Prince Albert has been that involved in the culture of the country.'

Speaking at the presentation of the Orange Prize for Fiction at the Royal Festival Hall in 2010, the Duchess confirmed as much. 'I firmly believe in the importance of igniting a passion for reading in the next generation. My father was a fervent bibliophile, and a brilliant storyteller too. Every night, he would read to us children – Enid Blyton and Lewis Carroll, Charles Dickens, Anthony Trollope and Baroness Orczy. And we would sit transfixed, disappearing up Faraway Trees, down rabbit holes, across Romney Marsh, through the stalls of Barchester Cathedral and into the depths of the Bastille. The power of a captivating story, a well-honed sentence or a beautifully crafted character is immense, not only taking the reader – or listener – to different worlds, but broadening and stimulating the mind too. A world without books is too hideous to even contemplate. I've yet to embrace the joys of the Kindle and iPad, but good writing is timeless, regardless of the medium upon which it is printed. Although it must be said that the old-fashioned book is blissfully unaffected by battery life!'

The Orange Prize, subsequently known as the Baileys Women's Prize for Fiction, was set up by a group of women in response to the 1991 Booker shortlist, which had not one female author amongst its six finalists – a fact that no commentator seemed to find strange. Had it been an all-women list there would have been an outcry. So they did a little research and discovered that 60 per cent of novels published were written by women and 75 per cent of novels sold were bought by women, yet fewer than 9 per cent of those shortlisted for major literary prizes were by women. So their books were being published and bought, but their achievements weren't being honoured in the same way as men's. The novelist and playwright Kate Mosse, the prize's co-founder and honorary director, says that the approach for Camilla to become involved, in 2008, came from her office.

Kate had met Camilla four years earlier at Ronnie Scott's Jazz Club, and hadn't known who she was. It was the launch party for Tom's first book, *E is for Eating: An Alphabet of Greed*. 'I remember standing in the queue for the loo with an incredibly nice woman who had a rather deep and infectious laugh and we had a bit of a chat. It was the women's locker-room moment. It was only later when someone said "Did you have a nice evening?" and I said, "Yes, I did. I talked to lots of people I didn't know, and I had a really hilarious conversation with a woman in the queue for the loo who was a complete hoot." They were like, "That's the author's mum, it's Camilla Parker Bowles."'

Kate has never mentioned that meeting to Camilla, but they did meet more formally at Windsor Castle after her engagement to the Prince. She remembers getting into trouble for putting her hand on the Prince's back when he came to talk to her; but also having a very animated conversation with Camilla and Helena Kennedy and once again thinking, You're really nice!

So, when the approach came, Kate spoke to a colleague: 'Very interesting, the Duchess of Cornwall's been in touch wanting to know if there was any support she might give to the prize and young people and literacy. And the person I was talking to was furious. "After everything she did to Diana! How could you …?" That was my first inkling that some, who didn't actually know any of these people, except through newspaper and media coverage, nonetheless had a strong emotional and personal engagement with them. It seems strange to me to judge people on those terms.'

They discussed what Camilla's involvement might be, and it was made clear that she wasn't merely after publicity. That year a youth panel of six teenagers, three girls and three boys, were reading the longlist for the women's prize and choosing their winner. 'The Duchess's people said, "Would you like to hold the judging at Clarence House?" And I thought that would be terrific. It was incredibly quiet and low key and there was never any "We would like to take lots of photographs" and use it in a way that was to do with her promotion rather than the young people. Some of them came from challenging personal environments, and suddenly they found themselves in the drawing room being served tea, and then Camilla came and sat down on the sofa and talked to everybody and was completely natural, was not patronising, was not let's-go-along-the-line-and-ask-each-young-person-what-they're-doing-and-what-their-ambitions-are. She just made six very overwhelmed teenagers completely at home. And they just talked about the books. Then I talked to her a bit and she said, "Oh, by the way, I really loved *The Winter Ghosts*," which was one of my latest novels. I said, "You've been very well briefed." And she said, "I have read it!"'

At a reception at Clarence House for the final of DJ Chris Evans's *500 Words* competition for young writers on BBC Radio 2, the Duchess explained her enthusiasm for stories. 'We all have our own favourites that we could read over and over again. For me, they were the stories my father read to me ... I can't guess yours – maybe Paddington Bear, Hairy Maclary, Harry Potter, Horrid Henry or Matilda?

'Like climbing through the wardrobe into Narnia, stories open doors into different worlds. They stretch our imagination and get our brains buzzing. We fall in love with heroes and heroines and can't turn the pages fast enough to find out what happens. We meet impossible people, travel to remote places and make hundreds of new friends. We look around with new eyes and recognise Horrid Henry next door and Professor Snape the chemistry teacher in the school down the road.

'Whether exotic or everyday, heart-warming or heart-stopping, stories help us to understand our world and the people in it. We can all see the differences in our points of view and backgrounds, but the best stories – just like those old tales – show us what we all have in common, what we all share.'

But it's more than the sheer pleasure of reading. As the Duchess said at the Man Booker Prize presentation in 2013, 'The world of books is, alas, not familiar to everyone. Those who cannot read and write are denied the pleasures and the opportunities which these skills can bring. That's why I became involved with several literacy charities.'

It was a scheme called Books Unlocked, run by the National Literacy Trust, that took the Duchess and me to HMP Brixton in February 2016. I was standing with a small group of media inside the main gates of the old Victorian men's prison in south London, surrounded by coils of razor wire. We were waiting for the Duchess's car – it's usually a black one – to draw up. The gates opened and everyone was poised for the shot when someone noticed the black car was an Uber taxi delivering a new inmate who was handcuffed to a prison officer. A few minutes later the right black car arrived, followed by a Range Rover, and there was the Duchess, accompanied by Sophie and her protection officers. Her solo engagements are always remarkably calm and simple; there's no vast entourage and no officious restrictions on the media. After greeting the governor, Giles Mason, she came across to us, smiling cheerfully, and said 'Good morning.'

I had been in Peterborough with her the day before, and seeing me again she said, 'Hello, Penny.' 'Hi,' I said smiling. It wasn't until later that I thought maybe 'Good morning, Your Royal Highness' might have been better – maybe even a hint of a curtsey – but she is so approachable and friendly and smiley that I said what I would have said to anyone I was pleased to see. To her credit, she was completely unfazed. As we were leaving an hour or so later, she came across and asked what I'd thought about the morning – and she was equally friendly when I saw her a couple of hours later at an event for the Poppy Appeal for veterans. I don't sense that it's calculated to make sure that I or anyone else write nice things about her. It is who she is, and I think it reassures her, as it would anyone, to find friendly, familiar faces amongst the sea of strangers that fills her working day.

In her hour she had met prisoners taking part in rehabilitation programmes. She'd sat in a reading group on national prison radio and, when asked what book she would recommend, she'd suggested *Anatomy of a Soldier* by Harry Parker, one of her own men from the 4th Rifles. She'd spoken to prisoners learning to paint and decorate, a project run by a charity called Bounce Back – and jokingly asked one of them whether he would come and paint the Palace. She'd met others learning to make bread and cakes in the Bad Boys Bakery and she'd had a cup of tea and a sit down in The Clink, a restaurant within the prison that's open to the public, and is almost entirely run by offenders.

Literacy is a huge problem in prisons. Sixty per cent of inmates are functionally illiterate. So they can't read job advertisements, letters, notices, instructions or newspapers. And if they can't live life as the rest of us do, it's no wonder they reoffend. As Kate Mosse says, 'We should be ashamed that there's anybody who hasn't got basic literacy in our country in this day and age. So Camilla putting her name to something like that really matters because it can help make that agenda more appealing to whatever government it is, and actually these are the things that help change society.'

The Duchess's day in Peterborough had also involved the National Literacy Trust. It's run by Jonathan Douglas, and Julia Cleverdon is chair. It was Camilla's 'phenomenal speech' at the Orange Prize that caught Jonathan's attention. Someone from the trust was at the awards and phoned him from outside the hall: '"Oh my goodness, this is really exciting. The Duchess of Cornwall has just said the following things ..." She basically channelled what we thought.' Jonathan contacted Clarence House right away and the Duchess came to an event in Devizes in Wiltshire. 'It went well: We've taken her to libraries and she's read stories to children, and she chooses stories she knows have worked with her grandchildren. There's no sense that she'll stand there awkwardly staring at people. It's not a staged relationship.'

The trust has set up four hubs in Middlesbrough, Bradford, Stoke-on-Trent and Peterborough, some of the most deprived areas of the country, where they are piloting ways of breaking the intergenerational cycle of poor literacy in partnership with local councils, and community, education, sporting, health, business, faith and voluntary sector resources. It's a strategy straight out of Business in the Community, where Julia Cleverdon cut her teeth. Three hundred schoolchildren were gathered in Peterborough Cathedral for a mini literature festival with readings and talks, each child proudly holding the flag of their country of origin. I couldn't begin to tell you what half of them were, but there were very few Union Jacks. Some of the children had taken part in a creative writing competition, *Our Stories: Celebrating the Cultural Diversity of Peterborough* – and each winner had their story read out loud and was presented with a certificate by the Duchess. It was a charming event, and afterwards she went up and down the pews chatting to the children.

Then on to Boots Opticians in the High Street. There were no security barriers. Her style is very relaxed. Her PPOs keep a close eye, but she happily stops and chats to people who have gathered to see her, and at times it's hard to see where she is amongst them. At Boots children were having their eyes tested, wearing green frog glasses to hold the corrective lenses. As Julia explains, 'We said, "A million kids can't read because they can't see," and the world said, "Are you sure about that?" So we sent Boots Opticians with 90,000 hours of ophthalmologists' time to go and test out kids' eyes in Bradford, Peterborough, Middlesbrough, Stoke and Liverpool, and we discovered that twenty per cent of kids whose eyes were tested couldn't see, because slightly chaotic families, or those where it isn't the priority, had not taken in that they should get their children's eyes tested – and it's all for free.'

The trust was very keen that their patron should be more than a name on a letterhead, but the feeling was mutual. The day the patronage was announced, in November 2010, the Duchess took part in 'a bus journey of reading' for thirty children aged nine and ten, who had gained their places by winning golden tickets like the children in Roald Dahl's *Charlie and the Chocolate Factory*. The trust commandeered a number 15 London bus, and at every tourist attraction along its route a famous author would be waiting to read the children a story. When the bus reached Trafalgar Square it deviated down the Mall and stopped outside Clarence House. The Duchess was there to welcome the children off the bus and took them all inside for some squash, while she read them a story by the fire. 'The kids were beside themselves.'

Other engagements have been tougher. 'We took her for a day to Middlesbrough, where there are really significant literacy problems, very much linked with socioeconomic background. She can talk to some very challenging families, but she's got an authority in terms of the conversation. What is so powerful about her is that she's authentic and she projects a strong image as to the importance of family reading. She's been really super for us, a good asset and a good friend.'

After launching a programme for the National Literacy Trust in 2012, with Theo Walcott, the Arsenal and England star, at the Emirates Stadium to use football as a means of encouraging boys to read, the Duchess set the trust a challenge. Walcott didn't start reading properly until he was ten because he was too busy mucking about with a football, so he was a good role model. What plans, she wanted to know, did Jonathan have for the Diamond Jubilee? He had none. 'Well, why don't you hold a competition

– and what about the Commonwealth?' The idea was that children should read their way round the Commonwealth, picking up facts about it and collecting air-miles for all the books they read. 'We put it out to the schools we work with and within twenty-four hours, two thousand schools had signed up.'

A year later, for their twentieth anniversary, the trust ran a project called Literacy Champions, designed to identify twenty people who had made the most difference to literacy, either in their communities or nationally. 'We ended up with this ragtag of extraordinary people, and one who we really hadn't anticipated was The Fonz' – in other words Henry Winkler, the American actor who played the renowned *Happy Days* character. 'Henry is dyslexic and had written a series of children's books – and has spent years, below the radar, going into schools and talking to children about the importance of reading and of not being afraid to ask for help when you're learning. So we invited Henry along to the reception at Clarence House to announce the winners, and everyone kept walking into the room and going "It's the Fonz!"'

In another twenty years I imagine Camilla's name will also be amongst those Literacy Champions.

35

Nothing to Prove

Camilla has good instincts. She doesn't pretend to be anything she is not. She is the age she is and she has no trouble with that. She might laugh – as we all do – about gravity taking hold and not being able to see anything without her specs, or work the remote control, but she is happy to be a grandmother, and to wear comfortable shoes and admit that she finds long days and foreign tours exhausting. She is not chasing eternal youth or dressing like a forty-year-old. She is happy in her own skin – which is refreshing – and, judging by the reaction of the people I've seen her meet, the public appreciate it. They find her genuine – down to earth, straightforward and approachable – and there is never the feeling that she is doing something because it would be good for her image. She may do things to publicise a charity she supports or an issue that needs airing, but never to promote herself.

Once she was married, she wanted no more slick PR tactics, no attempts to sell her to the public, and Paddy Harverson agreed. 'She's very smart,' he says, 'she knows that the still image is probably the most powerful one and that what works are a lot of consistently great shots of him and her together smiling, happy, enjoying themselves, working. Nothing more than that. It's actually very straightforward.'

The Queen has never given interviews; nor did the Queen Mother. As one of the household says, 'They are risky, and I think the public admire people who don't sit down and talk about themselves. Besides, what was she going to say? What would she be asked? Just imagine the first six questions and what those answers might be and you go, "No, this isn't going to work." I think less is more; she felt happy with that, it took away the stress.

'Then the building blocks for the work were around real, genuine themes of interest to her. If you're stepping up at an age when most people are getting ready to retire, you need to make sure it's authentic and true to you. So we let her get on with the job, we supported her enormously, we were very conscious the tours should be geared towards making sure she was comfortable.' They didn't overload the work, they made it clear from the start that she wouldn't do everything the Prince did; she wouldn't go to every event, she would have her own interests, they would do things together and then she would take breaks. 'As long as we explained it to everyone that was fine. There was a period where the media, needless to say, were asking how many engagements she had done, but that's a sort of numbers game you can never really win; it went well and she won people over through her personality and her charm and diligence. The public really appreciated the fact that she knuckled down and got on with it and there wasn't a slippery PR campaign to win them over.

'She married into the job knowing that it comes with a lot of work. A lot of great privileges too, a lot of benefits. But it's not like normal work. You don't go to an office each day; the office comes to you and you have meetings and briefing notes and folders.'

The Duchess and the Queen now get on famously. One of the most endearing moments of the Diamond Jubilee celebrations occurred during the River Pageant, the largest ever to be staged anywhere, when a flotilla of a thousand boats made their way up the Thames to Tower Bridge. As the royal barge, the specially built *Gloriana*, passed the National Theatre, the Queen nudged her daughter-in-law to point out Joey, the puppet realisation of Michael Morpurgo's War Horse, running along the roof beside them and rearing up in greeting.

The two of them were on sparkling form with real horses the following year when the Queen accepted Camilla's invitation to visit the Ebony Horse Club, of which she is president, in Brixton. Their first joint engagement, it was an ideal start. The club gives opportunities to disadvantaged young people in one of the poorest boroughs in London, teaching them to ride and care for horses. In the most unlikely setting, under the arches at

Loughborough Junction, overlooked by soulless tower blocks, are the stables for eight horses and ponies, a stable yard, a paddock and a floodlit arena.

The only shadow that darkens the picture from time to time is the memory of Diana. In 2007 it was the tenth anniversary of her death. Paddy worked closely with Jamie Lowther-Pinkerton, William and Harry's private secretary at that time, supporting the Princes in their determination that they and not the media take charge of the occasion. The Princes came up with a plan to both celebrate and commemorate their mother. They wanted a spectacular concert of music and dance with all the artists she loved most, to be held on what would have been her forty-sixth birthday, followed by a memorial service, again including the music she loved, on the date of her death. Seldom had the Princes been so demonstrative about what they wanted and how they wanted to do it.

The party was certainly spectacular. It was held at the new £798 million Wembley Stadium. When the Princes walked out onto the stage to rapturous applause, Harry simply said, 'Hello Wembley!' and 63,000 people got to their feet to stamp and cheer. The 22,500 tickets made available in December sold out within seventeen minutes. The six-hour marathon featuring all the top names in pop, along with pre-recorded video tributes from Nelson Mandela, Bill Clinton and Tony Blair, was broadcast in 140 countries to an audience of around 500 million people and raised a total of £1 million for charity.

To avoid any awkwardness, William and Harry had banned all senior members of the family from the concert. Instead, the royal box was filled with their cousins and friends, including Kate Middleton, now Duchess of Cambridge, William's wife, and her brother James. Discussions about their mother between the Princes and their father had always been very difficult. As one of their friends said, 'There is no doubt they love their father but from everything I've seen he is a complex man and difficult to be the son of sometimes, and his reactions to things aren't always as elevated as we might want them to be. Anything to do with their mother is really tricky. Their sensitivity about being seen to say anything about their mother is very noticeable. "Talk about our mother? Oh God, we don't talk enough about our dad." They are very careful of Charles's sensitivities and dance around them a lot. Like at the service. He was very sensitive about where he sat and what it said.'

The family – including Camilla – had all been invited to the memorial service. It was held at the Guards Chapel, and despite being in the middle of their annual holiday at Balmoral, they all came. This second event was designed in part to bring together the two sides of the family, which had been divided since Diana's death, and the seating was important – but Charles, via Michael Peat, made a meal of it. William gave up in exasperation. Finally it was Harry who said, 'F*** that,' picked up the phone and said, 'I want to speak to my father. Put him through.' He simply said, 'Right, Dad, you're sitting here, someone else is sitting there, and the reason we've done it is blah and blah. All right? Are you happy?' 'Oh yes,' said Charles. 'I suppose so.' Problem solved. William sat on one side of the altar, next to the Queen, with his father and senior members of the Royal Family, and Harry sat on the other side with the Spencers – Diana's brother Charles, sisters Sarah and Jane, and their spouses and children.

Camilla was the only notable absentee. She had accepted her stepsons' invitation and had intended to go, but just days before the service, Rosa Monckton, one of Diana's closest friends and the mother of one of her godchildren, wrote an inflammatory article in the press in which she said Camilla should stay away: 'I know such occasions should be an occasion for forgiveness, but I can't help feeling Camilla's attendance is deeply inappropriate.' Diana would be 'astonished', she wrote, at the presence of the 'third person' in the marriage. Camilla was prompted to issue a statement: 'I am very touched to have been invited by Prince William and Prince Harry to attend the thanksgiving service for their mother Diana, Princess of Wales. I accepted and wanted to support them. However, on reflection, I believe my attendance could divert attention from the purpose of the occasion, which is to focus on the life and service of Diana. I am grateful to my husband, William and Harry for supporting my decision.'

'I think the public would have been fine,' says Paddy. 'Once William and Harry had invited her, who were we to question that? My advice was to go, but looking back I think she was right. Our job is to advise and theirs is to decide. She's got very good instincts, very good intuitive understanding of what works, what's right and what's not.'

Several years before they were married, the Prince commissioned a portrait of Camilla from the artist Catherine Goodman. Catherine had come to know Charles and other members of the Royal Family though her friendship with his cousin, Sarah Armstrong Jones, Princess Margaret's daughter. She and Sarah had studied for many years together in the 1980s at Camberwell School of Arts and Crafts and the Royal Academy Schools, and had shared a flat. They are great friends, and as Catherine says, it was through Sarah that 'I came across this sort of strange world of the Royal Family.'

When the Prince opened his Institute of Architecture in 1991, she was asked to teach drawing to the students – while building her career as a professional painter – and swiftly found herself on the academic board. 'The institute started with a kind of Renaissance curriculum, students were going to do everything from philosophy to drawing, to building their own buildings.' When it closed at the beginning of 2000 – largely because there were too many conflicting ideologies within the organisation – they were left with a building in Charlotte Road in Shoreditch. Catherine asked the Prince if they could start a drawing school on the top floor, because the Slade and the Royal Academy were closing their life rooms and there were very few places in London for students to go to learn to draw. And so the Royal Drawing School was born, of which she is still artistic director.

Catherine came to prominence as a portrait painter after she won the BP Portrait Award at the National Portrait Gallery in 2002 and the gallery commissioned a portrait of Dame Cicely Saunders, the founder of the hospice movement, for its collection. She took over three years to paint Camilla. She would go down to Ray Mill at weekends, sometimes staying overnight, and got to know her subject very well. She also got to know Bruce, who was often there. 'He was a wonderful person, he had extraordinary dignity. He didn't like the press, he obviously had been quite traumatised by all the stuff that had happened. He had a good sense of humour like she does, but he was very reserved, had great judgement. I really got on with him, he really got the Drawing School, and he was very supportive of what I was doing as well. He sent me his book about being a prisoner of war, which he'd written for Tom and Ben, his grandsons.'

What surprised Catherine about Camilla was how caring she was. 'Actually, she's one of the more caring people I know,' she says. Catherine has a very disabled younger sister, Sophie, who lives in a care home and responsibility for her tends to fall on Catherine, the only unmarried one in the family. The Duchess, says Catherine, is 'amazing' with Sophie, sending her birthday cards and inviting her every year, on the Queen's official birthday, to accompany people who help her in her life, such as Philip

Treacy and her hairdresser Hugh, to gather at Clarence House and watch Trooping the Colour from the gardens. 'It's really sweet', says Catherine, 'because you know her disabilities can cause her behaviour to be challenging sometimes. And very few people say "Would Sophie like to come to something?"'

The portrait was worth waiting for. Camilla was very pleased with it, as was the Prince, and it sat for a long time on an easel at Clarence House on view to everyone who came to visit. It now hangs in the hall. It's very informal and depicts her wearing a simple blue shirt, looking dead ahead. 'It was kind of, "This is the new role I'm taking on" but also looking out at the world. In a portrait, if somebody is eyeballing you, they're eyeballing everyone who looks at the portrait. And she's got beautiful, very blue eyes.'

When Catherine had an exhibition at the National Portrait Gallery in 2014, Camilla came to open it. She spoke about their friendship and Catherine's style and how perceptive she is in her observation of the human character, but she also referred to her own sitting. 'Nowadays I'm reliably informed that her sitters can choose their favourite book tape and sit happily in silence whilst Catherine paints them. Which may explain why my portrait, minus book tapes, and plus a great deal of chat from both of us, took nearly three years to complete!'

36

In the Family

Camilla's ability to be so at ease with Sophie, and her understanding of the difficulties and strains imposed by having a profoundly disabled person in the family, came not just from her mother's volunteering at Chailey Heritage but from personal experience. Nic Paravicini and his first wife, Mary Ann, Andrew's sister, had twins in July 1979 who were born three and a half months prematurely. The little girl didn't survive; miraculously, the boy, Derek, did. But the equipment in the hospital was old-fashioned and he was given too much oxygen. His retina and part of his brain were destroyed. At six months they realised he was blind, and at two they discovered he had severe learning difficulties; he is also autistic.

Worried that when his older siblings were not there, Derek would rock back and forth poking his fingers in his eyes, Nanny Parker Bowles, who had come out of retirement to care for him and sang him nursery rhymes every day, went into the attic and found an old electric organ to amuse him. She discovered he liked music. She played a few notes and he shrieked with delight, his hands reaching for whatever was making the sound. Beside himself with excitement, he thumped the keys with ferocity. One Sunday his sister burst into the drawing room to find her parents. 'Quick, quick, come and see,' she cried. 'Derek's playing that hymn we sang in church!' The following week he was playing 'Molly Malone', one of Nanny's nursery rhymes, and more followed – anything he heard he would reproduce. He was just two years old.

As Nic says, 'The rest is history.' At nine Derek was playing jazz with the Royal Philharmonic Pops Orchestra at the Barbican. Since then he has played all over the world and has a repertoire of tens of thousands of pieces, all learnt very rapidly just by listening. In America, where he's played three times – on CBS's prestigious *60 Minutes* programme, at the Mandalay Bay Arena in Las Vegas, Nevada, and in Phoenix, Arizona for Muhammad Ali – he's known as 'The Human iPod'. In 2011 he played 'Rhapsody in Blue', a piano concerto written specially for him, at the Queen Elizabeth Hall, and he's played twice, at Buckingham Palace and at St James's Palace, for 'Aunt Camilla'. I would highly recommend Derek's TED Talk with his mentor, Professor Adam Ockleford, who has known him since he was four and a half.

That was the age at which the Paravicinis took Derek to look at Linden Lodge, a school in Wimbledon for the blind, where Adam was the music teacher. 'Derek could play things but he would use his nose and his ears and his chin and karate chops; he didn't know how to use his fingers,' says his father. Adam sat down at the piano with him, and in between having his hands karate chopped, taught him the scales. Afterwards, Adam rang Nic and asked whether he could come to the house at weekends to teach Derek. 'After a long argument I got him to accept his petrol, but that's the sort of man he is.' Adam is now Professor of Music at Roehampton University and has done a lot of work on the psychology of music, and how it can make a profound difference in all kinds of disability. Derek now lives with carers but Adam is still an important part of his life. They go on trips together, while Adam introduces Derek on stage and puts recordings together for him. And it was Adam's idea to start a charity to provide musical instruments and support for children like Derek. Thus the Amber Trust, which Camilla has supported from day one, was born in 1995. She is now president.

'I didn't ask her,' says Nic. 'We were having dinner at Highgrove and she started talking about it and I think she thought someone else was president.'

When Sister Frances Dominica, founder of Helen and Douglas House, the hospices for children and young adults in Oxford, approached the new Duchess of Cornwall to see whether she might consider becoming patron, she had no real idea what to expect. But again, Camilla's experience of Derek made her especially good at interacting both with the parents of severely ill and disabled children and with the children themselves. The Duchess of Kent, who had been a much-loved patron since Helen House opened in 1982, was retiring due to ill health and would be a tough act to follow, but Frances took a gamble. Helen House had grown out of a friendship between her and the family of a very sick little girl called Helen, whom she helped to look after. It was the first hospice in the world to offer respite and end-of-life care specifically for children with life-shortening conditions. There are now around fifty houses in Britain – and it has been an inspiration for the provision of paediatric palliative care all over the globe. Its sister building, Douglas House, opened in 2004 to cater for young adults between the ages of sixteen and thirty-five. Both houses were purpose-built in the grounds of All Saints Sisters of the Poor, in Oxford, where Frances had been Mother Superior, and are extraordinarily uplifting places.

'I wrote the appropriate letter to Clarence House,' says Frances, 'then I was given the OBE and when I went for my investiture it was Prince Charles conferring the honours. Before I could even do my curtsey, he said, "I understand you have invited my darling wife to be your patron." So I said, "Yes, sir, and we very much hope that she will accept our invitation." And he said, with a lovely smile, "She's looking on it." I came back absolutely thrilled because I thought that meant yes.'

Camilla has not only visited a number of times, endearing herself to families and staff alike, she has started a tradition of inviting a number of children and their families to Clarence House just before Christmas to help decorate her Christmas tree and have lunch. It has become the highlight of everyone's year, not just for those at Helen and Douglas House and at Clarence House but also amongst the media. Rebecca English, the royal correspondent for the *Daily Mail*, who has been following the Duchess for years, says it is 'the loveliest event of the year'. She never misses it. Camilla held the event in 2016 for the eighth time – and one year when she was ill, Charles was happy to stand in for her. Every year the routine is the same, and sometimes sick or disabled children supported by other charities are included too. In 2016, because the Duchess was patron of the centenary celebrations of the writer's birth, there were five who were supported by Roald Dahl's Marvellous Children's Charity.

Frances describes the day. 'We would all assemble in the Queen Mother's morning room and Her Royal Highness would come in. When she had met everyone, the double doors between the morning room and the small library would be opened, and there standing in the doorway would be a real live toy soldier in a bearskin, with ceremonial sword, the lot, and in scarlet tunic, of course, absolutely without movement. Everybody would be agog, and then he moved and the children realised he was real. Though I went quite a few times, it was always thrilling when the doors opened and there he was.

'The children would move through and usually the soldier would help to put decorations on the top of the tree with his long sword. The children would put decorations round the bottom, and Her Royal Highness would get down on her knees to help. When Prince Charles did it, he'd just come from an investiture, so he was in his ceremonial uniform, and there he was rolling up his sleeves, helping the children decorate the Christmas tree. Then the next set of double doors would open and we'd go through to the dining room. The children would sit round the big long table while the grown-ups stood. Her Royal Highness would have laid on sausage and mash, and the grown-ups had sausage and mash and champagne.'

Camilla is in full granny mode on those days – one year she talked about the fact that Laura was expecting twins at any moment. She hands round the plates – although in 2016 seven-year-old Millie, who suffers from cerebral palsy and epilepsy, handed hers straight back, obviously not a fan of bangers and mash, not even when arranged to look like a smiley face. Camilla just laughed and Millie ate biscuits instead. The table is always groaning with other options. Ronnie, six, who suffered from a bleeding disorder, wanted tomato ketchup, so Camilla arranged for a little bowl of it to be brought from the kitchen for him. Afterwards, she hands out party bags and they set off for home.

'What's so wonderful is it gives these children and their parents some very special memories,' says the chief executive, Clare Periton. 'It's not always easy to say but many of these children have terminal illnesses and will die, so it's very special for their families.'

The grandchildren's party in June is another that has become an annual tradition. This one is for Camilla's own grandchildren – and her children's friends' children, and her friends' and family's grandchildren. It is a huge party, growing every year, one that Charles also pops into. In 2016 there were about ninety children tucking into sandwiches, cakes and jellies and roaring around in the garden at Clarence House, having tugs of war and watching spellbound as magicians did tricks and entertainers made them laugh and funny people did clever things with balloons.

It's also an opportunity to catch up with old friends. Many of them hold back from phoning Camilla these days because of who she is. Her royal status has inevitably put a distance between all but the very closest, so they are particularly pleased to be invited to the party and find they immediately slip back into the old banter when they are face to face.

37

Bedside Manner

In July 2009, Harry Parker, whose book Camilla had recommended to prisoners in Brixton, was returning to camp from night patrol with his men in the Nad-e-Ali district of Afghanistan. He was twenty-six years old, a captain in the 4th Rifles, and that morning he made a decision that changed his life. He decided to take a short cut across a field, and he was unlucky. He stepped on an IED that exploded, blowing off his lower left leg and a finger and causing a host of other injuries.

Fortunately, an American helicopter was in the air nearby, and he was quickly taken to the military hospital at Camp Bastion; he needed to be resuscitated on the journey. From Helmand he was flown home to Selly Oak, the critical-injury military hospital in Birmingham, where they had to remove the lower half of his other leg because of infection. Heavily medicated, he was waiting to be wheeled into surgery when Prince Charles appeared by his bedside. 'There was this amazing moment when he came up and said "Hi". So we had this very strange conversation with me lying in bed and him there being charming and lovely. A few weeks later I had a letter from him saying "You won't remember, but good luck."

'It's weird,' says Harry, 'because when you're one of the people in bed, you feel slightly like you're on parade and as though you're still serving even though you've got no legs.'

Harry's father is General Sir Nick Parker, a very senior figure in the military, and his uncle Ed Parker was so shaken by the sight of his once athletic six-foot nephew lying in his bed in Selly Oak, reduced to four feet, that he was inspired to co-found the hugely successful charity Walking With The Wounded. It has taken wounded servicemen and women on expeditions all over the world – to both the North and the South Pole, and three-quarters of the way up Everest – to prove there is life after injury. Prince Harry has often walked with them.

From Selly Oak, Harry Parker went to Headley Court, the military rehabilitation centre in Surrey, and there for the next year on and off he learned to adjust, both physically and mentally, to life without legs. And it was there that his Royal Colonel came to visit him, along with four or five other members of the regiment. 'We sat in one of the break-out rooms,' he says, 'and had a coffee and a chat. She came across as very at ease, and I think she really cared about us and was interested in how we were doing and in what had happened to us.'

The next time they met was on a freezing cold day at Bulford, when Camilla presented Harry and others who had been injured on the tour of Afghanistan with their medals. As a thank you, he sent the Duchess a print of a painting he'd done during his tour in Basra. He had always painted and drawn – he'd studied fine art at university, and before joining the Army worked fleetingly in advertising, and the Battalion had commissioned the painting. 'It's not very good,' he says, 'it's probably gone into the cupboard under the stairs, but because of that she wrote to say thank you, and said, "My husband has a drawing school. Would you like to go? We'd love to give you a course there."' Harry snapped it up, went to meet Catherine, and – courtesy of Camilla – did one of their ten-week courses. It completely turned his life around.

After his recovery, Harry completed a Master's in international security at King's College and took a desk job at the Ministry of Defence in Whitehall. 'It got me back into doing art and it was the catalyst that made me realise I didn't want to sit behind a desk. You get institutionalised in the military and coming here was a good way of showing me there was more stuff out there.' Having finished the course, he applied for a place on the Master's drawing course, which entailed a year of full-time study. As soon as his place was secured, he left the Army and wrote *Anatomy of a Soldier*, a moving fictionalised account of what happened to him from the viewpoint of forty-five objects – a handbag, a helmet, a rug, a bicycle and so on. He's now married with a baby daughter; he paints and writes and makes it all look a lot easier than it is. 'The Duchess followed his progress all the way through the Drawing School,' says Catherine. 'She did it incredibly quietly, anonymously and everything, but it was definitely her link.'

As soon as she met Harry, Catherine wanted to paint him. 'I thought he was most extraordinary, so alive. And so intelligent, and so vibrant. We were in the lift going up to the Drawing School as I was going to show it to him, and I said "Will you sit for me?" I think he thought I was some kind of middle-aged stalker, he was a bit taken aback. It took me about six months, but I reeled him in to sit with me, and he came in and sat every Monday night for about a year and a half.' The painting hung in the National Portrait Gallery but is now in his parents' house.

When Charles and Camilla go on foreign tours, they take not only someone to film events for the Clarence House social media outlets, but also an official tour artist to record the atmosphere in sketches and paintings. Catherine Goodman has been on several such tours, and on long flights she and Camilla play Scrabble. 'She's a very good Scrabble player. I'm crap, it's not my thing, but she's very quick-witted. She makes puns and word plays and I suppose that's all part of it.'

Foreign tours are even more of a fandango than the normal away-days at home. On their tour of the Balkans in March 2016, a fascinating trip which took them to Croatia, Serbia, Montenegro and Kosovo, the couple's retinue comprised twenty-four people, including valet, dresser, hairdresser, secretary, private secretaries, press secretaries, security, equerry and doctor. They fitted snugly into a specially adapted Boeing 737 of the Royal Flight with a few spare seats, which on internal flights were available (at considerable cost, the taxpayer will be pleased to know) to the media. There were just five of us, and the atmosphere on the plane was chatty and upbeat. The Prince and Duchess are clearly good people to work for. They demand perfection and the team they've chosen to have around them provides it. No one is along for the ride. They work long hours, and from the minute the plane touches down everything is taken at a run.

I can't help thinking the pair are akin to a couple of swans, calmly gliding up river while beneath the surface, out of sight, legs are working frantically to battle against the current. They float effortlessly from presidential palace to church, to school, to hospital, to street market, to charity. Their car always takes them to the right entrance and is always waiting at the right exit, the convoy is in place, the press have vantage points from which to watch the proceedings and a bus laid on to whisk them on to the next event, the people who have been told they will shake a royal hand do shake a royal hand – and all of this is thanks to the support team, who race around desperately trying to keep everything together and to time. And seeing the team in action on a foreign tour – all of them, from the Prince and the Duchess to Andy Tibble, the jolly ex-military genius who handles the mountains of luggage, passports, paperwork and flight logistics – is an eye-opener.

It's like being part of a crazy roadshow where everything happens at top speed but with astonishing efficiency. Charles and Camilla sit at the front of the aircraft, screened off by the same sort of ill-fitting curtain that can be found on any plane. He holds her hand to help deal with the fear, which has been greatly eased since she's learnt to tap. This is a kind of do-it-yourself acupuncture, an ancient Eastern practice which involves tapping the body's energy meridian points with your fingertips to relieve a host of ills.

Everyone on the other side of the curtain is out of their seat, sometimes before the plane even lands, ready to grab whatever their job requires from the overhead lockers and run to the waiting car they've been allocated. At the front of the plane, the red carpet is ready, the local military awaits, the president is poised, the Prince adjusts his tie, the Duchess checks her make-up, and they are off. Hands are shaken along the welcoming line, the cars appear in great long convoys, and the moment the door is closed on the royal car, the couple are off at top speed with outriders to clear the traffic – if the route hasn't already been sealed – and local security fore and aft. In Belgrade I counted over fifteen escort cars including an ambulance, several police cars and a fire engine.

The Prince never stops. Camilla does far less than he does in a day but a tour is day after day, most of it on her feet, with dinners and receptions every evening. It's relentless; meeting dozens if not hundreds of different people each day, remembering briefing notes on the important ones, thinking of something worth saying to everyone, smiling at everyone, expressing interest in everything, listening to boring speeches and eating dodgy food.

'One time we were standing at a reception,' says Joy Camm, 'and there were a lot of speeches going on. She and I don't stand close together, we've got our eighteen inches of space, but she kept on getting closer. The next thing she was right next to me and she kind of pushed, so I thought I was in the way. So I moved a bit and she pushed again, and I kept on moving.

She was trying to find us something we could lean against because we'd been standing throughout these interminable speeches.'

It's rare, but things do occasionally go wrong – at home as well as abroad. The Duchess was once unveiling a clock specially commissioned for the Diamond Jubilee in the village of Colnbrook in Berkshire. It stood about twelve feet high and was covered in a heavy velvet sheet. There was no shortage of people: the whole village was out in force, dozens of schoolchildren, all eyes focused. At the critical moment, the Duchess pulled the cord with a flourish – and nothing moved. So she pulled again and again. Some other people gave it a tug and the cord snapped. It wasn't until a councillor found a long pole, whilst Camilla and the crowds talked amongst themselves, that the cover was finally, unceremoniously removed and the clock revealed in all its glory.

On another occasion, no one turned up. The Duchess was due to visit a new station medical centre at RAF Leeming in Yorkshire, and as always, the purpose was to meet people. But there had been a misunderstanding. When Laura Sullivan, from the press office, arrived ahead of the others she found the centre deserted. The only sign of life was a group of schoolchildren waiting outside, their faces obscured by police barriers. With just an hour to spare, she had to rapidly rustle up some bodies, move the barriers and behave as though nothing had happened. 'And then I bossily came in,' says Amanda, and said, 'This isn't what we planned!'

38

Abroad

When you are dealing with foreign countries, there's infinitely more that can be lost in translation. Sometimes even the best laid plans can go awry. In October 2006, the couple went to Pakistan, a country Charles had long wanted to visit. It was dubbed 'the terror tour'. 'I can't believe we got away with it,' says Paddy Harverson. 'That was the badlands. We'd recced it six weeks before and it's the only recce any of us had been on where there'd been gunfire.' Amanda, the mistress of understatement, was with him. 'I think it was probably leading up to quite a dangerous time. We had massive armoured cars in front of us and behind us, but do you know, I just thought this was rather normal.'

On day one, the government bombed a madrassa, killing eighty people they claimed were Al Qaeda terrorists. Tribal leaders insisted the victims were students, with the result that more than 20,000 people took to the streets to protest and the next day's visit to the northern frontier town of Peshawar had to be scrapped because it was too dangerous. They were told at a quarter past eleven that night, so they stayed in Islamabad and devised the next day's engagements on the hoof. 'The security was phenomenal,' says Amanda, 'but I think it was one of the most amazing tours we've ever done because the country was so beautiful and – I do sound a bit airy fairy, but everybody felt it – it was very mystical.'

The party flew up into the Himalayas to visit some of the villages where the Red Cross had been working since 75,000 people were killed in a massive earthquake the year before that made two and a half million home-less. Two years earlier, Camilla had attended a fundraising event for Brooke, an international animal charity that supports working horses, donkeys, mules and the people who depend on them. And here she saw them in action. The people scratching a life for themselves in the villages relied heavily upon donkeys but didn't know how to look after them. She was very affected by what she saw and is now president of the charity.

'Then we went even higher in helicopters,' says Paddy, 'up the Hindu Kush to visit a place called Altit [in the Hunza valley] with the Aga Khan, who is the spiritual leader of the Muslims who live up there. The Prince and Duchess were given a yak as a present and we all thought, We're not getting that on the plane! It's one of the highest towns in the world and people live longer there than anywhere else on earth. Fascinating diet and stuff. The Aga Khan is their spiritual leader, he's a living god. No one sees him in the flesh, so everyone burst into tears, including all the soldiers, who were Ismaili. Everywhere we went people were crying, and then they had a welcome with the old men in the village who were in their nineties, all dancing. It was great stuff.'

Catherine Goodman was the tour artist when they went to India in November 2013 en route for the Commonwealth heads of government meeting in Sri Lanka. 'That was rather poignant in some ways,' she says, 'because Mark Shand came and joined us. He was such a force of nature, such a lovely person, and also quite anarchic, and so I think Camilla was always a bit nervous that he was going to do something.'

The issue was the loss of the wild elephants' migratory routes. As Mark told the *London Evening Standard*, 'They might only be a quarter of a kilo-metre wide, but the elephants have been using them for thousands of years and they won't veer off them. That means if there's human habitation in the way, they'll just go through it … But that's a battle – between humans and elephants – that of course the animals won't in the end win.' The Elephant Family, the charity Mark co-founded in 2002, had spent £1 million on a single route in Kerala, and needed £50–£70 million to maintain them all.

So when the royal party were in Kerala, Mark took his brother-in-law to the jungle near Kochi in the hope of seeing some elephants. It was a futile and frustrating trip. They drove for two and a half hours, and when they arrived at the remote watering hole, there was nothing to be seen but hundreds of local police and troops drafted in to secure the area. What's more, it was pouring with rain, so they were drenched. 'On every other occasion in my life that I've gone to these things it's the same – it's the security that ruins everything,' said the Prince tetchily. 'It's Murphy's Law. Everybody always says, "The day before people saw God knows what."'

In the run-up to Prince William's marriage to Kate Middleton in 2011, the tabloids made much of a rather wayward uncle on her mother's side. Gary Goldsmith, a self-made millionaire, lived a colourful life on the island of Ibiza. He was caught in a *News of the World* sting cutting lines of cocaine at his house, La Maison de Bang Bang, and was repeatedly referred to as the black sheep of the family. Despite the publicity and the tattoos and the shaven head, Gary was invited to the wedding and said afterwards that Camilla was the one who had gone out of her way to welcome him. 'Camilla made a beeline for me,' he said. He plucked up the courage to say, 'I'm sorry for the bad press.' She simply smiled and said, 'Don't think twice about it. I get the same myself.' Gary is full of admiration: 'She was beyond amazing.'

Camilla and Annabel used to joke that Mark was their very own 'Casa Bang Bang'. He was no millionaire but he was unpredictable, as he was the first to admit, and although he had calmed down a lot in recent years, he told the *Standard* he was itching to go AWOL again. 'Don McCullin rings me up and growls, "Where are we off to, then?" But now, the elephants are my priority.'

Mark died at the end of an evening in which he had raised $1.7 million dollars for his beloved elephants. After the outstanding success of the Fabergé Big Egg Hunt in London in the spring of 2012 – when 200 two-foot-six-high fibreglass eggs, decorated by well-known artists and designers were placed all over the capital, including a Humpty Dumpty one which sat on the wall of Clarence House – he had launched the Fabergé Big Egg Hunt in New York. On 22 April 2014, thirty-six of them were being auctioned at Sotheby's in Manhattan. The main auction room had been packed with VIP collectors and celebrities who paid higher and higher prices – the highest was $900,000 for an egg decorated by the American artist Jeff Koons. And there were still 250 eggs to be sold by auction online. When it was all over, a triumphant Mark and about a dozen friends went to burger restaurant J. G. Melon, before heading to the official after-party at the Diamond Horseshoe nightclub. In the early hours, Mark and his creative director, 28-year-old Lexi Bowes-Lyon, went on to the Rose Bar in the Gramercy Park Hotel. They had a few drinks and danced to the Rolling Stones.

After about half an hour, they went out into the street for a cigarette. On the way back in, Mark motioned for Lexi to go through the door ahead of him, lost his balance and fell backwards, hitting the back of his head on the pavement. He lay there motionless and unconscious. At Bellevue Hospital he went straight to intensive care and was put on life support. Camilla was in Scotland with Charles when she heard the news. She immediately rang Tom and said, 'Mark's hit his head on the pavement. They're saying he's not going to make it.' Annabel spoke to the neurologist, who said, 'Your brother is 99.5 per cent brain dead.'

Mark and Clio were divorced by now, so nineteen-year-old Ayesha was legally his next of kin, but she wasn't left to make the decision on her own. Everyone hurriedly gathered at her cousin Kate Elliot's house and said to Ayesha, 'This is your father. This is your decision. But you know as well as we do that the idea of Mark as a vegetable – no way.' She agreed immediately. 'She was adamant and she was right.' So it was left to Annabel to call the neurologist at Bellevue and tell him to turn off the machines. 'That was the most horrible thing I've ever had to do,' she told Bob Colacello of *Vanity Fair*. Mark was pronounced dead at twenty-five minutes past eleven on 23 April. He had undeniably been drinking, but a post-mortem revealed that his skull had been unusually thin in places. Had it been thicker he may have survived.

The whole family was devastated. Camilla found it particularly difficult. She had never been as close to Mark as Annabel, but since her marriage to Charles they had made up for lost time. The Prince loved Mark, loved his madcap stories and his passion for travel and for India and for elephants. And he loved having him to stay at Birkhall, where he'd leap into lochs and swim across them. Their fondness for one another had brought Camilla closer to her brother, but Mark had said, ruefully, about a year before his death, that he had never once in his life had lunch or tea with Camilla by himself. And as in many families, there were difficulties between the sisters in the arrangements for his funeral. Camilla felt that Annabel was taking over again – she had felt the same way when their father died. But it was natural that Annabel should: both men had lived with her for some years before they died and she had looked after them. Mark's life had been difficult in the last few years and he had suffered from terrible depressions.

The funeral was again held at the church in Stourpaine, and afterwards at Annabel's house, where Mark had left in the garden an elephant made of wire and covered in ivy, and which they dressed up for the occasion. It was an intimate service with just family and close friends, with moving tributes, readings and beautiful music. Ben Elliot had asked talented tenor Hal Cazalet – grandson of the racehorse trainer Peter Cazalet – to sing a couple of songs. He and his wife lived in Dorset, but he had grown up at the other end of Plumpton Lane from The Laines. One of the songs Ben had asked him to sing was 'Wild World' by Cat Stevens, which Mark had loved and always used to sing with Ayesha. After he had put down the phone, Hal thought, I shouldn't be singing 'Wild World'; Cat Stevens should. So he rang back and suggested Ben try and get hold of the singer, who now lives in America. Now known as Yusuf Islam, he flew in specially; midway through the service, with no announcement, the Sixties legend slowly walked up the aisle from the back of the church with an acoustic guitar, singing his hit, which had been Mark's song. There wasn't a dry eye in the place.

Tom wrote a moving tribute to his uncle in the *Daily Mail*:

Uncle Mark is dead. Four words I never thought I'd write. It never even crossed my mind that Mark would cease to be.

Idiotic, I know, but such was the raw power of his personality, the blinding glare of his charm, the sheer force and magnetism of his character, that I never imagined life without him. None of us did. Other people die. Normal folk expire. Not Mark.

Death is for pencil-pushers, bank managers and pompous golf club bores. But now he's gone. Ripped from our grasp. Way before his time.

Because here was a man who'd brushed off cyclones, tsunamis, earthquakes, shipwrecks, pirates, bandits and malaria. An adventurer who relished nothing more than an old-fashioned punch-up in a torrid Jakartan dive; a dashing buccaneer who would have been dismissed by John Buchan as too far-fetched; a best-selling travel writer; and a conservationist renowned for his single-minded mission to save the Asian elephant.

He would have relished the irony of his demise. Not by poisoned arrow, or furious bull elephant in musth, rather the cold, hard, mundane pavement of the New York night.

And with Mark gone came the stark realisation that Camilla and Annabel were on their own and needed one another more than ever.

39

WOW

Jude Kelly is a most remarkable individual. She's not tall, but you wouldn't miss her in a crowd. She has her own funky style of dress and her hair (on the occasions I've met her) is a striking mixture of dark and platinum. She is a feminist, she has a heart of gold, and she is artistic director of the Southbank Centre in London, which incorporates twenty-one acres of concert halls – including the Royal Festival Hall – galleries, cafés, restaurants and open spaces. 'My grandmother left school when she was twelve, my mother left school when she was fifteen, and here am I,' she says, 'a girl from Liverpool in charge of one of Britain's biggest cultural institutions. Fifty years ago that wouldn't have been possible for a woman or somebody of my background. I might have some talent but that's not the story. The story is the opportunity and I thought I shouldn't be a leader as a woman unless I was going to use the platform.'

And so it was that I found myself a guest at Clarence House, in a room full of very different but all very remarkable women, including Theresa May, then Home Secretary, now Prime Minister. For the last few years Camilla has been president of WOW – Women of the World – the organisation Jude founded in 2010. And every year the Duchess hosts a lunch during the WOW festival at the Southbank. WOW grew out of Jude's frustration that despite decades of feminism, there is still profound inequality between men and women, which is not only 'a crazy waste of human potential' but a potential cause of violence against women.

As Jude explains, these are neither conferences nor symposiums. They are a chance to explore all kinds of ideas and subjects and meet women from many different backgrounds. They're an opportunity for people to draw attention to stories that are uncomfortable and difficult, as well as those that are triumphant but little publicised. There's music and poetry and dancing, and it's all a lot of fun.

'It's been overwhelmingly exciting,' she says. 'I was excited by thinking, do I dare? Feminism is supposedly not needed any more, do I dare create something which says the story's not finished?'

WOW has made a huge impact. In the first year, for example, they gave a platform to Leyla Hussein and Nimko Ali, both survivors of female genital mutilation. Nimko spoke. 'It was a fifteen-minute talk by a very inexperienced young woman, and the response was massive and that support led them to start The Daughters of Eve.' That's the charity that campaigns against FGM all over the world. 'She always says this happened because of WOW.

'WOW is very much an opportunity for people to enter at lots of different levels of experience; not everybody wants to start off with "What are we going to do about rape as a weapon of war?" It can be as simple as coming to one of the market stalls where they're doing braiding and hair care and talking about alopecia or recovering after chemo, or women's huge anxiety about going grey. I'm very keen that we don't police each other's language or tell each other how we ought to think about things, but I also think it's great to understand more than we do.

'My call to action is "Look, there are many things you will have seen and read and encountered during this festival and a lot of it springs from a society that is not yet confident that women are equal, or should be equal, or could ever be equal, but what would you like to do about that fact? Do you want to go home and readdress a few things in your own life? Do you want to help the victims of domestic violence?" My call is "Do something and change your language. Don't keep implying that there's nothing wrong, because the evidence is against that. Your life might seem perfectly adjusted and balanced, and we all operate so that we can live happily if we can, and we negotiate things and we're complicit in things and internalise things, otherwise we'd go mad. But how will you help make change happen?"'

Jude never set out to have a royal president for WOW. It was another serendipitous consequence of Camilla's appearance at the Orange Prize presentation at the Royal Festival Hall in 2010. 'Because I'm the artistic director here I welcomed her and we started chatting, and I instantly realised that she had read all the books. I'm not being disparaging about VIPs but often, for a number of reasons, they haven't done that, they have been given a text, but she had read the books and it was really interesting to watch her warmth, her engagement with the women authors that she talked to. She wasn't interested in being in the limelight, she didn't require status, she was very informal, self-deprecating in a jolly, humorous way and I liked her straight away.'

The upshot was the first of the lunchtime receptions at Clarence House, to which Jude was free to invite anyone she chose. 'It was a really great affair. She was unafraid to go and talk in depth about FGM.'

The Duchess has since been involved in supporting WOW groups around the world – they have now been established in fifteen countries, and by 2018 it's hoped they'll be in all fifty-three Commonwealth countries too – and in 2015, on WOW's fifth anniversary, she became president. 'Supporting the achievements of women – in all walks of life – is hugely important,' she said, 'and WOW plays a vital role in bringing the right people together. It takes a frank look at the obstacles that prevent women and girls from reaching their potential and provides a platform for discussions of issues that really matter.'

'People go away from those lunches feeling really respected,' says Jude, 'and they feel the warmth of her personality. She's lived her life and she's had to live some of it in public, and that's got a deeply painful aspect to it – and she's obviously transferred whatever difficulties she's had into a greater compassion for others. You can see that's what she does with it. Navigating that can't have been easy.'

40

Making a Difference

Finding Rape Crisis South London, in Croydon, is not easy. The building is an old bank in a pretty run-down part of the town, with traffic thundering past, and there is nothing outside to indicate you've arrived. This is deliberate. Not even the neighbours know what goes on behind the solid front doors. All they know is that women of all ages, all shapes and sizes, all ethnicities, come and go from it all day long. It is not a drop-in centre. Those women are here by appointment. They have all been raped or subjected to sexual violence – some of them recently, some of them historically, as children, by relatives, neighbours, people in positions of trust. They are all traumatised.

Inside it's surprisingly warm and comfortable. It's not like a medical centre or a hospital, it's like going into someone's living room. There's a big sofa to sit on, a coffee table with magazines on it and flowers, art work on the walls, and something feels indefinably safe here. It takes Yvonne Traynor, the remarkable woman who has been running it for the last twenty years, to explain what I'm feeling. It's the colour of the walls: they are painted terracotta, 'Because it was the only colour that survivors of the Holocaust felt comfortable sitting in when they were rescued.

'Survivors of sexual violence feel a huge amount of shame because this is violence against your whole being, against not only your external body but also the inside of your body. It's both external trauma and internal trauma, so it affects your spirituality, your self-worth, your self-esteem. It affects

248

your sense of safety in this world, because most women are raped by men that they know, whether they've known them briefly or whether it's someone they had come to trust, people they had made an evaluation about.

'Sexual violence isn't about sex; it's about power and control. And it's got to stop. We need to get the whole of society on board, because it's not just a women's problem. This is a male problem as well, so it's all of us getting together and saying this should not be happening in this day and age.'

Research into sexual violence invariably mentions the vulnerability of the women who are raped. This infuriates Yvonne. 'Being a woman is being vulnerable. Any woman can be raped, any woman can suffer from sexual violence, so the myths about whether they've been drinking or wearing short skirts, all of that should be debunked. The research should be into why men rape women. That's what needs to be looked at, not which women are raped. What makes these men think that they can rape women?' Male rape does happen – and not just to gay men – but the problem is far smaller. Ninety-nine per cent of victims are women and girls, and 99 per cent of perpetrators are men.

Today there are crisis centres for the survivors of rape and sexual violence in most parts of the country but public awareness of the issue – and sympathy for survivors – is relatively new. The attitude tended to be that girls who were raped were asking for it. Jimmy Savile's death, in 2011, brought sexual abuse onto the front pages. The entertainer everyone had thought so saintly, if creepy, turned out to have been one of the most prolific sexual predators Britain has ever known. Before that there was no funding and little specific expertise in the field of childhood abuse, or help for victims going through the criminal justice system.

Try as she might, Yvonne could find no one with a high profile prepared to come and look round the centre in Croydon, let alone lend their name to it. She had tried royalty, and she'd tried movie stars and actresses. None of them was prepared to engage. So when she wrote to Camilla in 2009 – two years before Savile, and a year before the first WOW festival – she wasn't hopeful. 'I was floored to get a reply from her office to say that she would be really interested in visiting. You could have knocked me down with a feather, really seriously.'

Yvonne had arranged for a couple of survivors to be there to meet the Duchess. But what impressed her before Camilla had even set foot inside the centre was the thoughtfulness of her office. They had rung to say that since the Duchess was well known, and it was an anonymous building, it might draw attention to the place if she came in through the front door. Might there be an alternative way in? They would ensure that the security cars parked somewhere else. And so Camilla arrived via the fire escape at the back of the building, bending down to avoid hitting her head on the metal door.

'It really inspired me and I was in awe of her from the moment we met. She was so warm, and she was just another woman that understood women, I think that was why I was so drawn to her. She didn't have airs and graces, she spoke to every one of the staff from the volunteer admin to the counselling coordinator, and then she went downstairs and spoke to our clients and she wasn't shocked. She spoke to them warmly, she asked pertinent but not intrusive questions, she was calm – everybody warmed to her, she was so open and so honest. I didn't feel she was doing this because it was a publicity stunt, and we've had people here who've done that.'

One of the survivors the Duchess met that day was Mia James, who had suffered the most horrific gang-rape by three men when she was sixteen. Camilla was profoundly moved by their conversation. Mia had self-harmed since the rape, she had attempted suicide, but now, ten years later, she was in therapy, and feeling strong enough to talk about it. 'If you can get help,' says Yvonne, 'and you have the courage to come forward to talk to a specialist, you can put it behind you and go on to lead a normal life, a better life than you're leading at the moment. But it takes courage, it's really hard just to utter those first words, "I have been raped." Many women push it down and try not to think about it, but of course that can lead to psychosomatic problems.'

Today, Mia has a daughter and has written a book about her survival, as well as a book of poetry, but meeting the Duchess that day was an important stage in her progress. 'She said afterwards, "I can't believe that somebody of her stature is taking an interest in me."'

Camilla's response to that first immensely affecting visit to Croydon was to do what Camilla does best. She held a reception at Clarence House, to which she invited everyone involved in the field of sexual violence, from the Home Secretary and NGOs down to the counsellors working in small rape centres. These people had never been together in one room before; they had been working in isolation, even if towards the same goals. 'She wasn't afraid of the subject, or of being associated with it.'

'This challenging and emotive subject,' said the Duchess, addressing them all, 'has been brought to the fore in recent months with some shocking news stories although it is by no means a "new" story. The findings of the government's recent report into sexual offending revealed once again that the number of victims reporting these crimes is only a tiny proportion of the total and even fewer of these cases end with a conviction.'

Yvonne Traynor is convinced that it was Camilla putting her name to the issues of rape and sexual violence that changed the political landscape. 'I am absolutely sure it put pressure on government. I have no idea how that happened. She's not somebody that gloats about her successes, she does everything low key, but soon after that the government took notice.' The Home Office and the Ministry of Justice began funding those who worked with the victims of sexual violence, while Prime Minister David Cameron mentioned Yvonne's work in a speech. In fact the Home Office then made a pledge to open thirteen new rape crisis centres. 'Based on that funding I've opened another centre in Crawley, and we were number thirteen. I honestly believe none of that would have happened without her.'

Camilla has now visited other centres, both in the UK and in other parts of the world. On her trip to India in 2013 she visited Asha Sadan, an orphanage and school in Mumbai for girls up to the age of eighteen who have been thrown out by their families after being raped or sexually assaulted. It was a very inspirational place, located in the middle of the slums but scrupulously clean and beautifully run. Camilla evidently told the Prince about it because that evening, at a dinner they attended for the British Asian Trust, he referred to the home in his speech. The BAT has since given the orphanage funding, and the hope is to bring the Indian women who run it to England to meet Yvonne Traynor and swap experiences.

Camilla constantly encourages her team to think of ways to maximise her impact and her influence. Women who have just been raped currently go to sexual assault referral centres for forensic tests and medical help. Here their clothes are taken away from them, they are given basic track suits and the most basic of toiletries with which to shower. Back at the office the Duchess pondered how they could improve the experience for such women. She came up with the idea of wash-bags filled with pleasant-smelling products. A little thing, but it made all the difference. For several years, Joy, Amanda and Sophie filled the bags in their office at Clarence House. 'The reaction from the women was overwhelming,' says Joy. 'They could not believe that this was for them, and for them to keep. It was the one positive experience to know that somebody was thinking about them.' As Yvonne says, 'This seemingly small gift helps survivors of sexual violence to feel valued and not so stigmatised and different.'

In most countries rape is about power and control, but in war zones it has for centuries been a by-product of conflict. Rape was condemned at the Nuremberg trials after the Second World War as 'a crime against humanity', but it wasn't until Bosnia in the 1990s that the charity Medicins Sans Frontières first came across it as a deliberate military strategy. A report by Amnesty International stated that 'systematic rape was used as part of the strategy of ethnic cleansing. Women were raped so they could give birth to a Serbian baby.' According to Unicef, 22,000 women were raped in Bosnia. Amnesty said, 'Survivors face emotional torment, psychological damage, physical injuries, disease, social ostracism and many other consequences that can devastate their lives. Women's lives and their bodies have been the unacknowledged casualties of war for too long.'

Alongside the American actress Angelina Jolie, special envoy for the UN High Commissioner for Refugees, William Hague began campaigning about the issue when he was Foreign Secretary in 2012. They jointly founded the Preventing Sexual Violence Initiative, and in 2014 co-chaired a global summit to end sexual violence in conflict at ExCel in London. It was the largest gathering ever held on the subject, with 1,700 delegates from 123 countries. During the summit, Camilla invited both Hague and Jolie to Clarence House for a private meeting.

However well-informed she was, though, nothing could have prepared her for the horrifying stories she heard from rape victims in Kosovo in 2016. The western Balkans had been a tough tour for Camilla. The visit was made 'to celebrate peace, reconciliation, youth empowerment and restoration' in a region where 100,000 people had died during the ethnic war in the 1990s. In five days they visited four countries – Croatia, Bosnia, Montenegro and Kosovo – and it was a full-on itinerary. She didn't do half of what the Prince packed into a day, but nevertheless it was impressive. Launching herself into formal presidential dinners and ambassadorial receptions, working her way round rooms full of strangers at the end of a day, must have been terrifying and exhausting in equal measure. But she performed with huge aplomb and everyone seemed enchanted. The British are apparently much loved in these Balkan states.

There was some light relief too. At an open-air market in Osijek, in Croatia, Camilla got the giggles – and infected the Prince – while watching a troupe of local dancers hopping about in brightly coloured traditional costume. A photograph of the two of them, composure just restored, with the dancers became their Christmas card in 2016. The Duchess visited the Dakovo State Stud Farm, where the famous Lipizzaner horses are bred and where she was well in her element, and the next day in Novi Sad in Serbia she had a wonderful afternoon at a Museum of Beekeeping; keeping bees herself (the honey of which she sells at Fortnum & Mason for charity), she found it fascinating. There was also plenty of local food and drink to be sampled in every country, especially the beautiful mountainous terrain of Montenegro – and as always she dived in enthusiastically, to the locals' delight.

But there were some very difficult visits in the schedule. In Belgrade, in Serbia, she met local women working with survivors of rape and sexual violence, and their work to provide psychological support and get justice for the women was inspiring and humbling. But the women she met in Kosovo had been unable to tell their stories, so there had been no support and no justice for them. Of all the countries on the trip, I found Kosovo the most affecting, and I suspect the Duchess did too. In Osijek – as we saw on the news – there had been buildings deeply riddled with bullet holes, and buildings with their sides ripped out by bombs, but there was a sense that those countries had moved on, they were now survivors not victims. In Kosovo the pain still seemed to be raw. Outside the parliament building in Pristina, the capital, dozens of people stood clutching ageing photographs of their lost loved ones, waiting to petition the royal visitors. Their sons, brothers, husbands had vanished during the 1998–9 war, when Albanian separatists fought against the Yugoslav regime led by Serb strongman Slobodan Milosevic. Sixteen years after the war ended, hundreds are still missing and their relatives have been unable to move on. These were very emotional scenes and when Charles and Camilla engaged with the people involved, having laid a wreath at the memorial 'To Those We Miss', they hugged the Prince and the Duchess. And, close to tears, the royal couple hugged them back, in a way I have never seen happen before. It was very moving.

The Prince had just emerged from a round-table discussion on the issue and he is good at following through. Out of sight doesn't mean out of mind.

Once he is involved he is like a terrier. A year later he invited representatives of the families to Clarence House with the director-general of the International Commission on Missing Persons to hear what progress had been made since their visit.

Camilla had been inside the parliament building too, to take part in a different meeting, and she was already very emotional. She had heard six rape victims describe their ordeals to her. One mother had been raped, along with her three daughters, then aged twenty, eighteen and thirteen, in an ordeal lasting seventeen hours. Another woman was brutally raped when she was eight months pregnant, and lost her baby. Another woman was raped in front of her elderly parents; afterwards, her mother threw herself down a well, and her father died not many days later from a heart attack. Joy Camm, who accompanied the Duchess, has never seen her so distressed. Everyone in the room was crying, even the translator.

Figures vary, but it is thought that about 20,000 Albanian and Ashkenazi women were raped during the war, and the outgoing President, Atifete Jahjaga, who hosted the meeting, had long campaigned for justice on their behalf. 'We were hearing things that no human being should ever hear about another human being,' says Joy. 'To get the women there in that room was quite amazing, they were very fearful. They can't tell anybody about it, they can't tell their men, their husbands or brothers or uncles because it's mostly a Muslim community so they are still, nearly twenty years later, bearing this awful secret that they can't share. So there's no way of getting better.'

In the corridor outside, Camilla had been shown two skirts hanging on the wall that had been worn by women when they were raped. They had written messages on the skirts: 'This skirt has a closed history since spring 1998' and 'I have a bitter experience.' The skirts were part of an art installation called *Thinking of You*, put together by the Kosovan-born artist Alketa Xhafa-Mripa. Five thousand women donated skirts which she hung on washing lines in the stadium in Pristina to encourage people to talk about the shame of the past, to literally 'air their dirty laundry in public'.

Powerless as I am sure she felt in that room, by listening to those women's stories and shining a light on such shameful acts of war, she will have done more good than she could know.

41

The Rubbish Picker's Wife

Eleven years ago, Elizabeth Gowing and her partner, Rob Wilton, went to Kosovo for six months. She had been teaching in a challenging school in Hackney, while he worked at the Foreign Office, and they wanted a year out. Rob was offered a job as adviser to the new Kosovan Prime Minister, which the Foreign Office was keen for him to take, and so the couple found themselves in Pristina.

They are still there and I suspect they will be for some time. They co-founded a charity called The Ideas Partnership, which has become a lifeline for a community that before Elizabeth accidentally came across it in 2011 was condemned to a cycle of poverty and illiteracy. It's an area called Fushë Kosovë, geographically just five miles from the jazz bars, hotels and restaurants of central Pristina – but for the Ashkali families, an ethnic minority, living there it is light years away. Traditionally, they've lived from hand to mouth on what they can scavenge to sell from a neighbouring rubbish tip and what their barefoot children can earn begging. But that is changing. Elizabeth and her volunteers are educating them and battling to get their children into schools – and a visit from the Duchess on her last day in the Balkans brought about an amazing breakthrough.

The schools were resistant to taking such children, partly because of racism and partly because they didn't fit the model. And they insisted that children over the age of nine have intensive classes to bring them up to standard. As Elizabeth explains, 'There's that sense of, We're on page twenty-three now, everyone should be on page twenty-three, if you missed page twenty-two that's not my problem, and tomorrow we'll be on page twenty-four. If you've got special needs, if you're visibly different, if you're poor and you haven't been to school and your parents can't help with homework, that's problematic. Fifty-five children had been waiting for seventeen months to get those intensive classes and the schools had been refusing to run them. I'd tried everything and was feeling powerless. The minister came out and said, "Yes, yes, we'll sort it," and nothing happened. We got the ombudsperson, we've done media stuff, we've written formal requests and submitted them through the government, we've done everything we could.

'When it came to the Duchess's visit, we were told by the embassy that we should consider inviting the Mayor to the tea party at the end of it. We said, "We're not going to invite him because he's the one who's stood in the way of these fifty-five children having an education." The ambassador said, "Well, then I could go and speak to the Mayor and explain to him that if these kids were in school by the time of the visit then he could come to the tea party – and if they weren't, we would make sure some journalists asked very publicly why it was that the Mayor had not been invited?" That meeting was on a Thursday and by the following Tuesday the children were in school. Which is sort of wonderful and sort of depressing, because if it was that easy, why wasn't it done by the municipality seventeen months ago?'

Elizabeth, who speaks fluent Albanian, is as adored by this community as she clearly adores them. It's a joy to watch. She has made a huge difference in the area and the secret of her success, she believes, is that she didn't go in with a clipboard and a list of objectives and a budget. She went in with a nine-euro tube of skin cream. She had wanted to find a deserving home for some surplus sleeping bags, which brought her to the door of one of the poorest families in the community, Agron and Hatemja and their five – now six – children. Elizabeth handed over the sleeping bags and they thanked her; then the mother came running out holding her three-year-old. She pulled down his track suit and said, 'You've got to help my son.'

The boy had tipped a pan of boiling water over himself a month before, while he was playing in their small, overcrowded one-room house, and had suffered burns to his legs and his groin so that he couldn't walk properly. When Elizabeth took the pair to hospital, she was told that the boy was too young for an operation. The best treatment was to massage cream into the skin every morning and evening to keep it supple. The family couldn't afford the cream so she bought it for them, and every two weeks went back to deliver a new tube. 'At first I just handed it over at the door, and then I was invited in, and then I was given tea and then the neighbours came round. So I slowly got to know this family in a very unplanned, organic way.'

Two older boys in the family weren't in school. 'I didn't believe it when their parents said it was because they didn't have shoes, I thought it was an excuse, so I said, "Okay, I'll buy you some shoes." And they've been in school ever since, so it really was just a pair of shoes. I thought that's easy, I'll just buy hundreds of pairs of shoes and we'll sort it, and then I met their nine-year-old sister, Gjelane, and discovered that even with shoes she couldn't go to school because the school said she was too old and too late.'

The girl needed to pass a test to get into school. 'It's like asking someone to get well before they can go to hospital.' So Elizabeth offered to teach her, and the little girl said, 'Can my friends come too?' The first week twenty-one children came to her class, the next week it was fifty, and she says teaching has never been more exhilarating. A group from the community then came to her and said that if she really wanted the children to succeed at school, it was no use giving them shoes at seven, or even getting them into school when they were nine. They needed to have pre-school and kindergarten experience. 'So we've set up a kindergarten. We now have sixty kids who go to pre-school, including the little sister and the brother of that family. So through that one family we've brought the whole community into school as well.'

Elizabeth once went out rubbish picking with Agron and Gjelane, just to see what their lives were like. After three hours, they each had a big bag over their shoulders, a wheelbarrow piled high and bags on each of its handles which they took to the depot to be weighed. Their earnings were two euros eighteen cents.

But in a three-storey, sparsely furnished, chilly building in the midst of this impoverished and rather menacing community, she is changing all that. With the help of nearly 150 volunteers, she has the kindergarten, catch-up classes to prepare older children for school, and literacy classes for adults. Women are taught to sew and make lavender bags, patchwork squares that are turned into cushions, soap, jewellery – things to sell to generate an income so they no longer have to pick rubbish and their children can stop begging and go to school. She teaches basic health and ante-natal care. And after a little seven-year-old boy was killed by a wild dog on his way to school past the rubbish tip, they now lay on a bus. Camilla met them all, including Hatemja, whose child had been so badly burnt, and in the kindergarten handed out a bag full of children's books she'd brought. It included one called *Does the Queen Wear Her Crown in Bed?*

Elizabeth and Rob still own a home in Port Isaac in north Cornwall to which they go whenever they are in the UK, and a lot of the support for The Ideas Partnership has come from there. Their slogan is 'It takes more than one village to raise a child.' Local women have knitted boxfuls of jumpers and blankets for the children; they've sewn curtains to hang at the windows in the education centre to keep the sun out of the children's eyes; they've bought baby milk and Haribo bars, and collected old shoes – all of which Cornish firefighters have taken out to Kosovo in lorry-loads. Some have raised money, others have been out to the country to volunteer their expertise. The response has been phenomenal. And when Camilla was in Cornwall four months later, on a beautiful sunny day, she went to the village hall in Port Isaac to meet Elizabeth and some of the local people who have been giving the Ashkali community such support.

Elizabeth had written to the Duchess after her visit to Kosovo to thank her, and had received a letter back inviting her to keep in touch. A month later, she was in England and was invited to Clarence House. 'When I told them our budget they were gobsmacked. They said, "Most of the charities we work with spend that much on their IT." Our budget is 120,000 euros a year – less than £100,000 – and we work in four locations. And that was really nice for me to hear, because we're battling with that budget. But the reason we can achieve so much with so little is because of volunteers. And I'm free. I survive from selling my books.' *The Rubbish Picker's Wife* is an inspiring read.

'Would I swap it for my life back in Hackney? No. It really is addictive. Every time I go to Fushë Kosovë there's a huge adrenalin surge of achievement, and seeing a child who is no longer begging or a mother who has had a safe birth – really life-changing things like that are just wonderful.

'We've helped thousands and thousands of people and literally saved lives. We took children to the hospital who had tuberculosis and who would be dead if it wasn't for us. Even that little boy, and plenty of babies would have died. It's wonderful to be able to transform the chances of survival in a community. Even if it was just one child it would be wonderful.'

42

Domestic Violence

On Sunday morning, 11 September 2016, the BBC Radio 4 programme *The Archers* was extended to an hour for the first time in its 65-year history. Millions of people sat gripped as the jury debated their verdict at the end of the five-day trial of Helen Titchener for attempted murder. After years of mental and physical abuse at the hands of her husband Rob, the young mother had stabbed him.

For three years the story of their abusive relationship had unfolded. The man who'd seemed perfect in every way, gradually, insidiously, coercively took control of his wife, isolated her from her family and friends, undermined her confidence, stopped her working, stopped her driving and even raped her. And this was the second woman he had destroyed. It was a nail-biting hour but the jury finally found her not guilty.

The public response was overwhelming. Thousands took to social media to applaud the BBC. One fan, Paul Truman, set up a JustGiving page 'because for every fictional Helen, there are real ones' that has raised over £150,000 for the women's charity Refuge. In thirty-three years, chief executive Sandra Horley had never seen 'such amazing public support for our work'. I would be very surprised if Camilla, an *Archers* fan, had not been listening.

Just months earlier, in Oval, south-east London, the Duchess had heard real-life stories about domestic abuse that were more harrowing than Helen's. Camilla cries easily. She's emotional and she's of a certain age. She may well up, but it's not often that she openly weeps during a public engagement. But that day at SafeLives she did. Twenty women sat on chairs in a circle and watched while one survivor after another told her story, holding an object that was relevant to the abuse. Until each woman got to her feet no one in the group knew who would be next, making the point that you can't make assumptions – anyone can be the victim of domestic abuse, no matter what their social status. One woman held the watch she had been wearing when the husband she was about to divorce after eighteen years of abuse burst into the hairdressing salon where she worked with a sawn-off shotgun and attempted to kill her. The watch was broken in the ensuing fight. He smashed her in the face with the butt of the gun, then took aim. She pulled her legs to her chest so that the first shot hit her leg, while the second narrowly missed her head. Six hours later her husband was found hanging in local woodland. Six weeks after that, while she was still in hospital recovering from the attack, her sixteen-year-old son hanged himself.

The last person to speak held a child's homework bag. She was the best friend of a young mother, Joanna Simpson, also going through a divorce after years of abuse, whose husband, a British Airways pilot, had bludgeoned her to death with a claw hammer within earshot of their children. He had been looking after them for the half term holiday and had hidden the weapon inside one of their homework bags when he delivered them home. He disposed of her body in a grave he had prepared beforehand. The dead girl's own mother was weeping while the friend spoke, and Camilla, also in tears, immediately went over to comfort her.

'It was not voyeuristic, just incredibly powerful,' says Diana Barran, who started SafeLives at her kitchen table in 2005. After a career in the City, she was advising philanthropists on where to give their money. She had chosen three small, local children's charities. 'I said to them, "If we hadn't given the money to you, who should we have given it to?" My criterion was that it should be the biggest human problem, the one that is hardest to raise money for, and all three of them independently said "Domestic violence".' So she investigated, spoke to charities, to the police, to social services. Their current focus, she discovered, was on removing women from their homes and placing them and their children in refuges, where they would have to live in one room, often at the other end of the country. Given the choice, the vast majority of these women would rather stay in their communities – indeed, of those who go into refuges, most return to their community very quickly, and frequently to their abuser, either for financial reasons or as a result of threats to them or their children. So her idea was to train people to advise at-risk women – and men, though there are far fewer of those – on how to stay safe in their homes, or at least their communities, and to work with the various organisations – housing, mental health, police – in their home town. 'It's not that we don't need shelters and refuges,' she says, 'we absolutely do, but they help a real minority of people.' In the past year these independent domestic violence advisers (IDVAs) have helped more than 67,500 high-risk victims and 76,000 children.

In the next ten years her plan is to think about the whole family. 'Domestic abuse doesn't happen in isolation. If we are exclusively focused on the adult woman, we miss the children and crucially we miss the abusive partner. We are now doing quite a good job of keeping the current Mrs Jones safe but we are doing nothing, as a society, to stop Mr Jones going off and getting a new girlfriend. The numbers vary but often men will go through five, six, seven abusive relationships and may have children in each one, so we increasingly feel we have to look at the family in the round.'

It was Catherine Goodman, a friend of Diana Barran's, who suggested the Duchess take a look at SafeLives, and before she left the centre in Oval that morning, Camilla said, 'I want to help in any way I can.' And so, just six months later, in July 2016, she convened everyone involved in the world of domestic abuse for another lunch party in the garden at Clarence House. As with the party for those involved in dealing with rape and sexual violence, it was the first time that all these people, who work towards a common goal with a common passion, had met one another in such a way where they were able to swap stories, compare experiences and make essential contacts. Louiza Patikas, the actress who plays Helen Titchener, was there, as were a smattering of high-profile ambassadors, including singer Alesha Dixon and actors Julie Walters and Sir Patrick Stewart (who grew up in an abusive household), but otherwise those present were victims – including some of the women Camilla had met at SafeLives – campaigners, lawyers, police, social workers and politicians.

In what many of those present considered to be a very brave speech, the Duchess said, 'Domestic abuse remains a hidden problem in our society. It is characterised by silence – silence from those who suffer, silence from those around them and silence from those who perpetrate abuse. This silence is corrosive: it leaves women, children – and men – carrying the burden of shame, it prevents them from speaking out about their abuse and it prevents them from getting help. And at its worst, it can be fatal.

'Now some of you in this room know, only too well, that coercive control nearly always is the beginning of domestic abuse. Some of you are already working tirelessly to try to eradicate it from our society. I hope very much that all of you will find a chance to make significant connections today and find new ways to bring this problem out into the open – so that together we can make sure that the voices of those who are living with abuse today are not silenced, but clearly heard.'

Every year about 2.1 million women in the UK suffer some form of domestic abuse, and everyone I spoke to that afternoon felt the Duchess of Cornwall's involvement was important – partly because they felt she connected well with ordinary women and partly because of the publicity she generates. And they thought she was brave to attach her name to such a taboo subject. They were particularly pleased that she had mentioned coercive control – which in 2016 became a criminal offence – in her speech. Society needs to understand that control is at the heart of domestic abuse. It's not always about physical violence.

Polly Neate, chief executive of Women's Aid, said, 'Everywhere I go I might as well have a great big badge on my head saying "Feminist" – and a lot of people are going to switch off to what I say because of that.'

Sandra Horley says, 'Domestic violence is a major problem that affects a lot of us and costs the state £16 billion a year – that's you and me, the taxpayer – so we need to be talking about it. We have 3,850 women and children in our refuges on any given day. Our helpline handles 400 calls a day.'

And as Polly says, 'If a victim has a copy of the *Daily Mail* sitting on her coffee table and sees the Duchess talking about coercive control she might start to think, hang on a minute, and then at the bottom of the article finds "Where to get help".'

Diana Barran confirms that the issue cuts across all sections of society. 'I think that the more isolated you are the worse it is, so there are parallels between the refugee woman who speaks no English and has nowhere to turn, and the upper-middle-class woman where it's deemed completely unacceptable socially, and nobody would ever talk about it and you cannot tell a soul.

'Invariably women feel they are partly to blame. That's because it's how we are as human beings, but also very often the abusive partner will tell them that they're to blame. "If only you did x, y and z this wouldn't be happening, you're forcing me to do whatever it is I'm doing." But it's also very true of children; they definitely think it must be their fault that their parents are behaving like that, which leaves all sorts of other scars. Sometimes I think both parents will believe that because the child is upstairs in bed they're not aware of what's going on. But of course they are absolutely aware of it, just as when you walk into a room you know what the atmosphere is. There's more and more research showing the harmful effect that living with domestic abuse has on children's brains as they develop, which is deeply worrying.

'One of the amazing things about the event the Duchess came to was the women she met who had been through differing degrees of incredible tragedy, and their absolute passion to try and make things better and the positivity that they brought to it. It's so humbling, you think, Oh my goodness, if she can dig that deep, we can all dig that deep.'

43

Mending Fences

Extraordinary contemporary architecture and cancer are not the most obvious of bedfellows. But thanks to a courageous and creative designer called Maggie Keswick Jencks, the two have become inextricably linked. In 1993 she was told that her breast cancer had returned and was now in her bones, liver and brain; she had two to three months to live.

She was lucky. Through her American husband Charles Jencks' contacts in Boston she learnt about a pioneering oncologist in Edinburgh. Under the care of this doctor at the city's Western General Hospital she lived for two more years. And in that time, in collaboration with her husband, a highly influential architectural critic who's written seminal works on post-modernism, and her oncology nurse, Laura Lee, she created the blueprint for a new type of care to help people live positively with cancer. Not medical care, but practical, emotional and psychological care, the kind that she discovered from her own experience was much needed. She envisaged colourful, light, welcoming places and spaces with professional staff on hand, where people could meet in a relaxed domestic atmosphere, chat, make themselves a coffee, get information about the disease, be given practical advice, massage or therapy, do yoga or just have somewhere quiet to sit and contemplate. She strongly believed that people should not 'lose the joy of living in the fear of dying'.

The result was an inspirationally converted stable in the grounds of the Western General designed by Richard Murphy. It opened in 1996, the year after Maggie died, but her memory and her ground-breaking ideas live on. Maggie's Centres have sprung up like mushrooms in the grounds of NHS hospitals all over the UK, and in a few other countries too, and in 2008, the Duchess of Cornwall became the charity's president. She was very keen to get involved, which is interesting given that each of the centres is designed by an internationally renowned architect – the sort that make Prince Charles shudder. Richard Rogers designed the one at Charing Cross Hospital in west London – and it's bright orange. Norman Foster's design at the Christie Hospital in Manchester, which Camilla opened in 2016, calling it 'another beautifully designed Centre', is almost all glass. There is no love lost between either architect and the Prince and they have had some very public spats, but while the designs may not be to his taste he would approve of the gardens over which each of them looks. Maggie loved and designed gardens herself and they are an all-important feature of each centre.

At the Manchester opening the Duchess said, 'Maggie's has gone from strength to strength, staying true to Maggie Keswick Jencks's vision of truly imaginative buildings whose design is an essential part of the Maggie's message ... Lord Foster ... has brought a personal understanding to this masterful design and its light airiness is matched by Dan Pearson's sensitive planting scheme. I cannot imagine a more welcoming or comforting sanctuary.'

'I think actually that she's had a healing influence in the architectural community,' says Laura. 'I think they've felt really rather pleased that, by association, their form of architecture is recognised. We've had no sense of "Why doesn't Maggie's use one of Prince Charles's architects?" Not once, not ever has that been a suggestion. Our architects are rather pleased.'

The association began in July 2008 when Prince Charles was making an official visit to the Western General Hospital, and Camilla asked whether she might unofficially come and visit the Maggie's Centre at the same time. 'I showed her around and we had a cup of tea, talked about what we did, and she said, "If there's anything I can usefully do to help, I'd love to." And so we invited her to become our president. As we walked her back across to the main hospital on that day to meet Prince Charles, we all kind of collided and he said, "I'm amazed that you're actually on time and on schedule." I remember that being such a normal moment, when you could just tell they were really happy.'

The official line was that the charity would see the Duchess no more than once or twice a year, but she has given them far more. Like all of us, she has lost friends to cancer, and has friends living with it, so the centres are close to her heart.

'She approaches Maggie's in a very professional, businesslike way, but what's wonderful about her is that her style is very appropriate to who we are as an organisation. Maggie's is about welcoming people.' A journalist arrived late and out of breath when the Duchess was visiting the Swansea centre. She teased him about his timekeeping – 'Where have you been? What time do you call this?' – before saying, 'Have a minute, take a seat, catch your breath, and Maggie's will get you a cup of tea.'

Being such a good judge of people and organisations, once she has committed to them Camilla is loyal and will go the extra mile. Even in snow. Most people looking out of the window to see four feet of snow would listen to the weather warnings and stay at home. The Duchess was due to open an extension at the National Osteoporosis Society – the product of a legacy, and a donation that she had personally secured – and overnight it had snowed heavily. Wiltshire woke up to a winter wonderland. The building is in the countryside, on a minor road at the bottom of two steep hills that had become impassable. 'I remember thinking, I can't see it unless she comes in on a sledge,' says Angela Jordan, then deputy chief executive, who had struggled in on foot. But there was no phone call. Mid-morning, to everyone's surprise, a four-wheel vehicle came slithering down the hill, accompanied by sniffer dogs. By this time the staff had been out and made snowmen in the garden. Next, a snowplough ground its way down the hill, then another and another, followed by a gritter truck, and finally by the royal party.

The NOS went through a troubled administrative patch for three or four years after Linda Edwards' death. The chairman at the time was Cyrus Cooper, now Professor of Rheumatology at the University of Southampton, who has been involved with the charity from its inception and is one of the world's leading researchers on musculoskeletal disease. He was involved in the decision to invite Camilla – then known to the public as the less popular Mrs Parker Bowles – to be president, and was strongly supportive. 'We had no qualms about this, and having her was the step change we needed.' But there were some like the Dean of the Faculty of Medicine who needed convincing. 'She's a fantastic champion. Just come and meet her and listen and I promise you, only good will come of the visit,' said Cyrus. Before the next visit it was, 'Oh brilliant, we really want her to come down,' and in 2016, she was invited to accept an honorary degree. So, on a sunny February day, dressed in a pale blue and red academic gown, the Duchess received an honorary doctorate of science from the vice-chancellor, Sir Christopher Snowden.

The charity stuck by her throughout the years of scandal, and when the tables were turned she stuck by the NOS. She expressed concern but didn't waver in her support. 'She's personally very loyal,' says Cyrus. 'Friends are friends in good times and bad.' The current chief executive, who quickly put the NOS back on course, is Claire Severgnini. Appointed in 2006, she remembers her first meeting with the Duchess, which took place over tea at Clarence House. She was offered some Duchy shortbread. 'I refused it on a couple of occasions and she said, "No, do have one, they're delicious." I was thinking, I know they are but I've got a dry mouth and I don't want to splutter crumbs. She said, "Well, have one for your bag on the way home." She was very insistent. I think I met Joy outside and sat chatting with her and then Amanda came in with me, so I was interviewed by everybody. But it didn't feel like an interview at all.'

Every time Claire has met the Duchess subsequently she has been impressed by her knowledge. And because people know the family history, they want to support her. For the charity's twentieth anniversary, Camilla raised £200,000 in sponsorship for a ten-mile walk around Loch Muick on the Balmoral estate.

The biggest single donation was of £3 million from the Freemasons, given to mark their 300th anniversary and presented at the Royal Albert Hall. The Duchess gave moral support to a very nervous Angela Jordan, then acting chief executive, who collected the cheque. 'Men. All in regalia, the Albert Hall absolutely packed to the rafters, more at another Masonic venue watching on screens and I had to get onto the stage and accept the cheque,' she says. '"I'm so glad it's you doing this," said the Duchess. "You must be so brave." I could barely breathe, I was so frightened. As we went to the exit afterwards and she was leaving, she had the grace to say, "You did that so well."'

Claire Severgnini had an NHS background, and her immediate obser-vation about the NOS was that while they were communicating with people living with the disease and raising money for academic research, they had little engagement with the health professionals who daily deal with the fractures and other consequences of osteoporosis. With the £3 million, and some clever negotiating, she has managed to get DEXA scanning machines, which measure bone density, into fourteen NHS hospitals, and has put £1 million into fracture liaison services within the NHS to detect those who should be scanned in order to pick up osteoporosis when it is treatable. Their best guess is that three million people may be living with the condition – there are 300,000 fragility fractures a year – and about half a million people on prescribed medication. 'Now we want to start talking about ending osteoporosis,' says Claire. 'Cyrus is working on preventing it in utero and hopefully we can look back collectively over our shoulder in thirty years and see we've moved some mountains.'

Three months after Angela Jordan left the NOS, Camilla invited her to Clarence House for morning coffee by way of a thank you. On the way out, Angela rather cheekily pointed out that Wroughton in Wiltshire, where she now ran Prospect Hospice, was not so far from Highgrove. If ever the Duchess wanted to visit on her way to or from London, she would be most welcome. She is now president and has visited several times, as well as opening an outreach centre near Marlborough. 'Local people don't have great expectations, so when somebody like the Duchess of Cornwall comes to visit an organisation like this, it means twice as much as it might elsewhere. People feel invested, they feel special, and after she's left, the atmosphere almost fizzes.'

And finally dogs. At the end of 2016, the Queen relinquished some of her patronages to younger members of the family, and one of those that came to the Duchess was Battersea Dogs and Cats Home. She has supported the charity unofficially for many years, both by visiting and by giving a home to two abandoned puppies. Battersea is a much-loved institution. It has taken in stray and unwanted dogs since 1860 and cats since 1883, and has always had royal patronage. It now has three centres, but the oldest is on a nine-acre site on the south side of the Thames, under the railway arches of Chelsea Bridge. It has around 500 animals in its care at any one time – and it sees the best and the worst of human nature. 'We cry many tears here,' says chief executive Claire Horton, 'happy and sad.' No animal in need is ever turned away, although for the most shocking cases of animal cruelty the kindest help is to put an animal to sleep. Its doors never close, it has eight vets, 30 nurses, 200 care staff, over 1,000 volunteers and gets 100,000 visitors a year.

In 2010 they built a smart new cattery, which Claire invited the Duchess of Cornwall to open. 'We knew she was a Jack Russell fan, and she then shared with us that she'd lost her older Jack Russell, Freddy, a couple of years before. You can't come here and say, "I suppose I'll get another one at some point, I do miss having Freddy around", because we'll be watching for the right animal and as soon as one arrives we'll call you. We had a little puppy called Beth come in, she'd been abandoned. She was exactly what the Duchess was looking for, a really nice little dog, so we rang up and said "What do you think?" I think she was at Balmoral. "Send me photos, send me photos!"'

Before an animal is re-homed, a home check is often carried out. Camilla insisted she should have no special treatment and so the inspector went down to Ray Mill, where she already had Tosca and Rosie. 'I said I thought we might get away with not home-checking Highgrove and that they were probably okay in Clarence House too. The puppy went down a storm.'

A year later, they gave her Bluebell. 'She was a small runty type of puppy who had been found in a park. She was in quite a poor state and spent several weeks here while we tried to rehabilitate her. The Duchess said "I'll definitely have her." A couple of weeks later the dogs were having a few squabbles and we panicked because we thought we'd sent her a Chihuahua-cross, and they can be a bit feisty. "I'm not sure if it's a Chihuahua or a Jack Russell or what," she said, "but don't worry, we're persevering, she's not coming back."'

A few months later Bluebell did come back, in style, in the back of a royal car, along with Beth, but it was only for a visit. 'We had a guard of honour,' says Claire. 'The car arrives, door opens, out pile these two dogs on a lead, sniffing. "Where are we?" And then, "Oh bloody hell, we're back," and they jump into the car again! So she tucks them under her arms and comes through and they were great. They met everyone, she met everyone, and it's the nicest thing for Battersea staff who look after the puppies and remember them to see them grown up, and happy with new lives in new homes – and they are really smiley, happy dogs.'

As pampered royal dogs invariably are.

44

The Future

Shortly before Charles and Camilla's wedding in April 2005, Helena Kennedy, in her role as chair of the British Council, was invited to a big event called Once Upon A Time, in Denmark, to celebrate the 200th anniversary of the birth of its most famous children's author, Hans Christian Andersen. Held in the national stadium, it was attended by the Scandinavian royal families and an audience of 40,000. Each of the guests was given a cushion to sit on, shaped like a book but tied closed. The title on the cover was *The Princess and the Pea*. The opening page read 'Once upon a time ...' and sewn into the soft material on the next page was a small hard pea.

'When we were invited to the wedding, they made it clear that they didn't want presents, but I came home with my cushion and thought this was the perfect present for Camilla. So I dropped it off at Clarence House, and I phoned Amanda and said "I've got a present that I'm sending in." I sent a note with it saying "And you are the real thing". She knew what I was saying to her. She loved it and just hooted with laughter when she received it, but she is the real thing. That's what I think about her, she's the real deal.'

The question, however, is whether when the time comes Camilla will be a real queen. Clarence House has always maintained that when Charles accedes to the throne, the Duchess will be known as Princess Consort. This was initially said at the time of their marriage to pacify those who were so hostile towards Camilla – but even now, although the mood in the country has changed, there has been no change in the official line. At the end of the day, it will be up to Charles, in consultation with others. The title taken by the wife of the king is not a matter of law, it is established through custom and practice. In the past, the wives of kings have been known as Queens Consort – but they have never arrived in that position via the divorce courts.

The husbands of queens, on the other hand, have never been known as kings. Queen Victoria's husband, Albert, was Prince Consort and the present Queen's husband was given the title Duke of Edinburgh – and neither was in any way diminished by it. I have little doubt that Charles is so proud of Camilla, and so grateful for everything she has done for him and sacrificed for him, that he will insist she gets the full title. Friends and family know it is not something she wants – she has said as much. She is in this position because of her love for the man, not because of her desire to be anything more than a support to him. The whole business of his accession is something she dreads and, in her inimitable way, is choosing not to think about.

Looking at the Duchess today, valued for her work, successfully juggling her roles of duty and family, beautifully presented, and stepping out serenely beside a much, much happier Prince Charles on the world stage, it is easy to forget just what she went through to achieve this. The pain of the past, the emotional damage wreaked by all those years as a figure of hate, worrying about the well-being of her children, living on her nerves, have taken their toll. She has health issues that are almost certainly a legacy of that time. And even today she is living on her nerves, particularly with the twentieth anniversary of Diana's death looming. Never knowing quite what lies ahead in a day's work, flying in aeroplanes and helicopters which still frighten her, meeting and greeting rooms full of strangers, knowing that everyone is watching her, listening to her, perhaps wanting to trip her up in some way. She has wonderful support, and she's surrounded by people who love her, but they can only do so much: she is the one with the title, the one everyone is waiting to see, the one whom people's expectations hang on, and that is an unenviable responsibility.

At least one member of her family doesn't want her to become Queen for fear of a backlash. 'I think it would be better for her if she became Princess Consort. I do so want her to be all right. And I do worry that she won't be. How is she going to be judged? That's the thing I feel fearful about.

Between Diana and the Queen is quite a hard place to be. People might go a bit wild. The Queen who's been in our lives for ever, the worship of Diana and suddenly Queen Camilla. It's going to be such a shake-up. I fear for them both.'

The Right Honourable Frank Field, MP for Birkenhead on the Wirral, is a great fan of the Duchess. And he doesn't think Charles gets enough credit for his work with the Prince's Trust. But he thinks there is a need to give one or two subtle pointers that it is the wish of the Palace that Camilla becomes Queen so there can't be an anti-Camilla campaign in the country on the basis that this is something that the Queen would never wish.

'Charles will try and press for her to be crowned Queen. And it is right that he should do so. We have no known basis of the wife of the King not being crowned Queen. It is how that goal is achieved which is crucially important.

'Charles wants to rethink the monarchy and who can blame him for that? But on this issue above all others it is important that he has a group of people advising him gently. The first aim must be to prevent Camilla being hurt in any way and the second that the normal precedent of the King's wife being Queen should follow immediately at the Accession Council.'

Frank has seen the Duchess on a few occasions in recent years. After a lifetime spent campaigning against poverty and low pay, he started a charity in his constituency called the Foundation Years Trust, which supports mothers who are helped to extend the life chances of children whose future would otherwise be blighted. It grew out of *The Foundation Years: preventing poor children becoming poor adults*, an independent report on poverty and life chances he wrote for the Prime Minister, David Cameron, in 2010. 'There was no indication until the very end of his period in government, that David Cameron had even read the report, so I thought I'd try and put it into action which governments might then lift.' The thrust of the report is that life chances are closed by the age of five for most children. Those are the formative years, cognitively, socially and emotionally, and are therefore crucial in determining whether a child will struggle in life or fly. The FYT has centred on three drivers where it is possible, Field believes, that work with mothers can prove more powerful than income or class – the mental health of the mother, the bonding between mother and baby, and the home learning environment. Camilla became patron of the trust in 2015 and

Frank has met her on occasions at Marlborough House, on her two trips to Birkenhead and at official receptions.

'She's brilliant. When she arrived on her first visit in Birkenhead there was mega wind – we're on the sea. Amanda was very worried about how she'd look and a room was arranged just in case. Well, she came in and shook her hair. Then she was with a group of young mums, talking about her role as a grandmother, then a dads' project, and to my joy, she had to be shoehorned away from the young dads because she was having such a good discussion with them about football. On another visit, the headmistress of a Birkenhead junior school that Camilla was visiting, had a shock of wonderful hair, dyed green that day, and Camilla couldn't believe this was the head, as she looked so young, and then joked about the whole thing. So it was immediate bond-making with the whole group and the families longed for their session not to end.

'Talking to a member of the Royal Family is a very unusual occupation and she gets it, she's as normal as she possibly could be. She's got all of Diana's abilities, although the expression of her human sympathy is on a more natural level. It's quite extraordinary how she can transfer back from the life in the royal circle she now lives, to the lives of the poor. One sees how lucky Charles is to have her as a partner, and you sense she knows full well the tram lines that he has to be in and she's always trying to push them a little bit to make life better for him. When I first met her – about the need to raise a million for the FYT – she said, "Oh come on, let's go up to my room. He keeps the temperature very low in here. I've got a roaring fire upstairs. Come on. How much do you have to raise?"

'"£1 million."

'"Well, a million's not what it used to be."'

Frank would like to see her as the nation's grandmother. 'When you talk to people, who do they look back on? Their grandmothers. They don't have to do the tough bit of parenting, they're the sanctuary a child can go to. I think we'll get the genuine article with Camilla, of which the Queen Mum was the prototype. Grandmothers aren't challenging, they're nurturing. I think as we lead up to the accession, the work she does plays a key part in preparing for her role in the new regime, in the country's acceptance.

'Her judgement is interesting. She brought in people she knew and could trust to be around, of whom Amanda is the most important. You're not swept up in, "Oh bye-bye everybody, I'm off to the Palace." Then there is her family. When she comes back from overseas trips you'll often read she goes straight to see her grandchildren. Her instincts are so good.'

Camilla also dashes off to see her grandchildren on Christmas Day. She has lunch with the rest of the Royal Family at Sandringham and once upon a time used to stay until after the Queen's speech was broadcast on television at three o'clock, but in 2016 she bolted for home straight after pudding, 'muttering something about grandchildren', to get as much time with her family as possible. Whether she will be able to keep her sanctuary at Ray Mill after the accession is another unknown, and something else she is not daring to think about. To lose it would break her heart. She needs it – and it costs the taxpayer nothing. She enjoys a lot of her new life, but not everything about it – which is perhaps what makes her so likeable – and having somewhere to escape to that is entirely hers and her family's, entirely normal, entirely stress-free, is not a luxury. It has helped her keep a sense of reality in the very unreal world she's now a part of. And I think people respond to that.

There will also be a question mark over where she and Charles will officially live. For the last few hundred years, the sovereign has lived at Buckingham Palace when he or she is in London, but it's not a home and none of the present incumbents like it. The Queen and Prince Philip were forced to give up Clarence House and move across the park when her father died, but she was very young and had a forceful Prime Minister in Winston Churchill, and was not in a position to protest. Charles, approaching seventy, is not likely to be such a pushover. He and Camilla are very happy at Clarence House and have made the private quarters a real home. Of course the house that is most like a normal home to them, that has no offices and no public rooms – and where they are at their best and most normal – is Birkhall. They love it there and the children love coming to stay. But as King, Charles will have to play host to more than friends and family. Might he have to forfeit Birkhall and use Balmoral Castle? There is also the Castle of Mey that he inherited from his grandmother.

And what about Highgrove, where he created his garden? It is owned by the Duchy of Cornwall, which will no longer be his. The Duchy provides an income for the heir to the throne, so when Charles becomes King, the estate and the title will go to Prince William, who will also become Prince of Wales. But will he and Kate want to use his childhood home? At the moment they are based at Kensington Palace, with George and Charlotte, and have the newly refurbished Anmer Hall, a gift from the Queen, at Sandringham. He may or may not want to use Highgrove. Then there is Windsor Castle, which the Queen is so fond of, and of course Sandringham itself.

That is a lot of property for a modern, scaled-down, cost-conscious monarchy and I am sure there are great minds wrangling with the matter as I write – although Charles has never been known for his frugality. The Queen herself gave the greatest indication yet of how the future might look at the end of her Diamond Jubilee celebrations in 2012. She appeared on the balcony of Buckingham Palace with just five others. The generations of extended family that normally fill the space were nowhere to be seen. It was the Queen, Charles, Camilla, William, Catherine and Harry – the Duke of Edinburgh was in hospital. A secure line of succession and no freeloaders.

'The Prince will be the best prepared King the country's ever had,' says Julia Cleverdon. 'He knows more about what goes on in the highways and byways and climate change and inner cities and everything else, he could not have worked harder at it – but Duty is the hound at his heels. In the end it comes back to his parents. Camilla's very good at the light touch and the funny joke. She lightens it all for him.

'The Prince is incredibly happy and contented and amused since Camilla came back into his life,' observes a friend, 'and I think she's very happy. They seem to be very keen on each other, they love each other, they've come to a contented happiness in their late sixties. Why not?'

The bonus is that this relationship is about more than a love affair, or two people being happy. Camilla has proved to be extraordinarily good at the job. No one is more surprised about that than she is, but friends say she is proud of being the Duchess of Cornwall. It's not just her people skills – the easy, open, friendly manner and sense of merriment – nor her ability to scrub up well, work a room, unveil plaques and glad-hand the public. She has put her stamp on issues that no one else was prepared to touch, doing it in such a way that it's the issues that get the attention and not herself. She is not on an ego trip, she's not seeking self-aggrandisement, she's not wanting to overshadow Charles's achievements. Within her pillars of interest – literacy, rape, sexual violence, domestic abuse, health – she is making a very real difference to many people's lives. In a small way, my own included. I was diagnosed with osteoporosis in 2016 thanks to one of the DEXA scanners put into NHS hospitals by the NOS. Without her commitment to the charity, the receptions she's held, the stars she's attracted, the profile she's given it and the donations for research and treatment that have followed, I may not have known I had the disease until I broke my spine – or lost eight inches in height like her mother.

She is utterly committed to the causes she's attached herself to, and she and her team are constantly looking for ways of joining up the dots, making a visit or a reception go further. Thinking laterally, connecting people and ideas. She has no doubt watched and learnt from Charles, who has worked tirelessly with a far wider portfolio his entire life. She admires what he has done and their views on many of the important issues are very similar. But she has one advantage over him. The Prince has not lived in the real world as she has. His approach is inevitably second-hand and based on theory and ideals. And although he has two children, there is only so far he could draw on that experience and be taken seriously. Camilla is quite obviously a hands-on mother and grandmother and can therefore relate to parents and grandparents in a more credible way.

One of the biggest problems with the charitable or third sector, as anyone who works in it will say, is the proliferation of small charities operating in the same field, competing with one another for recognition and for ever-diminishing funds. 'Somehow or other we have to work together,' says Jonathan Douglas, chief executive of the National Literacy Trust. 'By ourselves we can't crack it. The answer is collaboration, but by and large, everything predicates against that. What Clarence House, and what the Duchess is doing by adopting a group of charities in the same space, is convening and helping collaboration. And it's done subtly, through curiosity and through suggestion, but actually, that is the thing that makes us bigger than the sum of our parts. And it may be offering a footprint for how the third sector can increase its impact in the future.'

The other surprise is that Camilla has turned out to be a genuine asset to the Royal Family. She has given Charles support and encouragement – and belief in himself – that he's never had before, and that has made him much more likeable and therefore much more popular. And popularity is vital in a modern-day monarch. He's no longer angst-ridden and tortured; he's relaxed, he's humorous, he's teasing and he looks happy – and that comes through in the flesh and in the photographs of them together, and those of him with his sons. He's a Prince the public wants to engage with again. And she has made that happen, without in any way treading on his toes. Her pride in him and his achievements, which shines through in those photographs, has made people look again at him and appreciate him.

For so many years the Prince's extraordinary and in many ways visionary work has been buried by his scandalous private life. A television documentary to mark forty years of the Prince's Trust, presented by the cheeky Geordie pair Ant and Dec, went a long way to putting that right. And Camilla put her feelings into words. She described the energy that Prince Charles has and how hard he works for the charity. 'I think I'm really proud to be married to somebody who, forty years ago, aged twenty-seven, had the vision to put it together – I mean it was an incredible idea for somebody – he was very young then – to think of it and to think of these very disadvantaged young people who had literally been to hell and back and to find a way to give them a second chance in life.'

There are no longer calls, as there once were, for Prince William to leapfrog his father when the Queen dies. The debate is focused on Camilla's title, not on the Prince of Wales's moral authority to reign. I have no doubt William will be an excellent King when his time comes but it must be allowed to come naturally. Picking and choosing which member of the family we want next would set a dangerous precedent. The integrity of the British monarchy is based on heredity. Besides, William, at thirty-five, cannot hold a candle to his father in terms of preparation and experience – and he has young children. They need him during these early years of their childhood, lest they become casualties, like Charles, of parents consumed by duty too soon in life, and history repeats itself. And beautiful as Catherine may be, she doesn't yet have the maturity, the depth of experience of life, love, loss, pain and survival that gives Camilla such understanding and credibility.

In August 2017, a YouGov opinion poll indicated that both Charles and Camilla's popularity had plummeted. This was no surprise. The twentieth anniversary of Diana's death spawned countless tributes, and a plethora of documentaries nostalgically looking back at her life and tragic death. It was always going to have caused problems, especially since William and Harry took part in two of them – the one already mentioned, and *Diana, 7 Days*, which examined the week from her death to her burial. Channel 4, controversially, broadcast footage from private tapes that Diana had made during sessions with her voice coach in 1992; in *Diana: In Her Own Words*, she once again placed the blame for the marriage failure on Charles and Camilla. Swathes of the country were emotionally transported back to the dark days of her death. Expected or not, it was an uncomfortable time for both Charles and Camilla – a time when, once again, her strength kept his tendency to despair at bay.

It was almost certainly a blip; there is actually huge affection for them both amongst the public, but her family still worry for her. Amongst other things, they worry that she hasn't properly processed the grief of her brother's death and that she is still living on her nerves. She and Charles have become joint presidents of the Elephant Family and have secured £20 million to preserve a hundred elephant corridors across India by 2025. She is furthering Mark's dream, but she can't talk about him. Some in her family feel that there is a side of her that's trying to hold everything together, because she fears that if she allows the smallest chink in the armour, the entire suit will shatter.

'I think she's quite a brave person,' says Catherine Goodman, 'and you can't be brave without being frightened. But I think she's played it straight, and she's played it the only way she knows how to play it. And there's something within the British sensibility, you know, they kind of respect that in some ways. They may not have liked the story about what had happened in the past, but it's water under the bridge, and I think people instinctively know she's doing her best.'

By whatever title she is known, Camilla will no doubt carry on doing her best. She will be the strength behind the crown and do her husband proud, and I suspect history will be a kinder judge of their story than their contemporaries have been.

BIBLIOGRAPHY

I am indebted to the authors and publishers of the following works that I have consulted and in some cases quoted from:

Brandreth, Gyles, *Charles & Camilla*, Arrow Books, 2006
Dimbleby, Jonathan, *The Prince of Wales*, Little, Brown, 1994
Donaldson, Frances, *Edward VIII*, Weidenfeld & Nicolson, 1986
Ferguson, Josephine, *The Stuffed Stoat*, Melrose Books, 2009
Goldsmith, Annabel, *Annabel: An Unconventional Life – The Memoirs of Lady Annabel Goldsmith*, Phoenix/Orion, 2005
Gowing, Elizabeth, *The Rubbish-Picker's Wife*, Elbow Publishing, 2015
Hardman, Robert, *Our Queen*, Hutchinson, 2011
Hibbert, Christopher, *Queen Victoria*, HarperCollins, 2000
Holden, Anthony, *Charles: Prince of Wales*, Pan, 1980
Keppel, Sonia, *Edwardian Daughter*, Arrow Books, 1958
Morton, Andrew, *Diana: Her True Story – In Her Own Words*, Michael O'Mara Books, 1997
Shand, Bruce, *Previous Engagements*, Michael Russell, 1990
Shand, Mark, *Travels on my Elephant*, Eland, 2012
Shawcross, William, *Queen Elizabeth, The Queen Mother*, Pan, 2010
Souhami, Diana, *Mrs Keppel And Her Daughter*, Flamingo, 1997
Wilson, A.N., *Betjeman*, Arrow Books, 2007

Extracts on page 16 from Wilson, A.N., *Betjeman*
Extracts on pages 16–18 from Shand, Bruce, *Previous Engagements*
Extracts on pages 21 and 23 from Souhami, Diana, *Mrs Keppel and her Daughter*
Extracts on pages 22–3 and 24–8 from Keppel, Sonia, *Edwardian Daughter*
Extracts on pages 38–9 from Ferguson, Josephine, *The Stuffed Stoat*

Extracts on pages 59, 78, 80, 89–90 and 112 from Morton, Andrew, *Diana: Her True Story – In Her Own Words*

Extract on pages 65–6 from Holden, Anthony, *Charles: Prince of Wales*

Extracts on pages 71, 76, 102 and 107 from Dimbleby, Jonathan, *The Prince of Wales*

PICTURE CREDITS

ACKNOWLEDGEMENTS

This is not in any way an authorised biography. My views and my conclusions are my own, based upon conversations with dozens of people and many years of researching and writing about the Royal Family. Like any biography of this sort, it is only ever as good as the people one speaks to. Many of them are named in the text; others are not but they have all been invaluable and huge thanks go to each and every one of them for giving up their time so generously and sharing their memories. I am also enormously grateful to those people who read and checked the factual accuracy of the manuscript for me.

Many, many thanks also to Shana and James Wilby, who now own The Laines, for showing me around their beautiful house and garden. Also to Roger Broadbent for showing me around his remarkable house which was formerly Dumbrells school. And to Jenny Kirkbride and Pippa Creed for making the introduction and with whom I had a lovely day in Ditchling.

Particular thanks also to Andrew Morton for generously allowing me to quote so extensively from his unique material in *Diana: Her True Story – In Her Own Words*, and to William Shawcross for going to great lengths to provide the photograph of their families' outing to Newcastle so long ago. Also to Ian Jones for his wonderful images taken in more recent years – and John Stillwell for the snap of me with the Prince of Wales on our trip to the Balkans.

Huge thanks too to everyone at HarperCollins both in the UK and US who has helped bring everything together. In the UK, Arabella Pike, Lottie Fyfe, Julian Humphries, Katherine Patrick, Steve Gove, Zoe Shine and Arthur Heard. And in the US, Jonathan Burnham, Hannah Wood and Mary Gaule.

And to my agents, Jane Turnbull – a great friend for many years – and Daniel Conaway at Writers House, New York, a newer friend. And my husband, the wonderful James Leith, who makes everything possible, every time.

Last but not least, a big hug to William Yeoward for all his unfailing support and help, not just with my project but in safeguarding Luna (my very precious seventh grandchild), to whom this book is dedicated.

INDEX